DIVIDED WE FAIL

DIVIDED WE FAIL

The Story of an African American Community
That Ended the Era of School Desegregation

Sarah Garland

BEACON PRESS
BOSTON

Beacon Press
25 Beacon Street
Boston, Massachusetts 02108-2892
www.beacon.org

Beacon Press books
are published under the auspices of
the Unitarian Universalist Association of Congregations.

16 15 14 13   8 7 6 5 4 3 2 1

This book is printed on acid-free paper that meets the uncoated paper
ANSI/NISO specifications for permanence as revised in 1992.

Text design by Wilsted & Taylor Publishing Services

Library of Congress Cataloging-in-Publication Data
Garland, Sarah.
Divided we fail : the story of an African American community
that ended the era of school desegregation / Sarah Garland.
     p. cm.
Includes bibliographical references and index.
ISBN 978-0-8070-0177-6 (hardcover : alk. paper)
1. Parents Involved in Community Schools—Trials, litigation, etc.
2. Seattle Public Schools—Trials, litigation, etc. 3. Jefferson County
Public Schools—Trials, litigation, etc. 4. School integration—Law and
legislation—Kentucky—Louisville. 5. Affirmative action programs in
education—Law and legislation—Kentucky—Louisville. I. Title.
KF229.G37 2012
344.73'0798—dc23   2012027732

For my parents

The history of the American Negro is the history of this strife,—this longing to attain self-conscious manhood, to merge his double self into a better and truer self. In this merging, he wishes neither of the older selves to be lost. He would not Africanize America, for America has too much to teach the world and Africa. He would not bleach his Negro soul in a flood of white Americanism, for he knows that Negro blood has a message for the world. He simply wishes to make it possible for a man to be both a Negro and an American, without being cursed and spit upon by his fellows, without having the doors of Opportunity closed roughly in his face.

—W. E. B. Du Bois, *The Souls of Black Folk*, 1903

CONTENTS

PREFACE

On June 28, 2007, the U.S. Supreme Court handed down a ruling that officially ended the era of school desegregation that followed *Brown v. Board of Education.*[1] Five of the nine justices declared that race alone could no longer be used to assign students to a school, undermining the biggest civil rights cases of the previous century. Under the new interpretation of the law, school districts that had labored for half a century to integrate under plans once forced on them by the courts were told those plans were now unconstitutional.

Two cases led to the decision, one out of Seattle and another out of Louisville, Kentucky, the most racially integrated school system in America. The Louisville case had a long history. Ten years earlier, parents had gone to court to fight desegregation in order to save one school, Central High. The parents were angry about busing, the main tool used in Louisville's plan. Their children were being forced into the worst schools in the city while one of the best, located in their neighborhood, was being threatened with closure. They were frustrated that their children's educational fates were decided based solely on their race, with little attention to what parents and the community wanted for their kids. They believed the school system was violating their constitutional right to equal protection. They didn't care that their case might jeopardize a central cause of the civil rights movement, school desegregation; a few of the plaintiffs hoped that desegregation would be dismantled because of their efforts. Although they were not the first to bring a federal case challenging desegregation, they were the first African Americans to do so.[2]

To the plaintiffs and their supporters, the triumphant narrative of the civil rights battles that led to the long-awaited desegregation of the nation's schools ignored some ugly truths. Americans commemorated James Meredith's fight to attend Old Miss and the integration of the Little Rock schools, but they rarely talked about the mass firings of black teachers and widespread closings of traditionally black schools that followed. School desegregation reinforced assumptions about black inferiority, they argued, and it didn't succeed in closing the racial achievement gap.

Central High School, located in the inner city amid housing projects and industrial warehouses, was Louisville's traditionally black school. Under the district's desegregation plan, every school had to maintain a white majority, and Central couldn't attract enough white students to stay viable. It seemed the Louisville school district might close it. Represented by an ambitious personal injury lawyer, a group of African American plaintiffs, most of them Central alumni, won a district court case to end racial quotas at the school and keep it open. The victory opened the door for other lawsuits against the city's desegregation plan. Almost immediately, a group of white parents, angry that their children couldn't attend the schools of their choice, hired the black group's lawyer and took their cause to the Supreme Court.

The black parents' lawsuit was largely forgotten, but the white parents' case gripped the nation. Educators and civil rights activists worried that the justices were prepared to overturn *Brown*—that they would decide that thirty years of desegregation was enough to compensate for more than three hundred years of slavery and segregation. Others hoped the justices would affirm their belief that racial preferences were self-defeating and that American society had entered a "post-racial" era. Both sides argued that the other was turning back the clock to an era when racial discrimination was the law.

In the Supreme Court case, white parents fought against mostly white school officials, and white lawyers argued in front of a mostly white Supreme Court. Few people watching the national case unfold knew about the black parents in Louisville who had made it possible. This book tells their story.

Before I delve into the experiences and motivations of others, I should disclose my own reasons for writing about this case. When the Supreme Court case decision was published in 2007, my first reaction was to question why white parents would be selfish enough to tear down something that had changed the lives of millions of children across the country for the better, including mine. The era of desegregation corresponded with the largest leaps in black achievement in the history of American public education. Researchers had documented that desegregation held significant benefits for blacks, and no downsides for whites.

Like many families, white and black, mine had been deeply affected by the desegregation of the nation's schools. My grandmother volunteered to join the first group of white teachers assigned to the all-black inner-city schools of Oklahoma in the 1960s, where she spent the rest of her twenty-year teaching career. Her daughter, my mother, worked as a social worker at Samuel Coleridge-Taylor Elementary, an inner-city school in downtown Louisville, and also in the white, working-class South End, where she witnessed firsthand the upheaval and violence that busing wrought in its early years.

As for myself, I boarded a bus in my middle-class subdivision in Louisville's suburbs in second grade to attend the same school where my mother had worked a decade earlier, Coleridge-Taylor Elementary. The school was next door to one of the city's poorest housing projects, across the street from Central High School. Coleridge-Taylor was built like a prison, with narrow slits for windows and a tall fence around it. Fifteen years earlier, before busing, the students assigned there were all black. In the aftermath of busing, the school was transformed. By the 1980s, Coleridge-Taylor had installed an excellent Advance Program, Louisville's version of a gifted and talented track, with experienced and enthusiastic teachers. But throughout my twelve years in the Louisville public schools, there were never more than two black students in any of my classes, a pattern that was repeated across the city.[3]

After the Supreme Court ruling, I traveled back to my hometown to hear reactions from black and white residents, and to learn about the earlier case that had brought it about. For the most part, it was not that the black activists opposed racial integration. Several saw it as a highly desirable goal. What they opposed was how desegregation had so often worked as a one-way exchange, and the lack of concern about how the loss of their schools and their voice might affect their community. They wanted equal outcomes for black children and they also wanted equal power over the schools and over the content and trajectory of their children's education—something they argued that racial integration in the schools never produced. Desegregation had been framed as a way to make up for what black people lacked. They wanted recognition that the African American community also had something to add to American society, that their culture had strengths, not just weaknesses.

I was struck, as I listened to their criticisms of busing, at how similar their complaints were to the frustrations parents expressed with the current set of education reforms: the charter schools and accountability systems that replaced desegregation. As the era of desegregation ended, black communities across the nation were once again facing unilateral school closings and mass firings of black teachers. Many felt disenfranchised, wondering whether reformers cared about their own vision for their children's education. Some took to the streets in protest. Others filed lawsuits.

In the end, the dissatisfaction with the way desegregation was implemented—among both whites and blacks—toppled it. In the case of black parents, they wanted more from their schools than just test score gains. The story of Central High School in Louisville, and why black community members valued it so much that they helped overturn a half century of school desegregation, is not just a history lesson. It's also a message to education reformers today.

I

The Letters

Chapter 1

The letter Dionne Hopson had been waiting for came on August 15, 1996.[1] The oppressive heat of the Kentucky summer had lifted. School started in a week. On 28th Street in Louisville, the sounds of August in the West End—the bounce of basketballs in the abandoned lot next door, old ladies passing along the gossip from their front porches—would soon be replaced with the chatter of schoolchildren converging on Maupin Elementary across the alleyway behind her house. It was an old frame two-story, painted white, with a weedy front lawn and a small front porch—bigger than the shotgun houses down the block to the south, but smaller than the stately Victorians in various states of decay to the north. In these last days of summer, waiting for the mailman, Dionne found it hard to relax.

When the first letter arrived, back in May, Dionne had felt confident. It was from Central High School, the school she had dreamed of attending since middle school. Signed by Central's principal, the letter assured her that she was in the running to enter one of Central's magnet academies in law, business, computers, or medicine. They were the only such programs in the city, and out of 600 applicants, the school had chosen her. True, it put her on a waiting list, but she had excellent grades and the list was relatively short, only 107 students.[2] She hadn't thought twice about the part of the letter that explained the reason for the waitlist: "Jefferson County Public Schools policy is to keep all schools within racial compliance. No school can have a population more than 42 percent African American."[3]

Dionne picked up the pile of mail and flipped through, stopping at the envelope labeled with the rainbow logo of the Jefferson County Public Schools. The letter was addressed to her mother, Gwendolyn Hopson, but Dionne couldn't wait. She never opened her mother's mail, but this letter was about her. She tore it open. And then she read it several times. "Many students are still unable to attend Central High School . . . in an effort to provide a viable alternative placement . . . indicate if you would like this second choice."[4]

Central was Dionne's first and second choice. She had been daydreaming about her first day of high school for nearly three years. A year before the application was due, Dionne began writing her admissions essay and compiling letters of recommendation for Central's selective magnet program. She wanted to be a lawyer, and she was convinced Central High School's law magnet program was the ticket to her dream career. Dionne didn't know many lawyers, or what applying to law school entailed. But she had long been told she had the argumentative temperament that would make her perfect for the job.

Her mother was a cashier at AutoZone with a degree from the local community college and her father, who had divorced her mother and moved in with another woman a couple years earlier, worked the line at Louisville's General Electric factory. The people in her neighborhood were poor; many lived on welfare. But at Central, Dionne believed she would find her way to the next step. She called out to her mom as the tears of bitter disappointment began to fall.

———————

Dionne was accustomed to getting what she wanted. She was the youngest of five children, the rest of them boys. At age four, her brother Dejuan had jealously guarded his chubby-cheeked baby sister. "She's *my* baby," the little boy scolded admiring strangers who approached to coo at her. Her father, Thurman, doted on her, putting aside money from his GE paycheck so Dionne could have new clothes from Sears. Her brothers shared rooms in their modest white frame house on 28th Street, but Dionne had her own, filled with toys. Before she could walk, her uncles often dropped by the house to pick her up and plunk her on a blanket by the basketball court, where they could watch over her and show her off. Time with her mother, Gwen, was often spent shopping—Gwen wanted to make sure Dionne never felt the sting of the poverty that surrounded them. But in second grade, Dionne was removed from her sheltered life.

Under the desegregation policy of the Jefferson County Public Schools, which included Louisville and its suburbs, Dionne was assigned to an elementary school twelve miles to the south, in a white working-class village called Fairdale. Every morning for the next seven years, Dionne's mother shook her awake before dawn to catch the bus for the hour-long ride. On most mornings, she whined, argued, and stalled as long as possible. At age eight, Dionne was still a tiny girl, but she made up for it with her stubbornness. The view of the neighborhood elementary school from their windows added fuel to her griping. For first grade, Dionne had crossed through their yard to Catalpa Street to attend Maupin Elementary. Why should she have to travel to the outer reaches of the county when a school sat a few steps from their back door?

Dionne, her family said, got her strong will and strong voice from her mother. Arguments between them were frequent, and they were not for the fainthearted. Gwen's deep voice, trained from years singing in the church choir, dominated a room even when she wasn't annoyed. Yet Gwen's fierceness often dissolved for her daughter. She had always had a soft spot for Dionne, who was encouraged by the sympathy she detected in her mother's face.

Gwen's childhood had been similar to Dionne's—seven brothers protected her from most of childhood's difficulties. Girls didn't tease her and only the bravest boys asked her out. Her mother, who ran a home for orphans and foster children out of an old Victorian on Catalpa, buttressed the defensive dome surrounding her. When they shopped downtown or in their neighborhood, Parkland, her mother didn't explain why they couldn't go in the stores with the pretty mannequins except to say simply, "We're not allowed." When they walked to the back section of a diner to eat or to order takeaway at a lunch counter, the staff greeted Gwen's mother by name, as a cherished customer. Gwen never thought about the segregation that prevented them from sitting down or from taking a seat by the window. The boundaries between black and white that Jim Crow imposed on their lives didn't register, partly because in the 1950s, when Gwen went to elementary school in Parkland, suburban flight hadn't emptied the city of its white residents. Most of the students in her classes were white.

She had attended Maupin Elementary herself in the 1950s, walking a block from the three-story house where she grew up on Catalpa. Since she had attended, the school district had replaced the building with a modern new facility. Gwen was incensed that her daughter was forced to go to school an hour away when there was a brand-new school next door. She felt a pang each morning as she nudged her youngest out of bed and endured her arguments, but she never let Dionne skip school. Gwen wouldn't allow her daughter to miss out on her education. Every day, Gwen was out the door with the two youngest of her five children, Dionne and Dejuan, by 6:30 a.m., and she waited with them on the corner until the bus arrived and took them away to Fairdale.

After the bus picked them up, it circled through the shabby shotguns of Parkland and the Cotter Homes, a rundown housing project nearby. Children stood on corners loaded down with backpacks, expectantly holding their parents' hands. Once the bus was full, it rumbled away from Parkland's familiar streets, with their Baptist churches and fastidiously painted houses fighting the decay around them as well as those that had succumbed to graffiti and rot. The fastest route took them along the ring expressway, which passed through Shively, once a stronghold of white resistance to busing. From the expressway, Shively's small bungalows were hidden amid the trees. To the north of their route sat Churchill Downs; the storied racetrack's elegant white spires contrasted with the gritty urban neighborhood around them. Next they passed the acres of parking lots and bland hotel buildings surrounding the airport and fairgrounds. Finally, they entered the South End. Low windowless factory buildings and industrial parks gave way to flat patches of farmland. Stalled in the traffic going the opposite direction were commuters and buses filled with white children.

Dionne's bus exited onto an old two-lane highway that dipped and wound toward the ridgeline along the far southern edge of Jefferson County, which encompassed the city of Louisville and most of its suburbs. Trailer parks and vinyl-sided farmhouses sat back from the road. The traffic, mostly pickup trucks and rust-pocked Pontiacs, was light. Less than a mile from the county border was Dionne's school, Coral Ridge Elementary.

In 1989, on her first day at Coral Ridge in second grade, Dionne felt panicky as she watched the scenery changes through the bus window. The frilly, matching outfit picked out by her mother did not cheer her up—she cried when her mother waved good-bye, cried harder at the sight of tears on her mother's cheeks, then sniffled all the way to her new school. The alien landscape of Fairdale sparked a renewed outburst of tears as the bus slowed and turned into the school parking lot.

Beverly Goodwin, the principal of Coral Ridge, was ready for the forlorn band of youngsters climbing off the downtown buses.[5] Goodwin had greeted them each year for more than a decade, since the city's desegregation plan went into effect in 1975. The sight of her generally struck awe into her new charges. Dionne stopped crying when she saw the tall, elegantly dressed woman with a halo of bright blond hair and an equally bright smile. Many of the new students had already met her: Goodwin tried to ease the transition for the downtown students by holding meetings in their neighborhoods over the summer so that parents would be comforted by knowing who would be watching over their children and so the children would be comforted on the first day by a familiar face. After being promoted from guidance counselor to principal in the mid-1980s, Goodwin outfitted her wood-paneled office with stuffed animals and a worn-in couch that gave it the feel of a cozy living room. She made the rounds of all the classrooms most days, encouraging students and teachers in her Nashville twang. Soon Dionne began to settle in. Although she made it a morning ritual to protest the long trip to school, by her second year at Coral Ridge she was thriving.

Fairdale was a relic of Jefferson County's rural past that seemed more closely tied to Kentucky's distant Appalachian regions than Louisville's cosmopolitan center a few miles away. The town was an old farming village located next to an area known as the Wet Woods, once a hangout for bandits at the turn of the century.[6] It was all white and about as poor as Dionne's own all-black inner-city neighborhood. About three-quarters of the school's children had their lunches subsidized, and there was a high concentration of students with special needs—learning disabilities, emotional problems, and/or behavior issues. The school offered no classes for gifted and talented children, or even honors classes for a lower tier of high achievers. The school didn't enroll enough children from the wealthier families who generally demanded such programs. Yet Coral Ridge's test scores tended to be high for a school with concentrated poverty, and by fourth grade, Dionne stood out as particularly bright and driven.[7]

Dionne was talkative, sometimes too talkative according to her teachers, but she was also quick to learn, especially when it came to reading. She bonded with her classmates and teachers on camping trips to the nearby state forest, where Goodwin's husband was a ranger. By fifth grade, Dionne thought of Goodwin as a "mother away from home." Dionne stopped by the principal's office often to say hello. Sometimes she came in leading Gwen, who tried to visit the school as often as possible despite the distance.

Gwen was skeptical of Coral Ridge—she got a bad feeling from the white teachers, who, she believed, treated black children differently—but she tried to hide her opinions from her daughter. When it was time for Dionne to graduate from elementary school, after fifth grade, she didn't want to leave. In a note on her last report card from Coral Ridge, Dionne's teachers wrote that she "often escaped into a book," that her writing was "wonderful," and that she had "great potential that will be developed in her middle and high school years." At the bottom of the paper was a note from the principal: "I can't believe you're leaving us. You've been a joy and I'll miss you. Good luck in middle school, love, Mrs. G."[8]

Dionne had her own high expectations for herself. She believed her debating skills and her high marks in reading and writing made her a shoo-in for Central's law program, already her goal by sixth grade. But first she had to endure another three years of early-morning travel to Robert Frost Middle School, located in a thin peninsula of Jefferson County that jutted south along the Ohio River. The school was even deeper in the South End than Coral Ridge. Demographically, Frost was similar in most ways to Dionne's elementary school. Academically, the school didn't surpass the low expectations for a school with so much poverty, both white and black.[9]

The school was located at the end of a street in a subdivision of identical one-story houses the size of double-wide trailers. The blocks of homes were hemmed in by railroad tracks on one side and the Ohio River on the other. Nearby, Dixie Highway, the South End's main drag, led to the army airfield at Fort Knox. It was lined with fast food outlets, bait shops, and gun stores. Steep, forested hills surrounded Coral Ridge; at Frost, the skeletal skyline of the city's power plant loomed over the campus. All day, giant cooling towers belched clouds of white smoke into the sky and trains roared past on the way to drop off loads of coal. Levies hid a view of the river and an industrial waste pond a few hundred feet from the schoolyard.

More ominous to Dionne were the packs of white teenagers that roamed the subdivision's streets after school. During her years at Frost, Dionne ran track and often stayed after school for practice. To get home, she and a small group of other black students involved in after-school activities waited for a city bus headed downtown. Standing on a corner near the school, they were easy targets for high school boys cruising by in low-riding cars, screaming curses from their rolled-down windows. The one that bothered Dionne the most was, "Go back to your country, niggers!" She wondered where they thought she came from.

More than anything during her time at Frost, Dionne needed a haven where she would be loved and cared for. Her parents divorced when she was in middle school. Her father, Thurman, moved across town to Newburg, a black suburban neighborhood near the GE plant. Dionne remained close to her dad, but her mother loathed Thurman's new girlfriend. The conflict was devastating for Dionne. The only thing that might have hurt more was losing him for good. She began dreaming of going to Central around the time her dad left.

The magnet law program wasn't the only reason Dionne wanted to go to Central. It was a five-minute drive from her house in Parkland and, more important, the school was Louisville's traditionally black public high school. In the 1950s, Central had been an organizing ground for Louisville's civil rights movement and cultivated many of the city's leading black figures, from lawyers and intellectuals to boxing legend Muhammad Ali. It was the city's only black public high school until the 1960s. Tales of basketball and football victories from its early years, and the elaborate parades that accompanied them, were still repeated in Louisville barbershops decades later. The booming voice of its head disciplinarian for fifteen years, Maude Brown Porter, haunted Louisville's black senior citizens half a century after they had graduated.

Central was also the alma mater of Dionne's parents. Dionne grew up hearing stories from Gwen and Thurman about the legendary high school at West Chestnut Street and Ninth. Gwen could still conjure the mix of smells that met her each day as she filed to class—pressed hair from the cosmetology department, sawdust from the carpentry shop, and motor oil from the auto mechanic garage. She could hear the dignified click of Mrs. Metcalf's four-inch heels on the tile floors, see the grimace on her face as she glanced over Gwen's math homework and scolded her to study harder.

The school was all black when Gwen graduated in 1969, but she didn't notice the deprivations of segregation—the shabby secondhand books and aging facilities. What Gwen remembered was the fierce love of her teachers. It was their life's mission to help their students succeed in life.

To Gwen, this was the caring that she believed was missing from white-dominated schools like Coral Ridge and Frost.

Gwen had never thought much of desegregation as a cause, although as a child, she had grown up in a mostly white neighborhood. Her mother had inherited money from her husband, who had worked for the Louisville & Nashville Railroad, and after he died she moved her family to the house on Catalpa, two blocks from Parkland's town center. They were the second black family to move onto the street.

After they arrived, the number of blacks grew quickly as whites fled to new neighborhoods in the east and south. The white congregation of the Baptist church on the corner sold the building to a black congregation. In Parkland's quaint business district, the shops that had thrived as an alternative to downtown—the pharmacy, the bakery, and the A&P—stayed longer. Eventually, the Masonic hall was taken over by the African American division, the Prince Hall Masons. As the 1950s progressed, a few of the businesses closed, and some were taken over by black owners. To the north of Gwen's house, Virginia Avenue's Queen Anne and Victorian homes were subdivided, and swaths of buildings in Little Africa, a former black shantytown on the outskirts of the neighborhood, were razed to make way for housing projects. The Cotter Homes that replaced them in 1953 became known as the worst projects in the city.

The schools Gwen attended became increasingly black. When she started at Central High School in the mid-1960s, her classmates were all African American. In 1968, Martin Luther King Jr. was assassinated and the race riots sweeping the nation came to Louisville. Gwen was a junior in high school when the Black Panthers held a rally in Parkland. A few of the men came knocking on her mother's door and asked her to put up a sign of support in the family's window, but she slammed the door in their faces. Gwen wasn't allowed to leave the house for days. Instead, she watched on television as her neighborhood ignited in fury and flames. Two blocks away, shops burned and looters rampaged. When she finally left the house, she walked into a wasteland. Owners had abandoned their ravaged stores in Parkland and most never came back.[10] The business district stayed boarded up for nearly two decades, and many of the black middle class left, too, encouraged by the relaxation of housing segregation in the suburbs.

Watching her neighborhood disintegrate in the wake of Martin Luther King's death left Gwen angry. She looked around at her once close-knit community and saw a desolate ghetto full of strangers. She didn't understand where their fury came from, but she saw what the turbulence of the 1960s had done to her home. She had not thought much about racism before, but now she knew to look for it. She moved away from Parkland when she got married, but when her grandmother died and left her a house on 28th Street in the early 1980s, she came back.

By then urban renewal had come to the neighborhood, but to Gwen, everything seemed worse.[11] There were new apartment buildings, but Parkland's shops were still mostly boarded up. The streets were filled with idle people—gang members and hustlers and the elderly. The well-dressed church people came to the Baptist church on the corner and then left.

Gwen blamed the decline of the neighborhood partly on a school desegregation system that sent the neighborhood's children out to all parts of the city. She believed it undermined Parkland's already fragile community. In the 1950s, the neighborhood elementary school had been housed in an old brick building on the east side of Catalpa. Then it was called simply Parkland Elementary, after the neighborhood. A few years after the school district began busing in white students, a new building was constructed on the west side of the street. Perhaps to erase the uncomfortable memories conjured up by the name Parkland, the school's name was changed in 1985 to honor Milburn Maupin, Jefferson County's first African American central office administrator.[12]

After Parkland was looted in the riots, Gwen found security and comfort among her peers and teachers at Central. After what she had seen, a black school, where children would be insulated from racism and hate, made sense to her. Dionne's experiences at Frost showed her that nothing much had changed in forty years. When Dionne decided on Central as her first choice for high school, Gwen was relieved that her daughter would soon be enveloped in Central's protective armor.

Dionne's fixation on Central gathered force as her family fell apart. Not long after her father moved away, her worst fear came true. After years of stooping over refrigerator doors and washing machines as they slid down the line at the GE plant, Thurman was diagnosed with spinal cancer. He continued working at the factory until a month before his death. For Dionne, watching him spiral into dementia drained her of the spunk her teachers had praised her for in elementary school. After he died, Dionne, once the tiny girl with the big personality, became quiet and withdrawn.

Around the same time, a favorite aunt died suddenly of an aneurysm. The unfairness of the double tragedy was almost unbearable to Dionne. Gwen felt frantic as her daughter grew more distant. She didn't know how to help her, and she was grieving, too. Her older boys were struggling in high school, and Gwen—a housewife for years—now had to support all of them. It would get easier, both mother and daughter felt, once Dionne reached high school and finally came home.

To get into Central would not be easy. For seventy-five years, it had been the default school for all of Louisville's black students. But by 1995, as Dionne was preparing to apply, the school had been transformed into a selective magnet school under the leadership of a new principal, Harold Fenderson. The change had been implemented ostensibly to draw in more white students and to shed Central's reputation as a black school.

Fenderson, a Baptist preacher in his spare time, aggressively promoted the school and courted new partnerships with local businesses and universities to augment the school's programs, but his efforts seemed to be back-firing, at least when it came to attracting more whites.[13] Many of the career tracks focused on preparing for jobs, rather than for college. The business magnet included classes on managing a Super America convenience store, a Kentucky Fried Chicken franchise, and a bank branch. The medical program focused on nursing, veterinary science, and dentistry. The offerings did not necessarily evoke the sorts of careers that might draw elite white suburbanites whose sights were set on graduate degrees and six-figure salaries.

And most Louisvillians still thought of Central as the black school. The flow of white applications for Central remained anemic, but enthusiasm for Central among black students grew and applications poured in.[14] Under Louisville's desegregation plan, which was still in place twenty years after it had been implemented by court order in 1975, Central had to keep its percentage of black students under 42 percent. As fewer white students applied, more black students were turned away.

Dionne wasn't worried about her chances. It didn't occur to her that she might be turned down. She could already picture herself walking through the hushed hallways described to her by her parents and reading legal texts that would propel her toward a high-powered career in law. The thought that she would be able to sleep past sunrise on schooldays for the first time since second grade made the vision sweeter. Her mother called a church acquaintance employed at Central for advice. They attended a school fair, where they visited only Central's booth. She sent her application materials months early just to be safe. When Frost Middle School mistakenly sent Dionne's seventh-grade transcripts to their house instead of Central, Gwen wrote an urgent letter to the high school explaining the error to make sure it wouldn't affect Dionne's chances.[15]

The day Dionne received her rejection letter, Gwen began making phone calls. She called family members and the woman she knew from church who worked at Central, but there was nothing anyone could do. Another letter arrived a day later, this one from Pleasure Ridge Park High School, Dionne's assigned home school, a forty-five-minute bus ride away in the South End. The letter invited them to attend an orientation, but it had arrived late. The orientation had taken place earlier that week.[16]

Dionne was despondent. Gwen was angry. On August 16, the *Louisville Courier-Journal* ran an article about a protest at Central. Around a dozen black parents and community activists had gathered at the school to rally against the racial guidelines. Their picket signs read, "Let our children choose," and one protester told the paper that they were there to challenge a system that "always put the burden on African Americans."[17]

Not long after, Gwen received a phone call. The activists were meeting again to organize another protest at Central and Dionne had been identified as one of the students who had been denied admission. Parents who thought their children had been unfairly treated were invited to come and express themselves. Gwen promised that she and Dionne would be there.

Chapter 2

Ja'Mekia Stoner's first rejection letter had come a year earlier, in the summer of 1995.[1] It was stamped with the Jefferson County Public Schools logo and addressed to her mother, Jacquelyn, who had just arrived home on the bus from her job at a nursing home in time for the mail. The West End was steamy after days of rain, and a rambunctious crowd of cousins and neighborhood children was cooped up on the front porch that served as their living room in the summer.

Ja'Mekia and her little brother, La'Quinn, spent summer days throwing water balloons from the bathroom window at their cousins outside, playing ball in the street or, if no one was around to play with, hunkered down with a book in one of the shabby but comfortable blue chairs on the porch. Curfew was late, but they were confined to a range within sight of the house. The pulse of activity on the block contrasted with the shuttered and silent campus of Shawnee High School down the street. The truants and gang members who had spent school days lingering around its periphery were elsewhere for the season. Jacquelyn picked up the mail and rifled through to the letter with the rainbow logo. She slipped it open and read it to herself.

Jacquelyn decided not to show it to Ja'Mekia—she wanted to break the news more gently. She explained that it looked like there wasn't enough room for her at Central High School that year. Ja'Mekia was on a waitlist, but she would probably have to choose another school. The explanation did not satisfy Ja'Mekia. Central was a big school with plenty of space and she was in the Advance Program. She had worked so hard to ace her courses, usually as the only black student in class. What more did they want? Jacquelyn tried to comfort her daughter as she began to cry, and then to argue.

Jacquelyn was rail thin with a soft, tentative voice and an air of fragility. Ja'Mekia was stockier and more assertive, a poised debater who spoke in a precise but rapid-fire diction that could easily drown out her mother's more hesitant drawl. Jacquelyn didn't want to take the school's side in this fight. She didn't want her daughter to think she wasn't good enough. Ja'Mekia's grades were fine, she explained quietly, it was just that she was black. Ja'Mekia began to cry again, and Jacquelyn joined in.

Like Dionne, Ja'Mekia had attended a school in her neighborhood only briefly—for Head Start and first grade. Then the Jefferson County school system assigned her and La'Quinn to Eisenhower Elementary in the South End. When the children were young, Jacquelyn moved the family often, and each new home meant a new school zone. The family had most recently landed at a rented three-bedroom house at 41st Street and Market, near Shawnee High. The neighborhood had been a solidly white middle-class enclave in the 1950s, but its bungalows and cottages had gradually been taken over by middle-class blacks in the 1960s. By the 1990s, the neighborhood was home to the working poor. It resembled other clusters of once dignified but now decaying housing stock in the West End. The one difference was that the neighborhood's children were paired with the East End, not the South, under the city's busing plan. For the final grades of elementary school and for middle school, Ja'Mekia and La'Quinn were bused to the far eastern corner of the county, the wealthiest area of the city.

Norton Elementary, where Ja'Mekia attended fourth and fifth grade, was located across the road from the Standard Country Club and less than a mile from the lush campus of one of Louisville's most prestigious private schools, Kentucky Country Day. Ja'Mekia woke up at 5:30 in the morning to catch her first bus to the county depot, where school buses from across the county exchanged students. There, Ja'Mekia switched to another bus that headed past the downtown skyscrapers to the new brick four-squares and mini-mansions of East Louisville. In sixth grade, she was assigned to Kammerer Middle School, a short trip from Norton. Like Norton, Kammerer's black enrollment hovered below 25 percent, close to the minimum allowed under the desegregation plan.[2]

Ja'Mekia did well at Norton, and even better at Kammerer. Jacquelyn had her tested for advanced placement, and Ja'Mekia passed easily. At first, Ja'Mekia was nervous about being the only black student in most of her advanced classes. Louisville required its schools to maintain enrollments close to the actual percentage of blacks in the city—30 percent. Nearly all schools fell between 40 percent black on the high end of the spectrum to 20 percent on the low end.[3] But programs within the schools, like the Advance Program and special education classes, were exempted from the racial guidelines. The Advance Program—Louisville's version of an accelerated curriculum for students deemed to be "gifted"—was around 11 percent black. Ja'Mekia was afraid of being thrust into a white world, of being labeled the "black white girl" by her friends from the neighborhood. So what? her mother responded. Ja'Mekia stayed in the advanced classes.

Jacquelyn may have had a soft, tentative manner, but it disguised a steely determination to push herself and her children ahead. She encouraged her children, but she did not indulge them, particularly when it came to school. When La'Quinn passed first grade without knowing the alphabet or how to spell his own name, Jacquelyn rode the public bus to his school to talk to the administrators. Told he could catch up with his peers in second grade, she politely but firmly demanded that her son be held back. Assuming he could master two years' worth of school in one year was absurd, she argued, and letting him pass would most likely set him up to fall further behind each year. The school relented and let La'Quinn repeat first grade. And when the school system notified her that Ja'Mekia and La'Quinn would be bused to Fairdale, she moved the family to the rented house on 41st Street.

Jacquelyn's wariness about Fairdale came from firsthand experience. She had been assigned to Fairdale High School as a tenth grader in 1975, the first year of busing. Until then, she had attended schools near her house on Vermont Avenue, in the far West End near the river. She could have transferred voluntarily to a white school under the city's early version of a desegregation plan but, like most black students, she chose her neighborhood school, Shawnee. The school had once been all white, but as suburbanization accelerated, the school became mostly black. Unlike Central, however, Shawnee was never completely segregated. Many whites, most of them poor, still clustered in Portland, a neighborhood that hugged the West End's northern edge along the river.[4] They were the ones who couldn't afford to leave, even when cheap mortgages were handed out in the 1940s and 1950s. Jacquelyn's best friend growing up was white—one of the Portland holdouts. The two lost touch after tenth grade, however, when Jacquelyn was sent away.

On September 4, 1975, Jacquelyn boarded the bus to Fairdale, only vaguely aware of the decades of demonstrations and legal battles that had brought her there. But shortly after the bus turned off the expressway and headed into the country, the high stakes and emotional turmoil of the civil rights movement came vividly to life. A meadow in front of the school was filled with an angry mob waving picket signs and nooses. They screamed obscenities and aimed rocks and sticks at the windows of the school buses.[5] The welcome inside the school was only slightly warmer. In several classes, Jacquelyn sat alone as the only black student, a target for spitballs and whispered name-calling that she swore the teacher heard but ignored.

At the end of her first day, Jacquelyn climbed onto her assigned bus to head home. The other buses turned onto the highway and passed the crowd, but her bus, the last in line, stalled a few seconds too long before pulling away. The crowd surged. In a matter of seconds, angry whites surrounded them and clamored at the doors and windows. The bus driver held onto the door handle with both hands to keep them out. Frustrated, the crowd threw rocks at the windows, and then began to rock the bus. The students cried and cowered for over an hour before police dispersed the crowd and they were able to drive home. Jacquelyn's new pair of sailor-style jeans and flowered tank top, chosen especially to make a good impression on the first day of school, were smeared with grime from the floor.[6]

The next day, Jacquelyn's mother ignored her pleas to stay home. "You'll be all right," she said, "but call me if you need me." Jacquelyn boarded a bus to Fairdale every school day for the next three years, enduring taunting and harassment. Her mother listened to her reports after school each day, but the response was always the same: "You'll be alright." When the weather turned cold, white students rolled snowballs with sharp rocks embedded in them to throw at the black students as they passed through the hallways. The black students learned to travel in groups of at least five. Many of the boys were suspended or expelled for fighting. Black students didn't play sports or participate in clubs, and Jacquelyn did not attend her senior prom. She saw what Fairdale was like in the daytime. There was no way she was going there after dark.

Jacquelyn graduated in 1979 and vowed never to return to Fairdale. She certainly wasn't going to let Ja'Mekia and La'Quinn attend school there. But like her own mother, Jacquelyn was not the sort to hide ugliness from her children. She told Ja'Mekia and La'Quinn about Fairdale when they were young, and the story became family lore.

She also didn't shy from telling her children that becoming a single mother at the age of twenty-one had been her single biggest mistake. Her children were her life—she loved them intensely—but she repeated often that she had made herself a hard bed. Being a single mother meant she never went to college. Instead, she worked long hours at menial jobs to earn enough to get off welfare. For several years of Ja'Mekia and La'Quinn's childhood, she woke up before dawn each day to take a two-hour bus ride to the University of Louisville's suburban campus to work as a janitor. The money she earned was just enough to pay for rent, food, clothes, and the occasional splurge on popsicles from the ice cream truck. These were the consequences of her mistakes. She repeated often to her children that they had better not make the same ones. She expected them to do better, and being black and poor was no excuse. Her mother's sayings had become hers: Life wasn't always sunshine, but if you work hard, you'll be alright.

Jacquelyn's memories of Fairdale left her with more than a few misgivings about busing, but her children's experiences in the suburbs changed her mind. Alert teachers discovered La'Quinn had a learning disability, and they pushed him to overcome it. He never became an A student, but by the end of middle school, he was able to keep up. Ja'Mekia overcame her fear of being mocked as the "black white girl" and flourished both academically and socially. She went canoeing and camping with white friends and occasionally spent the night at slumber parties in the suburbs. By age twelve, Ja'Mekia decided she wanted to be a lawyer, and that Central was the best place for her to fulfill her dream. Jacquelyn was thrilled that her children seemed headed for a life better than her own.

Before the letter came, Ja'Mekia had rarely thought about race beyond her mother's stories and her nervousness over joining the advanced classes. Her mother's Fairdale story was dramatic, but it was a distant legend, an abstraction. To be told that the only reason she couldn't go to Central was because she was black was a shock. It seemed deeply unfair to her, as if she had traveled back in time to the Jim Crow days she had read about in school, when blacks weren't allowed to do anything. Worse, by the time the letter arrived, it was too late to apply for one of the city's other magnet schools, which tended to have the best reputations in the city.

Ja'Mekia was partly hurt, partly furious. She could try for a spot in a mediocre, nonmagnet school in the suburbs—probably in the South End— and face another four years of early mornings and long days. If she did nothing, she would be sent to Shawnee, down the street from her house. The school had a lingering reputation as a place for hopeless cases—the drug dealers in training and future dropouts—despite efforts at a turn-around in the early 1990s.[7] There was no Advance Program, so Ja'Mekia would have to return to regular classes. But Ja'Mekia decided she might as well stay close to home.[8]

Jacquelyn knew Shawnee was no place for Ja'Mekia, and she was frantic as she watched her strong, confident daughter deflate before her eyes. She made phone calls to Central, but she was rebuffed. She went in person, and she was turned away. She and her daughter still had hope, however. The letter had said that students not accepted their freshman year would be first in line the following year for any open slots at Central. That fall, Ja'Mekia applied for Central and also Fern Creek, an East End school with a com-munications magnet where several of her cousins went. Ja'Mekia wasn't interested in communications, but she figured some of the skills would be useful in law.

The letter did not explain that slots for black students rarely opened up after ninth grade since Central had trouble not only attracting white stu-dents but also retaining them. The school's administration and many of its teachers were interested in maintaining Central's legacy as a black school, and many white students, apparently, didn't feel welcome. In the summer of 1996, Jacquelyn received another letter. Central had refused Ja'Mekia again. Soon after, the story about a protest at Central ran in the newspaper. "Suddenly the system has become more important than the children," one of the protesters told the paper.[9]

The argument made sense to Ja'Mekia and her mother. The protest-ers were quoted in the newspaper as saying they would be meeting again soon to plan more action. Parents whose children had been turned away because they were black were encouraged to attend. Jacquelyn was curious. She couldn't afford a babysitter, so on the day of the meeting, she brought Ja'Mekia and La'Quinn along with her.

Chapter 3

The protesters called themselves Citizens for Equitable Assignment to School Environment (CEASE). The group had fewer than a dozen members. But those few people were already shaking the fragile foundations of racial harmony in Louisville. The city sat on the southern banks of the Ohio River, once the last barrier to freedom for slaves running north, but many white Louisvillians preferred to think of their city as northern at heart, more Ohio than Mississippi.

True, segregation had been enforced in schools, housing, train stations, buses, hotels, department stores, and restaurants, but the practitioners of Louisville's version of Jim Crow believed their system to be kinder than its counterparts in the Deep South. The Confederate flag might occasionally appear as a bumper sticker on a South End pickup truck, but Louisville was also a place where white Southern Baptists—staunch opponents of integration elsewhere—had once hosted Martin Luther King Jr.[1] The school system, the most racially integrated in the nation by the 1990s, was the bedrock of white Louisvillians' conviction that their city was racially enlightened.

Black Louisvillians were more skeptical about white good-will. Louisville was the city where a black family had been bombed when it tried to move into a white neighborhood in 1954. It was the city where rioters tried to outdo Boston's anti-busing zeal in the 1970s. The word *darkies* wasn't excised from the state song, "My Old Kentucky Home," sung every year before the Derby at Churchill Downs, until 1986.[2] In Louisville in the 1990s, whites and blacks who mixed at work and school parted ways each evening to go home to neighborhoods nearly as segregated as they had been a century earlier.[3]

Black residents who had been around in the 1950s scoffed at the idea that the city's discrimination against blacks had been more benign than elsewhere. One called the city a "bastion of polite racism."[4] Yet many were also proud of their city's progress. Yes, there were still many remnants of racism. But on most measures—test scores, graduation rates, numbers going to college—black students were far better off than they had been in the days before busing, and black leaders pushed back against occasional efforts to roll back pieces of the desegregation plan.[5] So far they had held the line, and most blacks in Louisville backed their efforts: When the school superintendent floated a proposal to end mandatory busing in 1991, a poll found that 70 percent of African Americans in Louisville disapproved and wanted busing to stay.[6]

But in the other 30 percent were those who measured how far blacks had come, and wondered how anyone could be so foolish as to call it progress. In 1996, CEASE, the group protesting Central's admissions policies, became their voice and their battle cry.

The group was led by a motley collection of outsiders and gadflies. One of the most outspoken was Carman Weathers, a former gym teacher and football coach. He was also a regular at school board meetings, and his rants against racial discrimination in the schools were occasionally published in the op-ed section of the *Courier-Journal*.

Weathers had begun his teaching career at a traditionally black school in the West End that was closed in the wake of busing so that black students could be sent to the suburbs.[7] He moved to another school, also a traditionally black institution, which was closed shortly after. Weathers ended up at Buechel, one of two alternative schools for children with discipline problems—the only schools in the system that were allowed to be majority black.

With his Don King haircut and beefy football player's build, Weathers made an odd companion for his fellow graduate of the Central class of 1953, Robert Douglas, a lanky art professor in the Pan-African Studies Department at the University of Louisville.[8] Douglas had been a community organizer in Louisville's housing projects in the 1960s before he went for his doctorate, and spent his free time painting and crafting sculptures of black nudes in a loft downtown. But the two agreed on most things, especially when it came to the dilemma of race and how to solve it. Like Weathers, Douglas believed blacks needed to reexamine their desire for integration and turn inward to uplift the race. Their main differences lay in style: Weathers had a tendency to turn friendly dinner party conversations into heated political debates, Douglas had a more Socratic way of making a point, asking questions that circled around his argument indirectly.

Although Weathers and Douglas were generally dismissed by leaders in the black community as outdated relics of the 1970s Black Power era, school officials had invited both men to join a committee of community groups convened in 1992 to monitor a new version of the desegregation plan—a gesture Weathers and Douglas assumed was a strategy to neutralize their criticism. If that was the plan, it didn't work. The two men became more disillusioned with and outspoken about the school system the longer they served, particularly as they learned more about the state of their alma mater.

On the committee they found an ally in Fran Thomas, a petite, jovial woman who directed the Kentucky Alliance against Racist and Political Repression.[9] An army wife who had spent most of her life in the white South End military enclaves linked to Fort Knox, on the surface, Thomas wasn't the most likely pick to lead an organization founded by Anne Braden, a civil rights activist once tried for treason because of alleged Communist ties. But despite her background, Thomas had always been rebellious. In 1968, when a real estate agent tried to steer her from buying a house in an all-white subdivision, Thomas called the colonel at Fort Knox. She told him her husband wouldn't be going to Vietnam if they couldn't buy a house in the same neighborhood as the white soldiers. A few phone calls later, the house was hers. They stayed in Valley Station, where she worked as a nurse for the base and the Veterans Administration until their daughter was sent to fight in the first Gulf War.

Thomas didn't believe in the war, and she didn't want her daughter risking her life for a mission she saw as an oil grab. Thomas joined an antiwar protest soon after her daughter was deployed. Not long after, she and her husband moved out of Valley Station to the West End, away from their shocked neighbors. Energized by a new calling, she became immersed in fights against police brutality and in the debate surrounding the selection process for a new superintendent of schools.[10] (Thomas, believing the school board should hire a black superintendent, later filed a federal complaint saying the board's choice of a white man was racist.)[11] The daughter of sharecroppers in Alabama, Thomas was also a Central graduate—class of 1946. She was convinced Central had saved her from a life of hard labor and poverty. Like Weathers and Douglas, she became more agitated about the school the longer she spent on the monitoring committee.

As committee members, Weathers, Douglas, and Thomas could ask for almost any data tracked by the school system. They examined graduation rates, enrollments by race and gender, school capacities, and test scores. One number that stood out to them in particular was the decline in the student population at Central. The school could hold 1,400 students, but the enrollment in 1994 was only 1,100.[12]

Their worries were confirmed by reports from the inside. A friend of Weathers and Douglas, Riccardo X, taught black history and world civilization at Central.[13] X grew up poor in Louisville's Little Africa neighborhood in the 1960s and had planned to join the military after graduating from Male High School. As a sophomore, however, inspired by fellow Louisvillian Muhammad Ali's refusal to fight in Vietnam, X dropped out of the ROTC. He became a teacher instead. In 1975, his first year on the job, he was assigned to Southern High School in Okolona, a working-class white neighborhood and a hub of anti-busing violence. The Bittersweet Shopping Center, across the street from Southern, was a headquarters for mobs of white protesters who screamed racial epithets and threw bottles as X arrived at work each morning. As the year went on, he became more immersed in the teachings of the Black Panthers and Malcolm X, eventually abandoning his European last name.

X moved schools every couple of years until he landed at Central. There, he finally felt at home. His classroom became known around school as the BCC, the Black Cultural Center. He decorated it with kente cloth and artifacts, articles, posters, and timelines outlining black history from the early Egyptians to current events in Louisville. His students worked in teams named for ancient African civilizations and studied a homemade textbook, the X Text, that he filled with excerpts from Maya Angelou and the architect of Afrocentrism, Molefi Asante. Like Carman Weathers, Robert Douglas, and Fran Thomas, X worried that Central's slipping enrollment would give the school board a good excuse to close it.

The group's concerns were still rather amorphous until September 23, 1994, when their cause suddenly came into focus. The *Louisville Courier-Journal* printed an article on the front page of its Metro section reporting that ten black students had been removed from Central High School.[14] The percentage of black students at the school had risen to 43 percent, pushing the school out of compliance with the school system's racial guidelines, which limited black enrollment to 42 percent of a school's population. The main problem was that Central couldn't hold on to its white students. Although the school was usually able to recruit an adequate number white freshman each year, they tended to leave at an alarming rate after their first or second year. As the white numbers were depleted, the school was forced to turn away more blacks. Sending away students in the middle of the school year was a first, however. School had already been in session a month, and some of the students had already attended Central for a year.

Fran Thomas convened the first meeting of CEASE in the living room of her three-story house on 47th Street in the West End, one of the only residential blocks in Louisville that overlooked the Ohio River. The neighborhood had once housed Louisville's white elite, but now it was an enclave of aging middle-class blacks who had raised their families there in better times. Robert Douglas lived around the corner, and Weathers lived a few blocks away. Also invited was Loueva Moss, a nurse and block watch leader who had helped Thomas in a failed run for city office, and a few other neighborhood activists. Most in the group were over the age of sixty, and several were members of the same Catholic church. The first order of business was getting Weathers to quiet down so the rest could speak, but eventually everyone got a chance to talk and agree on their mission: Central, the pride of the black community, was in peril, and they must save it.

None of them had attended integrated schools, and in their experience, integration had led only to violence and disappointment. Assembled in the creaky old house poised on the edge of the Ohio's southern banks, they agreed that their principal enemy was the desegregation system that had never lived up to its promise of uplifting the black race. Mixing white and blacks students together was supposed to bring equality, but in Louisville and across the country, equality was still as elusive as ever. In their eyes, black people had not yet crossed the river to freedom, and desegregation was the chain that was holding them back.

Black students were still relegated to the worst schools; they had seen

the numbers to prove that low-performing schools such as Fairdale enrolled many more blacks than the city's top-tier magnet schools. The numbers told them that "choice," the new education reform buzzword, really
just meant choice for white students. Too few blacks could be found in
accelerated tracks such as the Advance Program, and their test scores still
lagged far behind whites. Worst of all, the one school in Louisville that
had long taken blacks from the ghetto and propelled them to success was
threatened. They were not against integration, but it always seemed to
entail compromises that hurt black interests. It no longer seemed worth
it to them.

On October 24, a month after the ten black students were forced out
of Central, the fledgling group had the chance to make its argument in
public at the monthly school board meeting. The room was packed. On
the agenda was a presentation by a professor who had studied the city's
desegregation plan and drawn up a list of suggested improvements—
among them, a proposal to allow for at least one majority black school.
But the study was pushed aside when Riccardo X, along with three of his
students, stood up to make his case. "Central's existence is now dependent
on whether white students choose to go there," X said. "And under your
rules only white students get to choose."[15]

X sat down, and an elderly man stood and began to shuffle toward the
podium. His craggy, elongated features were hollowed with age. But most
in the room recognized him. Lyman Johnson was X's predecessor as Central, for years its most radical and most beloved teacher. As a young civics
teacher at Central in the 1940s, Johnson—like X—taught an unvarnished
version of Western civilization, telling his students that he hoped "old
Leopold, that devil Belgium king, is still roasting in hell for the way he
forced black people in the Congo to bring rubber sap into the villages."[16]
Outside of school, he brought his most devoted students along with him
to lunch counter sit-ins. (Later, he would admit embarrassment that he
was never actually arrested, despite his best efforts.)[17] In 1949, Thurgood
Marshall and the NAACP sued the University of Kentucky on his behalf,
and he became the first black graduate student admitted to the state's flagship school.[18]

He had always believed deeply in integrated education. In 1956, he
accused the Louisville school superintendent of being "a cheap, peanut"
politician in a letter to the *Courier-Journal* after a desegregation plan was

enacted that led to only token racial mixing.[19] In the early 1970s, he was a plaintiff in the lawsuit that forced the city to begin its busing program, and later joined the school board to see his legal victory implemented in policy.

Johnson reached the podium and turned to face the crowd: "I feel like asking all of you to leave the room and just let me cry for a while. I just want to cry." Johnson talked about Central in the old days, reminding the room of when Central's campus had been devoid of trees. When the white students came, trees were planted. Central finally got the swimming pool it had requested thirty years earlier. Windows were replaced. New books were bought. The broken seats in the auditorium were finally fixed. It got an Advance Program and new science labs. As Johnson saw it, forced desegregation might not be the ideal way to achieve equality, but it was the only realistic one. "For 60 years, I've tried to get my people out of the cotton patch . . . and some of them are trying to get to go back to the cotton patch," he said. "And I'll tell them right to their face, they haven't got the sense God gave chickens."[20]

Johnson sat down. Riccardo X's face was impassive. Fran Thomas was up next. She was feeling a bit weak. Thomas had graduated from Central in 1946, during the time that Johnson was rising to prominence as one of the city's leading civil rights figures. Although she never sat in his classroom, Thomas, like many older Central graduates, claimed him as her teacher. Later, she had met him at political demonstrations, and now they exchanged Christmas cards every year. She made her way to the podium.

"I'm not going back to the cotton patch," she began. She was tired of black children having to bear the brunt of a busing system that had not brought them equality yet, she said. The facilities might be better, but the level of education was just as poor. "Dr. Johnson hasn't been in the schools in years. I love him. I appreciate him, but you've got to listen to us now. It's a new day."[21]

A year later, Fran Thomas's defiance would seem less shocking. Across the country, an old strain of black politics was rising to the surface once again. Black Nationalism was back. In 1995, the leader of the Nation of Islam, Louis Farrakhan, called for a new March on Washington. The black men who answered his call far outnumbered the 250,000 who attended Martin Luther King Jr.'s 1963 march.[22] Although Farrakhan was widely denounced in the mainstream media for his homophobia and anti-Semitism and dismissed as a "sect leader," to many blacks, his talk of self-help and racial independence inspired. As one housing project resident in Washington, DC, put it, when Farrakhan spoke, "Black people listen."[23] Dennis Walcott, then the president of the New York Urban League and later chancellor of New York City schools, described the march as representing "the true beliefs of blacks for years: self-determination, strengthening families."[24]

Three decades after the peak of the civil rights movement, a host of worsening social problems overshadowed black gains, including significant increases in income and educational attainment for blacks. Under Reagan, African American unemployment spiked, the wealth gap widened, and crime in inner-city neighborhoods exploded, eventually peaking in the early 1990s.[25] Black test scores stopped climbing in the mid-1980s, leaving black students still stuck far behind whites.[26] Families appeared to be on the brink of collapse. Single mothers headed nearly half of black households, up from 18 percent in 1950.[27] By the 1990s, many blacks were fed up. In the midst of all these crises, it could be hard to remember what good desegregation had done anybody.

Just as the message of Marcus Garvey, who advocated for blacks to join together and return to Africa, had been embraced during some of the worst years of Jim Crow—as the Ku Klux Klan was flourishing in the 1920s and millions of blacks were abandoning the South—the mounting troubles in the 1980s and '90s corresponded with a rise in Black Nationalism. A 1996 survey found that 12 percent of blacks ascribed to nationalist views.[28] More than a quarter had beliefs that were "neutral," falling in between integration and nationalism.

One of the survey questions asked whether blacks should attend Afrocentric schools. A quarter of African Americans agreed that they should.[29] The question tapped into a movement among blacks starting in the late 1980s to revive the connection between black Americans and Africa, thus enhancing their racial pride. In this vein, Jesse Jackson proposed a new name for blacks, African American, at a national conference in 1988, after he failed in a run for president.[30] By the early 1990s, Afrocentric schools were opening across the nation.[31] Many operated privately, but public schools with an African focus became increasingly common.[32]

Although most advocates of Afrocentrism publicly eschewed black separatism, in practice, Afrocentric schools inherently bred racial isolation. Most schools offering the curriculum were majority black, a function of the fact that many such schools were opened in black ghettos or in districts that had resegregated after their desegregation orders were lifted. In one California school, students said a pledge each day to "think black, act black, speak black, buy black, pray black, love black, and live black."[33]

In Louisville, only Carman Weathers openly advocated for the creation of all-black schools. The rest of the nascent group believed integration was a fine goal, but equality was more important. In meetings held in living rooms and the basement of the Catholic church, the core group grew to half a dozen. They came up with the name CEASE, and they crystallized their demands: The school system's upper limits on the percentage of blacks per school should be raised to 85 percent—the same as it was for whites.[34]

In the summer of 1995, less than a year after news broke that Central had kicked out ten of its students, denial letters went out to more than two hundred black students, including Ja'Mekia Stoner.[35] The students met all of Central's entrance requirements, except for their race. The following June, another round of letters went out denying more black freshmen, among them Dionne Hopson. Fed up, the members of CEASE formalized their organization. That summer, they lined up a series of meetings with school board members, state senators, and civil rights organizations to seek support for their cause. For the most part, the response was icy. The next step was direct action, and if that didn't work, then they would sue.[36]

First, they needed willing plaintiffs. From his position within the school, Riccardo X was able to help identify some of the students who had been denied. Others were found by word of mouth, flyers, and the publicity from the newspaper stories. The students and their parents were invited to a meeting at Robert Douglas's home, where the CEASE members gave speeches and urged the parents to join their cause for the sake of their children. They passed around a petition demanding that "the ratio of African American students to White and other students be changed to allow African American students their right of choice."[37] They also asked parents to sign a "request for enrollment," agreeing that if their children weren't allowed into their school of choice, they would "join with other outraged and unfairly treated parents to pursue legal action against the Jefferson County Public Schools for denying my request because of my child's race."[38]

The arguments appealed to Gwen. Why shouldn't there be quality schools in the West End? Why did everyone assume her child had to sit next to a white child to learn? Why did their lives still have to be defined by their race? When the group asked who would be willing to join a second protest outside of Central High School on the first day of school, Gwen promised that she and Dionne would be there. CEASE marked her as a potential plaintiff.

Jacquelyn sat through the meeting accompanied by her two restless middle schoolers. She was not particularly impressed by their arguments— she thought they were putting too much emphasis on the barriers faced by blacks. She wanted Ja'Mekia and La'Quinn to focus on what they could accomplish, not what stood in their way. But she also badly wanted her daughter to get into Central. The first year at Shawnee had been worse than Ja'Mekia had feared. The teachers seemed to regard her classmates more as problems to be managed than students to be taught. Bored and humiliated, Ja'Mekia often didn't arrive at school until around 10 a.m., but she made Bs in her first two classes of the day. Sometimes she didn't go to school at all. Jacquelyn knew her daughter wouldn't make it if she didn't get out soon, so she gave CEASE her name.

The protest was mortifying. Ja'Mekia couldn't meet the eyes of the students filing into school. She was sure everyone was laughing at her, assuming that her grades weren't good enough to get in, and that here she was skipping school to whine about it. It was nearly as bad as the shame she felt sitting through class at Shawnee.

Dionne felt numb. She was spending her first day of high school at Central, but instead of embarking on a legal career, she was on the outside, holding a picket sign. In their matching deep altos, Dionne and her mother bellowed chants along with Fran Thomas, Carman Weathers, and the others for the television cameras. But Dionne was already thinking about the following day, when she would be starting school at Pleasure Ridge Park, a few miles up the road from Frost Middle School. When a white student stomped out of Central and yelled to the picketers that someone could have her seat, Dionne winced. It wasn't a seat she could have. The next day, Dionne woke up early to catch the bus to the South End. Ja'Mekia headed east to Fern Creek. CEASE began looking for a lawyer.

II

Our Beloved Central High

Chapter 4

Lyman Johnson was born in 1906, a grandson of slaves who talked often about the hardships of plantation life. He was the youngest of eight, skinny, with a long, serious face, and wavy, thick hair. He learned to be self-sufficient after his mother died and he was left to tend to the housework for his father. The family lived in the cabin his grandfather had built in Columbia, Tennessee, not too far away from the plantation where he was born. By the time Lyman lived there, white families had moved in nearby. His father was principal of College Hill School, the one-room schoolhouse for black students in Columbia, and he instilled in his children pride and ambition.[1]

In comparison to many Southern blacks, Lyman's family was well off, but as a teenager, Lyman had his first inklings of how difficult it was to protect one's dignity in a segregated world. On a school day in 1921, Lyman's father sent him on a quick errand to the local white high school to retrieve some papers from the superintendent.[2] Lyman trotted over to the school and reported his message to a clerk, who told him he would have to wait for a few minutes. Lyman perched in an office chair next door to the superintendent's door. As he sat, the black janitor passed by the doorway to the office.

Lyman knew him as Mr. Graham, a friend of the family. Mr. Graham peeked in, his eyes on the school clerk. When she looked away, the janitor gestured to Lyman. "While you're waiting, don't you want to walk around with me?" he said.

Lyman was confused, but he decided that a tour of the white school could be interesting. He followed along as the man stooped to pick up trash in the halls until they reached the school gymnasium. The wood floor glared with polish. There was a roof overhead. Lyman had never seen anything like it. At his school, recess was held outside and the students learned to shoot baskets while dodging stones jutting from the field. College Hill didn't have a cafeteria with hot lunches as the white school did—the black children who could afford a midday meal ate from brown bags outside. Lyman's school lacked plumbing and children used fetid outdoor toilets that were eventually closed down by the state health department.[3]

Lyman remembered that tour as he prepared to graduate from College Hill in 1924. Of the one hundred students in his class when he began in first grade, only nine graduated. Lyman was the only one to go to college. Even then, he had to spend two years at a remedial boarding school because College Hill's courses ended in eleventh grade, not twelfth, like the white school. He buckled down, learning Greek and calculus. But history was his favorite subject.[4]

He was particularly obsessed with the history of the black struggle for education: After blacks were freed following the Civil War, most stayed on the plantations where they had worked as slaves.[5] Progress for blacks overseen by Northern troops during Reconstruction—including the election of black politicians to local and national offices—eroded after only a decade, when Rutherford Hayes pulled out the Northern army in return for Southern electoral votes in the election of 1876.[6]

Despite these circumstances, Southern blacks forged ahead to build an education system for their children from scratch. There was no movement for integration with white schools because in the immediate aftermath of the Civil War, there were no public schools at all.[7] Independently from whites, black communities opened schools in churches, family homes, and buildings donated by Northern philanthropists and churches. And although help from white Northerners allowed for the construction of new black schools, they were sustained by the efforts of black parents, teachers, and administrators.[8]

They were proud of what they built. The community and the school were symbiotic, sustaining a sense of pride, culture, and history in the children and the adults, generation after generation. Although black schools often lacked plumbing, heat, textbooks, gymnasiums, cafeterias, school buses, and sufficient classroom space, the principals and teachers worked hard to make up for these deficits. Even if the schoolbooks were old, curriculum in some schools was state of the art, with offerings ranging from Latin to black studies.[9] In a seminal case study of one segregated black school in North Carolina, historian Vanessa Siddle Walker wrote that in many of these schools, there was not a choice between "learning and not learning."[10] Failure was not an option. Expectations were high. Black teachers and administrators cared deeply about their students—they were the children of neighbors, friends, and family. They often saw their work as a religious calling.[11] Their job was to uplift the race.[12]

The black southerners' efforts awakened whites to start demanding a public school system, too. The white schools soon had the upper hand, with better facilities, better supplies, and better-paid teachers. The tax systems that eventually funded both school systems, white and black, were usually heavily weighted toward white schools. But though the white teachers were better paid, they were not always more qualified. Many black teachers, especially in the early years, were assigned to schools only a few years after graduating from elementary school themselves. Before the 1930s, only about 9 percent of black teachers had a degree.[13] After 1930, however, 42 percent of black teachers had some college. Black normal schools and colleges, also funded by sympathetic northern whites, churned out a formidable force of highly trained professionals who had no other options but to teach.

In 1896, the Supreme Court handed down the *Plessy v. Ferguson* decision.[14] In the case, Homer Plessy, who was "seven-eighths" white, boarded a whites-only train car in Louisiana in protest of the state's segregation law and refused to leave. The Court decided in favor of Louisiana. Southern states soon applied the Court's decision to all facets of public life. Racial separation in schools became law, but for many blacks, integration was not a desirable goal. The most prominent black voices during this period instead called for black independence from whites. Booker T. Washington, who said he believed in integration, but only once "the Negro learned to produce what other people wanted and must have," became the face of black America for the white world in 1895, when he gave a speech in Atlanta calling for blacks to accept their segregation from whites and to "cast down your buckets where you are."[15]

Although many cringed at what they saw as Washington's capitulation to white supremacy, his support for separate black schools reflected the sentiments of many ordinary blacks in the South. Reacting to the overt racism of southern whites and the condescension and paternalism of northern whites, a large swath of blacks in the South favored "black teachers for black children." They were encouraged by the two most powerful church denominations in the black community, the African Methodist Episcopal Church and the National Baptists, which had both followed a separatist agenda after the Civil War and carved out their independence from the white church.[16]

Lyman admired Washington. As the president of the Tuskegee Institute, Washington had convinced wealthy white patrons in the South to fund the education of thousands of black students. But in the early years of the twentieth century, as Lyman was immersed in his studies, new black voices out of the North were calling for change. The National Association for the Advancement of Colored People appeared in 1909 to oppose Washington's ideas and to fight for equal rights through integration. That message spoke to Lyman.[17]

For Lyman, the academic star in his small-town school in Tennessee and the second generation in a family of teachers, a career seemed set. He would be a schoolteacher. But Lyman wasn't willing to settle. He wanted to move beyond the expectations of both his community and the white world. He had kept track of the daily humiliations that the grown men around him suffered: When white vegetable peddlers refused to call his father by his last name, insisting instead on calling him "Uncle." When his uncle, a dignified college professor, had to ignore the white farm boys who called him "nigger." When a classmate of his was lynched after being falsely accused of raping a white woman.[18]

After graduating from high school in the mid-1920s, Lyman headed to Virginia Union for college. The school was cut in the mold of northern liberal arts schools—a place where philosophy and Greek took precedence over the vocational training offered at many other southern black colleges. After he graduated, he applied to graduate school: Yale, Michigan, and Iowa. All accepted him, but he couldn't afford Yale, where he had planned to study theology. He settled on Michigan, and a history degree instead.[19]

Lyman's journey north coincided with the path followed by tens of thousands of other black southerners in the 1920s.[20] Few came from an advantaged background like Lyman's. Many were former sharecroppers.

But they moved for the same reason he did: to find better jobs, dignity, and freedom.

The early waves began in the first decade of the twentieth century. Northern industrialists, in need of workers to replace soldiers off at war, enticed the migrants with jobs that paid more than double what they could make down south. The black newspaper founded in 1917, the *Chicago Defender*, lured them with biblical allegories of Exodus and the Promised Land. Many found their way to Chicago and other northern urban centers. Others made shorter journeys: Southern cities, including places with more progressive reputations and growing industries, such as Louisville and Nashville, saw their black populations swell. From 1890 until the Great Depression, Kentucky lost blacks to out-migration, but many more entered the state.[21] And thousands moved internally, away from the state's rural tobacco fields and isolated mountain hollows into the cities.

Among the tide of young men, women, and families traveling north was Fran Thomas, who at age seven made the journey alone. Fran made it as far as Louisville, officially still the South, but with a friendlier reputation. She wasn't looking for a job; she wanted to go to school.

Fran was born Frances Newton in 1928 on a farm in the northeast corner of Alabama, outside the town of Florence. She and Lyman grew up in similar circumstances: in a small cabin inherited from family members who had worked as chattel. Fran's great-grandparents had been slaves, and her family also acquired its own land after the Civil War. In contrast to Lyman's experience, however, her family, along with an extensive network of uncles, aunts, and cousins, lived in an all-black community called Bailey Springs. Town life centered around the one-room schoolhouse, built and maintained by the community, and the church.

Lyman's father, as a teacher, was an elite in the black community. Fran's parents worked as sharecroppers. Her family lived in a log cabin of two rooms divided by a breezeway. One served as a bedroom, the other as a kitchen. Fran was an only child, but her parents still struggled to support her. They had attended school until sixth grade, but hoped for more for their daughter. The local school was five miles away, and in those days, a ride on a school bus was a privilege reserved for white children. Her mother walked with her because she was so young, but the farm's success depended on both parents working from sunup to sundown. After a couple of years, the family decided that if Fran was going to continue her schooling, she would have to leave home.

In the 1930s, Fran, a pale, freckled girl still in elementary school, made the journey north on the Louisville & Nashville Railroad, alone. She followed family, and many in her town, who had already headed north. The train was dirty—blacks were forced into the car nearest the engine's grimy smoke stack—and it was crowded. On the other end, in Louisville, Kentucky, she was met by a teenage aunt who had found work in the city as a housekeeper.

The two girls lived in an apartment a few blocks west of downtown, but Fran never ventured far from her new elementary school on 16th Street, in a black neighborhood known as California. Louisville, to her, was the small area of the inner city that blacks were confined in, although as the country came out of the Depression and headed into World War II, that area in Louisville was growing.

Chapter 5

Louisville was built along a two-mile stretch of waterfalls and rapids at an N-shaped bend in the river, the one interruption on the Ohio's smooth, southwesterly meander toward the Mississippi. Locks were constructed in the 1820s to tame the rapids, and the city boomed.[1] The river was the state border with Indiana, and it served to constrict the population's northern expansion. To the south was a marsh, and to the east were hills. But to the west, curled into the river bend, was a flat expanse of lush, forested floodplain.

At the end of the nineteenth century, this floodplain was gradually being built up as one of Louisville's first white suburbs. In 1937, after days of rain, the river broke over its banks, turning the West End into a lake.[2] When the waters receded, the houses were rebuilt. But this disaster, along with the end of World War II, accelerated a transformation. Whites headed for new suburban frontiers to the south and east, many with the help of housing loans from the federal government. The wealthy concentrated in the hilly sections to the east of downtown. Poorer whites headed south, where the floodplain extended until it hit a ring of steep hills and the village of Fairdale. By the 1950s, black families had moved into the bungalows and old Victorians that whites had left behind.

During this first half of the twentieth century, Louisville was slightly more welcoming to blacks than Alabama. Blacks owned their own businesses and a significant black middle class was up and coming. But they were not allowed in public parks, hotels, restaurants, or stores. In 1914, the city passed a law barring blacks from moving to white residential streets, which the Supreme Court declared unconstitutional three years later.[3] The reversal of the law made little difference in practice, however. During the Depression, blacks were still largely confined to the shantytowns formed by ex-slaves: Little Africa, deep in the West End; California, the neighborhood just west of downtown where Fran lived; and Smoketown, just east of downtown. Their numbers were growing, however, as blacks fled the Deep South and the tobacco fields of Kentucky and Tennessee.

Forced to settle in segregated inner-city ghettos, these migrants were discovering that racism was endemic outside of the stifling plantation culture, too. During the height of the Great Migration, integration was not the dream embraced by most blacks, however. The NAACP's platform, at least at first, had to compete with the much more popular Black Nationalist movement of Marcus Garvey.[4] Garvey's Universal Negro Improvement Association (UNIA) reached its peak in the 1920s, with a membership estimated at between 1 million and 6 million members—more than half the population of black Americans at the time.[5] The UNIA rejected integration as an undesirable and foolish ideal. The organization's goal was to promote "pride in race."[6]

Fran's world in Louisville was all black, but she didn't notice. No one had a car, but everything she needed was in walking distance. Her neighborhood had its own skating rink and swimming pool. The streets were lined with black-owned barbershops, funeral parlors, clothing stores, and even a movie theater. The Great Depression had hit its peak just a few years earlier, sending African American unemployment soaring to 37 percent in Louisville, but the city was relatively resilient compared to other places.[7] The cigarette and alcohol industries—two of the city and the state's biggest—were booming.[8] The factories near Fran's apartment hummed with activity.

Her new elementary school was an improvement on the crowded schoolhouse back in Alabama. There, the education for girls included cooking lunch for the rest of the students. Still, at Fran's new school, books were hand-me-downs, and the building was old. Eleanor Roosevelt visited the schoolyard during her travels in 1938 to investigate the nation's poverty.[9] And Fran missed home terribly. She took the grimy train, or sometimes the bus, back to Alabama each summer to visit her family. But her parents insisted that she return: the black high school in Alabama didn't have the same reputation as Central.

Louisville's Central Colored High School, as it was called at first, originally opened in 1882 in a three-story brick building south of downtown.[10] It quickly outgrew its facilities. The original 27 students ballooned to 185, and the number kept expanding. By the time Fran enrolled in the 1940s, the school was on its third building, which was still too small.

Like its books and desks and chalkboards, the structure, an edifice of heavy stone and Greek revival columns, was secondhand. The building had originally been built for Male High School, Louisville's pride and joy, the first public high school west of the Allegheny. Male, for white boys only, had moved on when the city built it an expansive new facility farther away from the encroaching black neighborhoods downtown. After a half century of use, the hand-me-down building was decrepit. The hallways were so dark students bumped into each other while changing classes. In an annex built to hold the overflow of students, the gas heaters spewed more fumes than warmth. Rats infested the basement and the maid had to double as the school nurse. On one occasion, a student who began hemorrhaging blood during class died as the cleaning woman helplessly held him in her arms in the school bathroom. The death didn't prompt the city to assign a nurse to Central.

Fran's homesickness faded when she began attending Central. Among her classmates, she was something of an anomaly: Many of the students who made it to Central were from Louisville's black middle classes. Poorer students often had to drop out and work full-time. Left to fend for herself for most of her childhood and teenage years, she reveled in the fierce embrace of Central's teachers. Just as Central drew its students from as far away as Alabama, it also attracted some of the South's brightest teachers. They mixed maternal love with a strict discipline code that students dared not break.

Maude Brown Porter, the assistant principal, stalked the hallways in cat-eye glasses and ugly black shoes, sending students skittering into class at the sound of her low but powerful voice.[11] She was tiny, but it was rumored she had the strength to lift up a basketball player twice her size. The students loved and feared her. They felt the same about their teachers, who on Saturdays and Sundays visited the homes of students who were absent during the week or doing poorly in class. The classes ranged from

Latin to physics and from typing to woodshop. Many of the teachers held multiple master's degrees. A few had doctorates. The goal at Central was to bolster Louisville's growing black middle class—with or without the help of whites.

Academics were rigorous, but sports were key to Central students' sense of identity, engendering fierce loyalty and love among the school's alumni.[12] Until 1919, the school didn't have fields or basketball courts, but as soon as the school gained a gymnasium, the Central Yellowjackets began winning games. Central won the National Negro High School Basketball Tournament twice. The second time Central came home with the trophy, in 1952, the Louisville mayor threw the high school a parade, complete with a brigade of fire trucks and a key to the city. In Kentucky, basketball was king, but football at Central was big, too. Under one beloved coach, the Yellowjackets football team racked up a record of 280–30 during the 1930s and '40s. Thousands of black Louisvillians lined the streets for the Thanksgiving football game each year to belt out the refrain of the Central High School song: "Long live Central, our beloved Central High. Ours till we die."[13]

Fran graduated from Central in 1946, fulfilling her parents' dream. She missed home, but no longer saw going back as an option. Florence, Alabama's plantations were giving way to factories, including a Reynolds aluminum plant. The foundry was nicknamed the Pot, and the men who worked there—most of them black—were worn down by the brutal conditions. They often came home with severe burns, and they died young. Beyond manual labor and farming, Florence offered few opportunities; a black woman could help tend the farm, work for a white family, or maybe teach. Central had pushed Fran to think bigger: she was going to college.

She enrolled in the Louisville Municipal College for Negroes, a black school linked to the University of Louisville.[14] Municipal had a few excellent teachers, but struggled with meager resources compared to its white sister school. Fran's education there went beyond academics, however. During her college years, she met Alberta Jones, who had graduated from Central just behind her. Jones—who eventually became the first woman to pass the bar in Kentucky and Muhammad Ali's personal lawyer—was bold and defiant.[15] She became a role model for Fran and introduced her to activism through a group called the Independent Voters Association, which trained and registered black voters. Fran also began attending forums on open housing, a growing movement to fight housing segregation organized by black activists, ministers, and a handful of white liberals.

Marriage whisked Fran away from her first steps as a budding activist, however. Before she graduated, she married a maintenance man in 1947 and they moved to Beecher Terrace, a decade-old housing project built to look like a village, with peaked-roof multifamily houses and small lawns surrounding a park. Fran had five children in quick succession, but the marriage was troubled. By the mid-1950s, she got a divorce, staying on in Beecher Terrace to raise her children alone. She worked long hours as a nurse, saving enough to enroll her children in Catholic school. The public schools available to black students in Louisville were better than the ones in Alabama, but despite the *Brown v. Board of Education* decision in 1954, the options were still bad. Like her own parents, Fran wanted better for her children.

Chapter 6

As he began his history studies at the University of Michigan, Lyman's pride was challenged as much as it had been in the South.[1] In Tennessee and Virginia, he had never doubted that he was as good as or better than white people. At the university, however, he encountered white students for the first time, and he was the only black person in many of his classes. On his first day, he had trouble holding his head up and worried that everyone assumed he was inferior. His abiding fear was to be mocked for asking a "Negro question" or giving a "Negro answer." One professor, giving him a C, told him it was a "good grade for a Negro."

Eventually, as he got more comfortable, Lyman's dignity returned, and he began to push back. At least one of his professors encouraged it, and soon Lyman was thriving, challenging his professors in class and writing papers that questioned conventional wisdom. He graduated at the height of the Great Depression, however, and there were no jobs. He moved to Louisville to stay with his sister, initially scratching out a living doing handyman jobs.[2]

In 1933, Central's civics teacher left. Hired for the job, Lyman threw himself into the work. He turned his classroom into a forum where he could preach about civil rights. Kentucky had the oldest black teachers' union in the South, and within five years, Lyman had joined the National Association for the Advancement of Colored People and been elected president of the Louisville Association of Teachers in Colored Schools, which had as its main goal the attainment of equal pay for black teachers.[3] The campaign was a part of a huge effort by the NAACP rolled out in nearly every Southern state to bring black teacher salaries up to the level of whites.[4]

The strategy was bold: The teachers didn't ask nicely, making a request through labor arbitration hearings—they sued for equal pay in court. It was a risky tactic. The jobs of black teachers were at the mercy of white school boards. But the movement built on both the economic desperation of blacks and a growing restlessness with the American racial order. The Great Migration and the two world wars had introduced new horizons and new possibilities, and increasingly, blacks were willing to demand their fair share. By the 1930s, the black teaching force had become overwhelmingly female, and the wages reflected the low status of both their race and their gender. (After the Great Migration, many black men had moved into better-paying factory jobs.) In 1930, black teachers earned 45 percent of what white teachers earned in the South, a percentage that had actually declined for black teachers from 60 percent at the turn of the century, when more men were in the profession.[5]

The teacher-pay movement fit into a wider effort by the NAACP to challenge Jim Crow that had begun in the 1930s. A black sociologist, William Edward Burghardt Du Bois, had founded the organization in 1909. Du Bois was, in the words of journalist Richard Kluger, "a lonely, terribly proud black man."[6] He grew up sheltered in a mostly white New England town, attended Fisk, the elite black university in Nashville, as an undergraduate, and Harvard for a PhD in history, and made his name attacking the accommodationist strategy of Booker T. Washington. With his pointed beard, pale skin, and white gloves, Du Bois cut a sharp physical contrast to his Southern adversary, who had been born into slavery in a plantation kitchen. Reflecting his own experience along with his observations as a sociologist, Du Bois argued that education, not hard labor, was the best strategy for extricating blacks from their lowly position in American society. On Lincoln's birthday in 1909, he helped to launch the NAACP with the help of a group of like-minded white liberals.

Du Bois busied himself writing the NAACP's mouthpiece, the *Crisis*, a sharp-tongued publication dedicated to boosting black pride and pushing the cause of black equality. Within two years, the organization had turned its focus to fighting for blacks in the courts. The NAACP's first

Supreme Court victory was won against the City of Louisville, Kentucky, overturning the housing law banning blacks and whites from sharing the same neighborhoods.[7]

The organization took on all kinds of cases as the membership and its experience in the courts grew. Its lawyers, led by Charles Houston and his protégé, Thurgood Marshall, fought for black criminal defendants accused in rape and murder cases across the country. But by the 1930s, Houston and his colleagues were shaping a strategy to attack segregation in schools, where the discrepancies between blacks and whites were the starkest—and the most potentially damaging for the future of the black community. They hoped equalizing education would topple the other pillars of racial discrimination in the South.[8]

They targeted graduate schools and then moved gradually down to public elementary and high schools, reasoning that the legal argument to desegregate graduate schools was easier: If a black student was barred from attending the state law school, there was usually no alternative option, or a very poor one. It was also more likely to be politically and emotionally palatable to white judges. Mixing young adult students was less emotional for whites. Racial prejudice was largely rooted in and justified by deeply held, irrational sexual stereotypes about blacks, and they knew convincing the South to send little white girls to school with blacks would be a difficult battle.[9]

At first, the NAACP's strategy was not to challenge directly the Supreme Court's 1896 decision, *Plessy v. Ferguson*, which required that schools and other public services be separate but equal. Instead, they would push states to make good on *Plessy*'s promise that black schools and students be given the same quality of books, facilities, teachers, and other resources as white schools. Actually maintaining a dual system of equal schools would be expensive, and the lawyers assumed financial pressure would be more likely to persuade school boards to integrate than a moral argument against segregation.

After a victory in the equal pay campaign in Louisville, Lyman Johnson volunteered to be a plaintiff in this new strategy. In March 1948, Lyman, represented by the lawyers of the NAACP, sued the graduate school of the University of Kentucky, the state's flagship school.[10] The story made the front page of Louisville's afternoon paper, the *Louisville Times*. The *Times*, owned by the same family as the more stately morning broadsheet, the *Courier-Journal*, was relatively liberal on race, as was its sister paper. But the front-page treatment was rare; the reporter on the story, a rookie education reporter named Anne Braden, had pushed her editors for a top billing and won.[11]

Anne, born in 1924, was the daughter of one of Kentucky's oldest families. She was thin and elegant, with deep, sad eyes offset by a fringe of short, jaunty bangs. Her grandmother had been a proud slave owner. But in her work as a journalist, Anne began to question her family's heritage. As she covered criminal justice and education in Alabama, she was shocked at the mistreatment of blacks in Southern courtrooms and schools. When the Louisville paper offered her a job, she headed north, thinking she would soon be settled in a more reasonable, tolerant city.[12]

Lyman's case horrified and fascinated her. To avoid legal trouble, the state paid for blacks in Kentucky who wanted a graduate education to leave the state and go elsewhere.[13] For the story, Anne visited Central to meet with Lyman. After the meeting she became more immersed in the troubles of the black community in Louisville. Later that year, Anne married Carl Braden, a labor reporter, and not long after the two quit their newspaper jobs to become full-time activists. Anne joined the Civil Rights Congress, traveling to Mississippi to get arrested in support of a black defendant who had been accused of raping a white woman.[14] But it was a seemingly innocuous gesture that thrust the Bradens into the spotlight and made them local symbols of the decade's racial turbulence.

In March of 1954, a young, black World War II veteran, Andrew Wade, approached Anne and Carl Braden to ask a favor. The couple lived in a compact brick bungalow on a quiet residential street in the West End. The neighborhood was still all white and largely hostile to blacks, but Wade knew about the Bradens' work and he was desperate.[15] He was looking for a house for his wife and baby daughter. After serving his country and saving money from his job as an electrical contractor, he believed he had earned a nice, roomy home the suburbs. The Bradens were sympathetic. Wade explained that he had almost closed on four houses, but each time, once the real estate brokers realized his family was black, they pulled out of the deal.[16] The Bradens agreed to act as dummy buyers. They would sign for a house, and then pass the mortgage over to the Wades.

The Wades found a house they liked—a one-story ranch made of limestone—in the small, incorporated city of Shively, just south of the

Louisville city line along the border of the West End.[17] The little city had started as a village of farming estates, but by the 1950s, the city was attracting new sorts of residents. Large tracts of land had been converted into two- and three-bedroom bungalows after the war, and a flood of young families filled the neighborhoods fast. Some came from the city, but many came from the country in search of jobs and the suburban lifestyle that had become the new American dream. This dream did not include blacks, but the Wades ignored the taboo.

So did the Bradens. Anne had thrown herself into fighting the state's school segregation edict, known as the Day Law. It was less than a month before the Supreme Court would hand down its decision in *Brown v. Board of Education.* And so, distracted, the Bradens went through the motions of buying the house—a tour, a visit to the bank, a signing—and then handed it over to the Wades. A few days after the Wades moved in that May, a mob of local whites gathered on the lawn of their next-door neighbor.[18] After several hours, they left, driving to the Bradens' house, where they found Carl alone with the couple's two children. "You better watch out," they warned. The Bradens and the Wades ignored the threat. They couldn't predict the waves of anger and violence that the Supreme Court was about to unleash.

Chapter 7

In 1949, Lyman Johnson won the case against the University of Kentucky that Anne Braden had first written about in the *Louisville Times*.[1] He was admitted to the school but attended only a class or two.[2] He looked down on the university as inferior compared to out-of-state places he had studied. Nationally, the NAACP's schools strategy had been moving along in fits and starts for more than a decade. By 1950, Thurgood Marshall was prepared to take a risky new step: attack *Plessy v. Ferguson* head-on.[3] The lawyers found five segregated school districts across the country and five willing plaintiffs, among them Linda Brown of Topeka, Kansas.[4]

On December 9, 1952, standing in front of the nine justices, Marshall was cautious in making his case: "The only thing that we ask for is that the state-imposed racial segregation be taken off, and to leave the county school board, the county people, the district people, to work out their own solution on the problem to assign children on any reasonable basis they want to assign them on."[5]

The NAACP lawyers hoped for a slim majority in *Brown v. Board*. The judges themselves seemed reluctant to make a decision in the case. They stalled, ordering the lawyers to come back in 1953 to reargue the case.[6] Then, in September, Chief Justice Fred Vinson died.[7]

Dwight D. Eisenhower, newly elected as president, made an unexpected choice for his replacement: the governor of California, Earl Warren. In 1947, Warren had repealed school segregation in his state in response to a state court decision, *Mendez v. Westminster,* brought by Mexican American plaintiffs.[8] Warren, a talented politician, corralled the cantankerous group of justices into a unanimous opinion in *Brown.* In particular, Warren had to contend with an elderly justice with old-fashioned ideas about race, Stanley Reed, another Kentuckian. But in the end, Warren prevailed. On May 17, 1954, he convened the press to read a decision signed by all nine justices.[9]

The ruling was short and mostly to the point, but Warren had been forced to compromise. There was no time frame for schools to implement desegregation.[10] The ruling gave no instructions to school districts about how to go about dismantling school segregation. Warren barely addressed the 1896 *Plessy v. Ferguson* ruling.[11] The *Brown* decision simply concluded that "in the field of public education the doctrine of 'separate but equal' has no place." In a subtle but important omission, the decision also didn't mention the lone dissent in *Plessy,* written by a judge from eastern Kentucky, Justice John Harlan.

In 1896, Harlan had made two arguments that would later become critical points of tension in the country's struggle over racial equality in schools.[12] He wrote that the Constitution could not abide the subordination of one group of people to another, but also that it was intolerant of classifying people by race. One of his phrases came to have as much weight in civil rights law as *Brown* itself: "In the eye of the law, there is in this country no superior, dominant, ruling class of citizens. There is no caste here. Our Constitution is color-blind, and neither knows nor tolerates classes among citizens."[13] These two ideas would later come into sharp conflict: how could the government uproot the effects of systematic subordination of blacks without identifying them as black and carving out special treatment for them?[14]

Although the *Brown* decision didn't mention Harlan's dissent, this idea of color blindness was foundational to the reasoning behind it: The schools must not classify children by race, because doing so created a caste system in which one race would inherently occupy a superior place over the other. But to undo this caste system, it would be necessary to identify those who had been harmed by it, to make sure that the dual system didn't continue. As Warren constructed his opinion, he either could not foresee these complications, or he chose to ignore them.

He also left out any hint of the mechanisms that the Court would approve for taking apart the segregated school system, perhaps in part a recognition of the cherished American notion of local control of schools. And possibly, Warren understood that in order for *Brown* to be a decisive turning point in American history, it had to be vague on many points.[15] He got across the main idea, "Separate but educational facilities are inherently unequal," and left the other details—the how, when, and where—to be hashed out later.

As Warren was getting ready to announce the *Brown* decision on the afternoon of May 15, 1954, a group of men gathered next door to the Wades' house in Shively to burn a cross. That night, a gunshot shattered one of the windows in the house.[16] The next day, *Brown* was trumpeted across the country as a new, clean slate for America. The reality, of course, was much different. On the streets of Louisville, the decision came down amid a wave of racial hatred. The *Courier-Journal* blamed the Bradens for stirring up trouble. The local Shively paper, the *Shively Newsweek*, launched a campaign arguing that the Bradens were a part of a Communist conspiracy to provoke racial conflict. They were flooded with hate mail and threatening phone calls. Police set up a guard at the Wades' house, which was augmented by friends of both couples.

Lyman was one of the men they recruited to stand guard.[17] On a Saturday night in June, he was stationed at the couch by the house's front window. Others were spread around the house, but the evening was quiet. At 9:00, everyone left except for a couple of men who had agreed to stay on through the night. They chatted with the Wades, who had been out for the evening and come back late, on the porch. The Wades' daughter was staying with her grandmother, as she did most weekends. A police officer, there ostensibly to guard the Wades' home, stood in the next-door neighbor's yard. Suddenly there was a flash and an explosion. A pile of dynamite tucked under the foundation had ripped open their daughter's room, collapsing half of the house into rubble.

The city's reaction was as stunning as the blast. The *Shively Newsweek* printed a letter by Milliard Grubbs, who had alleged links to the KKK, accusing the Bradens and the Wades of being part of a Communist conspiracy. Perhaps the bombing was "self-inflicted," the paper suggested. That fall, a state prosecutor announced that he, too, believed the Bradens were Communist schemers, and that the bombing had been a plot to sow racial conflict in the suburbs.[18] Six months after the bombing, the couple was charged with sedition under state law. In December, an all-white jury convicted Carl Braden of sedition, and shipped him off to jail for a fifteen-year sentence. Anne was left behind, waiting to hear if she would be next.

To many blacks living in the South, this reaction to an attempt at residential integration didn't seem so farfetched. After *Brown*, blacks were both joyous and apprehensive. The idea that whites would passively accept desegregation without a fight was naïve, and many were terrified at the idea of sending black children as frontline soldiers in the upcoming battle.[19]

For the decade after May 1954, when the *Brown* decision was handed down, Gallup polls found some ambivalence about desegregation among black Southerners; the percentage of those who agreed with the decision fluctuated between 30 and 70 percent between 1954 and 1961. The poll findings were based on a small sample size, which partly explained wide variations between years, and black respondents living in the South may have been reluctant to express their true views. The numbers contrasted starkly with the 95 percent approval rating among black Northerners, a number that remained steady in the decade after *Brown*.[20] By 1962, about 70 percent of American blacks, North and South, favored school integration, slightly more than the proportion among whites.[21]

W. E. B. Du Bois, the founder of the NAACP, was among the skeptical. In what seemed a shocking about-face from his earlier days as Booker T. Washington's nemesis, Du Bois had published an article in 1935 titled, "Does the Negro Need Separate Schools?" A year earlier, Du Bois had left the NAACP in part because of his dispute with its new leaders over the best way to uplift the race.[22] Du Bois no longer thought integration was the most practical solution.

In his article, he argued that in the face of white hostility, the black student needed the "sympathetic touch" of a teacher who understood "his surroundings and background, and the history of his class and group." His conclusion was not necessarily that segregation should be maintained, but that it was beside the point: "Theoretically, the Negro needs neither segregated schools nor mixed schools. What he needs is Education. What he must remember is that there is no magic, either in mixed schools or in segregated schools."[23]

Fear for the well-being of black children was not the only reason blacks in the South were uneasy about integration in the lead-up to and the immediate aftermath of *Brown*. Black teachers and principals feared for their jobs. In a 1953 poll of 150 black teachers from the South, only about half said they would prefer desegregation to the segregated system.[24]

The ambivalence about *Brown* in some communities was deepened by the fact that quite a few black schools were doing much better during the years leading up to the ruling. In many places, white school districts poured money into black schools both preemptively and in reaction to lawsuits forcing them to live up to *Plessy*'s separate-but-equal clause. The black schools in Hyde County, North Carolina, were a prime example. Before *Brown* was handed down, and just after, the white school board of Hyde County constructed new buildings, science classrooms, libraries, and gymnasiums for the black schools in a flurry of belated good-will.[25] Blacks were wary about sending their children to white schools in a place where the Ku Klux Klan was not only alive but very active. They were also proud of the schools they had built and maintained despite meager school board investments during the many years of white neglect.

Hyde County reacted to the desegregation order by proposing to close the traditionally black schools and transfer their students into the traditionally white schools. The black community was livid. They didn't want desegregation if it meant losing everything they had worked for. Rather than give up, they chose to boycott: for two years, black children in Hyde County were kept home from school.

In Louisville, Central High School also appeared to benefit from growing white apprehension over the tide of NAACP court victories in the early 1950s. Years earlier, when Fran Thomas was still a student, the Louisville school board had promised Central a new building. The only step that was taken, however, was to choose a site already occupied by dilapidated houses of the black poor in the California neighborhood. The board stalled for years on the new construction, however, because members said they were reluctant to start evictions, although, at the time, thousands of blacks were being uprooted from "slum housing" under urban renewal plans.[26]

Atwood Wilson, who had become principal at Central in 1934, fought for the new building and more money for programs at the school for much of his tenure. Wilson was a quiet but awe-inspiring figure at the school.[27] He had a degree from Fisk University, and master's degrees in education and chemistry from the University of Chicago and the University of Colorado. He considered a doctorate, but he didn't want to be away from his school for the amount of time it would take him to complete it. He pushed his faculty to extend their education, however, and some took off for Columbia University and other northern schools during their summer vacations.

Wilson was single-minded about improving Central for black students. In the 1940s, he asked the teachers to draw up lists for the classrooms, labs, and equipment they would need in a new facility, and put the architecture teachers to work drawing up plans. The result was a ninety-five-page report that included plans for an ROTC unit, a swimming pool, a gymnasium, an auditorium, and a stadium. Wilson's dream was to create spaces and programs for students across the spectrum of class and ability. Central would focus intensely on college prep, but the school would also expand its vocational offerings, which already included carpentry, tailoring, dressmaking, and mechanics. In 1947, he gave the plan to the school board for consideration.

A year passed with no response, and Wilson took Lyman with him to confront the board. The costs had risen with inflation, and the board members said they would need to consider the plans in light of the new expenses. Meanwhile, the school's 115-year-old building was oversubscribed by five hundred students, and the roof had begun to leak. Construction finally started three years later. In 1953, a few months after the school desegregation cases were argued in the Supreme Court, the new Central building opened. Board members dubbed it the "South's finest high school for Negros," and it probably was.[28]

The school had its own radio studio and shops for tailoring, dressmaking, pressing and cleaning, sheet metal, carpentry, and auto mechanics. It also had a "beauty school . . . to offer training in beauty culture."[29] A space was left for a swimming pool, although it would take another two decades for the board to get around to having it built. The two-story building took up a whole city block and was constructed with yellow brick. In contrast to the heavy stone structure the school had previously occupied, there were lots of windows. There were no rats in the basement, and the roof didn't leak.

A year after the *Brown* decision came down, even as students basked in Central's new, state-of-the-art facilities, the school was preparing for a new era of integrated schools. It seemed like the country had suddenly, unexpectedly made a huge leap forward in its race relations, and things were changing fast.

Chapter 8

Early in the morning of September 10, 1956, the superintendent of the Louisville public schools took his position in front of the stone arches and columns surrounding the doors of Male High School, a sprawling brick building just south of the city's downtown business district.[1] Male, the all-boys' school opened in 1856 that had handed down its old building to Central, was Louisville's best, and proud of it. In 1950, protests had broken out when the city announced that Male would have to admit girls. It took two years to force the school to open its doors to female students, and the district was never able to make the school give up its name.

In 1956, just a few months after its hundred-year anniversary, another of the school's cherished customs was about to be challenged. That September, for the first time, black students would cross under the arches and take their seats in the school's venerable classrooms. The protests against admitting girls had taken place mostly in the confines of school board meetings. This time the superintendent, Omer Carmichael, was prepared for violence in the streets. The mayor, the police chief, and the school board president joined him at his post. Newspaper and television reporters dispatched by national media outlets waited nearby to witness the violence firsthand.

Louisville was one of the only Southern cities that had set a timeline to desegregate in the wake of *Brown*.[2] Carmichael was an unlikely maverick, however. He was a farmer's son who had graduated from a one-room schoolhouse in Clay County, Alabama, just southeast of Birmingham in cotton country.[3] Carmichael started out as a teacher in another one-room schoolhouse, but quickly moved up the ladder. He became superintendent in Selma, where he made a few small efforts to combat the inequities of segregation, including banning the practice of addressing black teachers by their first names. He moved to Tampa, where the KKK was "in its heyday," and then to Lynchburg, where he adjusted the teacher-rating system that determined salaries and was heavily skewed against black teachers. Blacks were still paid less than whites, but he was proud that he had raised their salaries somewhat, and pleased that by the time he left, black principals ran all of the black schools.

On the day in 1954 that the Supreme Court handed down the *Brown* decision, Carmichael took a bolder stance, perhaps encouraged by the Kentucky governor's public approval of the ruling.[4] Without checking with the school board first, Carmichael announced that Louisville would comply with *Brown* by 1956: "There will be problems but they are not insurmountable . . . the group to suffer most will be the Negro children in the early stages of integration. The real problem will be with the adults, however, not the children."[5]

Louisville held tight to its racially tolerant image, keen to sell this image to the outside world. Just as the United States was struggling to hide its racial troubles as it competed with the Soviet Union for the world's allegiance in the Cold War, Louisville was fighting to attract industries and workers to revive its fortunes in the post–World War II boom. The chamber of commerce had launched a big push to lure trade shows and concerts to the newly built fairgrounds, and the city was in the midst of demolishing slum housing to clear the way for the redevelopment of the downtown.[6] The bombing of the Wades' house—two days before Carmichael made his announcement—threatened the city's carefully laid plans.

After the *Brown* decision and his promise that Louisville would comply, Carmichael spent the next two years frantically working on a viable desegregation system and fielding angry questions from white parents. The education department held question-and-answer sessions with PTAs, recruited ministers to preach the value of integration from their pulpits, and posted notices in the newspapers. Teacher training didn't go as smoothly as hoped. Carmichael discovered a deep-rooted racism and anger among many in his teaching force. Some called the prospect of teaching black children a "bitter dose" or "simply repulsive."[7] The NAACP also complained—that the school district was moving too slowly. The biggest worry, however, was caused by the White Citizen Councils.

The councils had formed across the South to hold the line against integration in the wake of *Brown*, and Milliard Grubbs, the man who had germinated the idea that the bombing of the Wades' house in Shively was the work of Communist infiltrators, founded the Louisville branch.[8] Members included some of the Wades' white neighbors. In the lead-up to the first day of school, meetings were held calling for the assassination of the Supreme Court justices and crosses were burned on school property, including in Parkland, where white parents were agitating to have their middle school district lines redrawn to keep out blacks.[9]

So as students trickled into Male that morning in September 1956, Carmichael was nervous. Some of the students lingered to watch and pose for photos. More arrived, some of them black. They walked up the stairs and disappeared through the doors. The officials waited for something to happen. Nothing did. The five hundred police officers patrolling other schools around the city called in their reports. Nothing. A handful of picketers from the White Citizens Council showed up briefly at education department headquarters, then disbanded. Carmichael was elated. Louisville could reclaim the mantle of racial tolerance and progressivism, and bury the uncomfortable tensions provoked by the bombing in Shively. The city's track record on race could now be a role model, not an embarrassment.

Elsewhere, desegregation of schools in the South began terribly, if at all. In a few smaller towns, the transition went smoothly, but elsewhere, violent mobs blocked black students from attending white schools.[10] It was becoming clear that in the majority of Southern cities, the order of things would not be too disrupted by pronouncements coming out of the Supreme Court. A year after the *Brown* decision was announced, the justices handed down a second decision, *Brown II*, outlining how they expected school desegregation to be carried out: with "all deliberate speed."[11] Southern school districts interpreted the line to mean "slowly," and as years passed, it seemed clear many hoped to get away with "never."

School districts dragged their feet with the blessing of state governments; the federal government expressed little interest in forcing them to act.[12] In 1956, President Eisenhower was in the middle of a contested reelection campaign.[13] The Suez Canal crisis and a catastrophic drop in agricultural prices had taken precedence over the South's intransigence on desegregation. Race was a problem that Eisenhower generally tried to avoid. He, along with his opponent, Adlai Stevenson, publicly supported *Brown*, but the president was wary of pushing the issue any further during an election year; racial justice was never a winning campaign issue for presidential candidates.[14] The Supreme Court, after all, had not set any deadlines for the South to comply with its decision.

Nevertheless, in the few places in the South that did attempt to comply, the violent reaction captured national headlines. The Eisenhower administration knew the president needed a stronger response and a positive angle.[15] At a White House press conference on September 11, 1956, a reporter asked Eisenhower if he had any plan for making desegregation work. He was prepared with his response. He said he deplored the violence, and then pointed to Louisville's success story: "I think Mr. Carmichael must be a very wise man. I hope to meet him, and I hope to get some advice from him as to exactly how he did it, because he pursued the policy that I believe will finally bring success in this."

The next week, Carmichael received an invitation to the White House. He was suddenly a national celebrity. The *New York Times* praised him in an editorial, and *Time* magazine lauded his success in an article titled "How To Integrate." The superintendent spent forty-five minutes with the president explaining his strategy, and Eisenhower emerged from the meeting impressed. Carmichael had handled the desegregation mandate in "the truly American way," the president said.

Eisenhower's words were prescient. Carmichael's strategy to integrate schools looked good from afar, but it had little effect on the deep racial divide between Louisville schools. Although all of the city's schools were opened to black students, and by the next year 78 percent of students were in a mixed-race school, many of those schools held only one black student or only one white one.[16] Ten schools were still all black and eight were all white. Fewer than half of Louisville's black students went to integrated schools in the years after the program was implemented. Only eighty-seven white children out of more than thirty thousand in the city went to a school that was previously all black.

This discrepancy between the hype and the reality in Louisville was rooted in the choice provision of Carmichael's plan, which ensured that no white parents who objected to integration would actually have to send their children to a school with black students. The lesson whites took away from the reverberations of the unfortunate Shively incident was that pushing blacks and whites together too fast was unwise. The best strategy, many believed, was gradual change, letting whites become comfortable with the idea of sharing their schools with blacks, and perhaps someday, their neighborhoods.[17]

As a key part of this inch-by-inch strategy, the school choice provision allowed parents to request transfers away from their assigned school without explanation. Of white students assigned to traditionally black schools, 85 percent requested a transfer. Black parents were also hesitant to send their children to white schools. Of black students assigned to traditionally white schools, 45 percent requested transfers. More than 90 percent of transfers were granted. In addition, teachers in Louisville were not integrated, meaning black teachers taught only the handful of white children who went to the traditionally black schools. The black students who acquiesced to integration entered environments that were entirely white except for their fellow students. At Central High School little changed in the aftermath of Carmichael's decision. Except for one white student, the school remained all black.[18]

As the limits of Carmichael's program became clear, local civil rights activists realized that the struggle for school integration in Louisville was just beginning, as it was across the South. The school choice strategy pioneered in Louisville was also a favored strategy of other Southern cities. The policy allowed districts to open schools to racial mixing, but in practice, most white parents were allowed plenty of wiggle room if they didn't want their offspring mixing with blacks. The plan had another weakness: It covered only the schools inside the city limits. Jefferson County was a separate district. Whites who moved to the suburbs were beyond the city's reach, and most of the county schools were still lily-white.

As the 1960s progressed, the South's slow-and-unsteady approach to integration became untenable. In the courts, the NAACP was pressing dozens of cases calling for the rapid and proactive desegregation of the schools.[19] At the same time, a new movement, emboldened by the Supreme Court's overturning of *Plessy v. Ferguson* in the *Brown* case, had taken to the streets to push for the integration of everything else.[20]

In April of 1961, Martin Luther King Jr. was invited to preach at Louisville's Southern Baptist Seminary, where he repeated his now-familiar call for blacks to rise up in nonviolent resistance: "We've made the world a neighborhood, now we must make it a brotherhood. We must all live as brothers or we will all perish together as fools," he told the audience.[21] The same day, forty black students—most of them younger than eighteen—followed his instructions and were arrested at sit-ins in segregated restaurants downtown.[22]

The sit-in movement had jumped into the national spotlight a year earlier, when college students in Greensboro, North Carolina, began a wave of protests targeting downtown lunch counters.[23] The tactic had spread like wildfire across the South, mostly among college students, but in Louisville, it was high school students who were leading the protests.[24] Most attended Central. Encouraging them was the young and fashionable publisher of the local black newspaper, Frank Stanley, the NAACP, and, of course, their teacher, Lyman Johnson.[25]

As early as 1956, Lyman had taken a group of Central students, many of them members of the NAACP's Youth Council, to conduct sit-ins in drugstores.[26] Four years later, he had been incensed at the irony of a segregated theater that banned blacks from coming to see the Gershwin opera *Porgy and Bess* about a black community in South Carolina. He and his students helped form a picket line outside of the show, and eventually attendance dwindled enough that the show's run was cut short.[27] The pickets moved on, and so did Lyman and his students, to the Blue Boar Cafeteria, an inexpensive plate lunch place catering to downtown office workers.

The boycott and pickets carried on for months, a victory in itself for the black leadership. The sit-ins brought together the black community "as nothing else in the past had," one *Courier-Journal* reporter wrote.[28] But, as in other places across the South where blacks were becoming bolder about challenging the old power structure, whites were slow to give up their privileges. It took two years from the climatic 1961 sit-ins for Louisville's board of alderman to finally criminalize racial discrimination in public accommodations.[29] The same year, Johnson won another victory: the public school system agreed to desegregate teachers.[30]

Black leaders, most of them drawn from top echelons of the community, or, at least, from the squarely middle class, had forced immense progress in just a little over a decade. In theory and usually in practice, blacks could walk into any restaurant and expect service; they could send their child to any school inside the city limits; they could ride on buses, read at the library, and swim in the pools, just like anybody else.[31] Most blacks didn't spend weekends golfing at the Shawnee Golf Course, but just knowing that they had fought and won the right to do so was a point of pride. Yet the day-to-day realities for many blacks had hardly changed at all. Everything was different, and yet nothing was.

For Fran Thomas, who had graduated from Central, the upheaval seemed distant. After years of struggling to support her children on a nurse's salary and keep them out of the public schools, in 1966, she married an army officer, Virgil Thomas, and the family moved to Fort Knox, an army post south of Louisville. Fran left the black cocoon she had been raised in and entered an entirely white world.

The United States was increasing its involvement in the Vietnam War, and only a year after their marriage her husband was deployed. The G.I. Bill meant the couple could afford a home, though. Fran was nervous about the idea of settling permanently outside of the black community, but she went looking for houses before Virgil left. At the far tip of the county, the G.I. Bill had stimulated a suburban growth spurt. Many young military families found their ideal spot in Valley Station, a neighborhood situated along Dixie Highway near the halfway point between Louisville and Fort Knox. As the influx reached its peak in the early 1960s, the schools strained to accommodate all of the new children.[32]

Fran found her dream house there, on a quiet street off the main drag. It was a freshly built one-story ranch with a façade of white stones. There were hardwood floors, a full bathroom and a half bath, three bedrooms, and a big backyard. She stopped to see it one evening and talked to the realtor. Perhaps he was fooled by Fran's light skin or by the dim light, but he agreed to show Fran and Virgil the house the next afternoon. When they arrived at 2 p.m., the realtor took another look at her and refused to let them in. "There are no blacks in this subdivision and there will never be," he told them, shooing them away.

Fran was furious. The realtor had sparked the rebellious side that had led Fran to dabble in civil rights activism during college. Before she had been reluctant to move to Valley Station; now she was determined. She made an appointment to see Virgil's colonel at Fort Knox. The colonel was surprised to see her, but cordial. The military had long been in the vanguard of racial progress, ever since Truman had integrated the military on executive order in 1948. Fran got down to business quickly: "If I'm not going to get the house I want to live in, then my husband is not going to Vietnam. He doesn't have anything to go over there and fight for."

The colonel looked at her, and then told her he would make some calls. He informed the real estate company that if Fran and Virgil Thomas couldn't have their house, then it would have trouble selling any more houses in a neighborhood that was financed with government money. The threat worked and the realtors relented. A few days later, Fran went to sign for her new home.

Virgil left soon after; he would eventually be deployed three times to Vietnam. When her son was old enough to fight, he was sent to war, too. Fran was left alone with her younger children, once again working as a nurse at the Veterans Affairs Hospital. Fran's neighbors were tolerant, if not too friendly. Many were also in the military and were more used to the idea of sharing their space with blacks. It was a new decade. As the 1960s dawned, the trauma of the house bombing had been largely forgotten; Shively was still all white, but Carl Braden had been released from jail after Kentucky's sedition law was overturned, and charges were dropped against Anne. Louisville had reached "a most enviable position" when it came to race relations, according to the city's mayor, Bruce Hoblitzell, a gentlemanly former sheriff who addressed both men and women with an affectionate "Honey."[33] Enormous, unimaginable progress had been made over the course of just a few years. Still, there was a long way to go.

III

With Our Own

Chapter 9

Riccardo X liked to say that he stopped believing in Santa Claus at a very young age. The apartment where he was born in 1953 had no chimney. It was in the College Court housing project, the oldest public housing in Louisville.[1] To get to Riccardo's stocking, the jolly old white man with his bag of toys would have had to make it through the projects without being mugged—an unlikely prospect.[2]

In the mid-1960s, his mother moved Riccardo and his sister across town to another public housing project, Southwick, built a couple of years earlier on the land where Little Africa, the former enclave of freed blacks in the far West End, once stood. Southwick had been envisioned as a village of two-story, brick apartment buildings with modern plumbing and tidy green spaces where mothers could garden and children could play, all centered around a shopping complex that would carry the neighborhood into the modern era.

The shine rubbed off quickly. The shopping complex never materialized.[3] With no investors interested in developing the area, the new residents were left marooned at the edge of the city, with their businesses and churches destroyed and nothing to replace them. Louisville's school desegregation plan was in its tenth year, but Riccardo's elementary school was all black. It was about as rough as the surrounding projects. He recalled his fourth grade teacher drinking beer at her desk as her students copied multiplication tables. He, as class clown, was a frequent recipient of the paddle.

The nearest store was two blocks away, and when Riccardo ran errands for his mother, he had to pass through another housing project, Cotter Homes, where gangs waited to beat up the Southwick kids who walked alone. In summer, the rivalry between the two projects turned into an all-out war, with rock throwing and knife fights, until the arrival of autumn cooled things off. The violence among the adults was more intense. At age thirteen, Riccardo watched a man shoot another in the head after a game of craps went bad.

This was not the way it was supposed to be, of course. In 1957, before Southwick had been built, the chamber of commerce invited Louisvillians to go "slumming" in the city's black neighborhoods to see the poverty and decay infesting the city.[4] In Little Africa, visitors would have seen seven hundred black homes, some of them dating from the 1800s, when the first black settlers had claimed the area for their own. There was poverty, but in the intervening years, residents had built sturdier houses, paved the streets, added sidewalks and mailboxes, and built up a significant business district. They established six grocery stores and a similar number of churches.[5]

Many old shacks still remained, however, and the chamber of commerce saw only "cancerous blight" that the city couldn't afford. Its members vowed that soon Louisville would get a "new look."[6] Over the next decade, more than two thousand acres of the city were razed in pursuit of a modern new cityscape. Politicians and chamber of commerce members called it "urban renewal," but its supposed beneficiaries, nearly all of them black, called it "urban removal."[7]

Urban renewal had been intended to correct a problem of the federal government's own creation. The Roosevelt administration, during the Great Depression, had set up a system to make home buying easier and less risky for average Americans. During the next several decades, the Federal Housing Administration insured billions of dollars in home loans, mostly for new houses being built in rings around core cities.[8] "Average American" didn't mean black. Up until 1950, the federal government essentially had a policy against making and insuring housing loans in black neighborhoods, arguing their presence hurt property values.[9] Even when the agency dropped the policy, blacks still faced huge obstacles in getting a loan or finding a real estate agent who would sell to them.[10] As cheap loans, new expressways, and expanding industry pulled whites out to the suburbs, most

African Americans were left behind, isolated in neighborhoods that no one was willing to invest in.

As inner cities became poorer, the federal government set out to mitigate the blight it had given birth to through the Federal Housing Administration's mortgage program. Cities like Louisville eagerly applied for federal grants set aside in 1949 and 1954 for what was at first called slum clearance. The main condition attached to the funds was that cities would find new housing for the people living in the homes that were destroyed.[11]

In Louisville, thousands of people and small businesses in "old tumbledown buildings" were displaced to make way for new roads, shops, hospitals, and office buildings and funneled into more "sanitary" homes overseen by the government.[12] About half of the ten thousand homes that were eventually torn down in Louisville were unoccupied. But tight-knit neighborhoods organized around church and school were also dispersed.[13] Slum clearance dissolved the warmth and caring that Fran Thomas remembered from her youth in Louisville's black community. In the area west of downtown surrounding Central where she had lived, three hundred acres of existing structures were demolished, 1,000 families plus 900 individuals were moved, and 560 businesses were closed.[14] In many cases, black homeowners were forced to sell their homes, but the payouts were rarely enough to allow them to buy elsewhere. Instead they became renters, often in the subsidized public housing that eventually replaced their neighborhoods.[15]

Usually, it took a while for the government to get around to building the new homes. Near Central's new building, the city demolished thirty-four acres of housing and left the area sitting empty for five years.[16] At one point in 1965, an aerial photograph showed the school standing nearly alone in a vast desert of empty lots spanning dozens of square blocks.[17] Some lots were never filled in. As one woman who was forced to sell her house put it at the time: "They're supposed to be helping poor people, but urban renewal is helping to make people poor."[18]

As blacks were displaced, many moved further west, to the dismay of the whites still rooted in the West End. The flow of whites to the suburbs became a flood in the 1960s. Realtors took advantage of the panic, scaring white residents into selling cheap with the news that blacks had moved to the block, then reselling their homes to blacks at a profit. Some white liberals, including the Bradens, fought back by holding protests and posting signs in their yards declaring that they would refuse to leave. A few of them still lived there half a century later.[19] But these holdouts couldn't stop white flight. Louisville's urban developers, in their efforts to root out the ghetto, had simply spread it across a larger swath of the city.

Starting in the 1970s, the conventional wisdom about urban renewal shifted. The federal government, finally noticing the disastrous consequences of slum clearance, began to emphasize rehabilitation over demolition.[20] But by then it was too late for the black communities in Louisville and in cities from Newark to Chicago that were already gone.

The civil rights movement gathered steam in the context of this huge shift in the landscapes of cities. The era of sit-ins and the dawn of busing corresponded with the new era of suburbs and white flight. Activists claimed victory after victory in the bloody battles to end Jim Crow, but as the suburbs filled up and cities emptied, these victories would eventually seem anachronistic. They won the integration of public transportation systems, but before long, there weren't that many whites taking the bus anyway; they drove their cars into the city from their homes in the suburbs. They forced the integration of downtown department stores and lunch counters, but whites no longer shopped there; they could be found in the new strip malls and shopping centers beyond the city limits. In cities that had yet to integrate their schools, which was most of them, there were fewer and fewer white students to integrate the black students with.

In Southwick, ten-year-old Riccardo X watched children not much older than he attacked by dogs and hosed down by police in Birmingham on the evening news. But more thrilling to a black child growing up in a Louisville housing project in the 1960s were the battles fought by Muhammad Ali.

Ali was born in 1942 on Grand Avenue in the West End, about ten blocks north of where the Southwick projects would be built. Relative to many blacks in Louisville, his parents were comfortably middle class. His father had regular work as a sign painter and occasionally did murals for local Baptist churches. His mother raised her two sons and worked as a housekeeper for white families when the family was stretched for cash.[21] Their block was a pleasant stretch of one- and two-story frame houses with porches, mowed lawns, and large trees near the unofficial border between the black and white West End. Ali wasn't sheltered from the racial struggles shaking the city and country as he was growing up in the 1940s and '50s, however. The newspaper pictures of Emmett Till, a boy about his own age who had been murdered after allegedly flirting with a white woman, put into focus the threat that always hung over the head of a black man in the Jim Crow South.[22]

Ali attended Central High School in 1957. Although he ostensibly could have chosen another high school under the city's new desegregation plan, like most black students that year, he didn't. He was indifferent to school (as he would tell reporters later, a high school diploma was still likely to lead to a dead-end for a black man), but the principal, Atwood Wilson, was patient with him. Already at that age, Ali was winning a name for himself as a boxer. Wilson ignored his abysmal grades and embraced Ali's bragging, even repeating at school assemblies the teenager's boasts that soon he would be heavyweight champion of the world. Ali would eventually be Central's "claim to fame," Wilson told faculty members who were reluctant to grant him a diploma.[23]

He was right soon enough. In 1960, a year after graduating, Ali won a gold medal at the Olympics and made his triumphant return to Louisville.[24] The mayor and three hundred other fans, including the ebullient Atwood Wilson and a group of Central cheerleaders, drawn away from their duties rooting for the school's championship football and basketball teams, greeted him at the airport before he paraded to his alma mater.[25] Before he was famous, Ali had vowed that he would always be nice to his fans once he became a celebrity, and nowhere was he more beloved than among the youngsters of the black West End. In the weeks after his victory, he rode the streets of Louisville in an open pink Cadillac, shouting, "I am the greatest!" to his ardent fans.[26] His brashness was daring and inspiring to his young fans, but in an era of sit-ins, marches, water hoses, and police dogs, Ali wasn't pushing very hard against the boundaries of the Southern racial structure—yet.

Ali's celebrity did not, unfortunately, improve Central's stature in Louisville. In fact, Ali's success corresponded with a major shift at the school. In the past, when Fran Thomas had attended and Lyman Johnson taught there, Central had been more like a prep school for the city's black middle and upper class. In the 1960s, thanks to the new building, Wilson met his goal to open the school to more students through a wider array of vocational offerings. Students made bookcases and cedar chests in advanced woodshop, learned welding and jewelry making in the machine shop, and served lunch to school officials in the commercial foods class.

Upholstery and dry cleaning classes came in 1967, around the time the school introduced a vocational orientation course, which a school official said was intended "to help the under-achiever into the mainstream of education." Students like Gwendolyn Hopson studied art and took home economics. A co-op program, which allowed students to leave school to work in the afternoon, typically at clerical jobs, also opened in the same year.[27] The programs were welcomed and needed, but they did not necessarily burnish the school's reputation for academic excellence.

By this time, more and more blacks from lower income levels were pursuing a high school education. Many black parents who had moved from the Deep South or the countryside seeking better opportunities for themselves were even more determined to find better opportunities for their children. The newcomers were mostly funneled to Central. At the same time, the opening of the white schools to blacks led some in the higher strata of black society to send their children to schools like Male, Shawnee, and even Atherton, a school on the eastern edge of the city limits that served the city's old-money neighborhoods.

Although Central was also adding new foreign-language classes and electives in journalism, Shakespeare, and the short story, its reputation was shifting along with its student population. Central was increasingly seen not only as the city's black school, but as a school for a lower class of blacks. The stereotype was cemented by urban renewal: The acres of vacant lots surrounded the school were being filled in with public housing projects that, in look and feel, closely resembled their dismal counterparts in Southwick.[28] The businesses the city promised would flock to the area never came. By the end of the 1960s, Central High School found itself situated in the heart of a new black ghetto, which, as a result of government good intentions gone awry, was more isolated and fragile than ever before.

Riccardo X would have liked to follow his hero, Ali, to Central, and most of Riccardo's friends from the Southwick housing projects were going there, but his mother was reluctant to let him go with them. In her eyes, Central had become a school for hoodlums. She wanted her children to get out of the projects eventually, and Central seemed like it would lead them straight back. Ali was influential among Louisville's young people, but the most important African American figure for many middle-aged blacks was Martin Luther King Jr.

Martin's brother, A. D. King, was the preacher at Zion Baptist Church, one of Louisville's most prominent churches. He had marched through the West End to promote open housing, and had spoken in the city many times.[29] Riccardo's grandfather was a Baptist minister, so weekends and many weeknights were spent in church. The adults around him revered Dr. Martin Luther King Jr. and muttered about the heresy of his rival, Malcolm X. Like many of her generation, Riccardo's mother, who had grown up as Jim Crow was in full swing, believed in King's integrationist goals and his nonviolent strategy. She wanted her son to take advantage of what Dr. King had been fighting for, and to her that meant going to a desegregated school. Riccardo didn't put up much of a fight. He was consoled by the fact that he could join the ROTC at Male, which would help him pursue a plan to join the military when he graduated; Central didn't have the ROTC.

Male High School, a long public bus ride away from Southwick, was not the picture of successful integration that Ricardo's mother imagined. As suburbanization drained the city of whites, schools in once-mixed neighborhoods like Parkland, Shawnee, and Old Louisville, a once-wealthy enclave south of downtown, became all black. Male sat on the outskirts of downtown, in a neighborhood that was also swiftly changing over. When Riccardo entered as a freshman in tenth grade, the school was roughly half white. Three years later, when he graduated, only a handful of white students were left.

Riccardo didn't much notice, nor did he mind. He realized the white people were probably leaving because of him, but he didn't have any desire to be around them, either. He was commander of the drill team and focused on becoming a soldier. After a childhood of battling in the streets, it seemed like a reasonable career choice. He often got into fights, but at the same time, he didn't want to end up like the guys who shot craps on the street corners in Southwick and Cotter. His mother was strict about school; she grounded him if he received a bad grade. Every afternoon, he marched in drills and saluted the flag with the Male ROTC. He channeled his energy and anger into academics and pickup basketball games.

In the evenings, he watched the news over dinner with his mother and sister. Opposition to the Vietnam War was gaining in fervor. Starting in 1965, every summer was punctuated by a new series of riots in black ghettos from Los Angeles to Newark. In Oakland, a fledgling new group, the Black Panthers, had created an alternative police force.[30] In the fall of 1967, two police officers were shot and one was killed in a confrontation with the Panthers' leader, Huey Newton.[31] For Christmas that year, every kid in Southwick wanted a black leather jacket and a beret. So did Riccardo, who was intrigued by the Panthers and their ideas.

Also gripping his attention were the changes happening in his hero, Muhammad Ali. In 1964, Ali had changed his name from Cassius Clay and made his membership in the Nation of Islam official.[32] For Ali, the association with Muhammad and Malcolm X's Nation of Islam, which the white media had characterized as a hate group, was a grave career risk. But to him, the Nation of Islam's take on America's race problem, and what blacks should do about it, made sense. It also gave him the purpose he had been looking for since the Emmett Till murder. "Black people were in trouble; we needed to help ourselves first," he later wrote.[33]

The ideas were old; the Nation of Islam simply repackaged them and sold them to a new generation. The message borrowed both from Booker T. Washington's arguments that the black race could be uplifted only in conditions of self-isolation and internal struggle and from Marcus Garvey's movement to reclaim Africa—and all its achievements and heritage—in order to ignite pride among African Americans.

Young men like Riccardo X, who grew up in the desolate landscape manufactured by urban renewal, where dignity was hard to come by and respect was earned with your fists, saw Ali's beliefs as revolutionary. Here was their hero, a black man unabashedly promoting himself, demanding respect and shamelessly declaring that he was the best and that he was beautiful. He didn't back down when white people, his parents, the newspapers, or even Martin Luther King Jr. disapproved. His bravery inspired awe.[34]

Most jarring and transformational for Riccardo was Muhammad Ali's refusal to fight in Vietnam. Riccardo had always admired Ali's rebelliousness, but had never thought too deeply about his political ideas as an adolescent. He started paying closer attention in 1966. "I ain't got no quarrel with them Vietcong," Ali declared to reporters when he had learned he would be drafted.[35] Riccardo, who often donned his military uniform to wear to school, was caught off guard, and also mesmerized. Ali stood to lose everything, including his heavyweight title, but he had not backed down. The news was a major jolt to Americans, both white and black. "My hero is not going to this white man's army," Riccardo thought to himself. "The black man's fight is here, not over there."

In the summer of 1967, blacks rose up in riots in cities across the country again. Even some of the city's pro-integration activists were fed up. The civil rights movement was splintering. Some were angered at the slow progress and the compromises that black leaders like King and others were forced to make with whites. In 1967, one group in Louisville, the West End Community Council—founded as a progressive homeowners' association—made "black power" its mission.[36]

The organization was racially integrated, counting among its members Anne and Carl Braden, and many of its members still espoused integration. But as their original goal became increasingly elusive, they turned to fighting against the degradation of the black ghetto. To further the mission, the group created a youth organizing arm staffed by young people employed with federal funding from the domestic Peace Corps, VISTA, one of President Johnson's War on Poverty innovations. The staff included a young art student and Central graduate from Smoketown, Robert Douglas, who would later be a founding member of CEASE. They called themselves the Black Unity League of Kentucky—BULK. Although two of the leaders, Sam Hawkins and Robert Sims, were drawn from Martin Luther King's Southern Christian Leadership Conference, they said their mission was to teach "black people to think black" in order to instill "self-pride into Negroes."[37]

As if to confirm to Riccardo that nonviolence and integration were doomed ideas, in the spring of 1968, Martin Luther King Jr., who had called for calm the summer before, was shot in Memphis. King's assassination unleashed another wave of violence in urban ghettos. That afternoon, Riccardo was outside hanging out with his friends when parents began appearing in apartment doorways calling for their children to come inside. The Southwick courtyards emptied quickly as families gathered around the television. Riccardo joined his mother to watch the news unfold. That night, riots erupted across the nation. In Louisville, the streets stayed quiet, but the calm was temporary.

A month after King's death in April, a black teacher and a real estate agent accused Louisville police of beating them during a traffic stop. The police officer admitted to slapping and hitting the real estate agent, Manfred Reid, who had stopped by the side of the road to see if his friend needed help. But Reid was arrested and charged with assault anyway; the police officer wasn't charged.[38]

Louisville's black community was outraged. The mayor, Kenneth Schmied, reacted by eventually suspending the officer, but a few days later, the civil service board overturned the officer's suspension.[39] BULK swung into action. The young men, now even more disillusioned with non-violence in the aftermath of King's death, called for a rally to protest the release of the officer the following Monday, May 27.[40]

On Monday, about two hundred blacks gathered at an intersection in Parkland for the protest. The two BULK leaders, Hawkins and Sims, took their place on top of a car parked in the middle of the street so they could be seen and heard. Joining them was an out-of-town guest, James Cortez, a member of the Student Nonviolent Coordinating Committee—SNCC. Cortez said he had also invited Stokely Carmichael, SNCC's leader, who had recently linked forces with the Black Panthers.[41]

In his speech, Cortez told the group to be proud of their blackness, and then broke the news that Carmichael wasn't coming: he said Carmichael's plane had been blocked from landing.[42] The crowd was furious. Sims stood up to speak, directing his wrath at the mayor. Schmied, a short, round man nicknamed "Cannonball," owned a business that sold furniture in the West End.[43] He was a Republican and a Nixon supporter who had opposed an ordinance banning racial discrimination in housing.[44] In his speech, Sims told the crowd that Mayor Schmied, whom he had met with that morning, had insisted to him that he understood what it was like in the West End. His furniture trucks drove through "everyday."[45]

"I'm not preaching violence, but if it was me, I'd turn those trucks over," Sims said. "The reason we're up here is that the honky policemen have been brutalizing our black brothers. We're going to tell the mayor that the next time this happens, he's going to see smoke signals coming from the west."[46]

Sims and Cortez climbed down from the car. People began to walk away.[47] Then, a bottle hit the pavement and smashed. A few seconds later, another hit. The people who had been strolling away began to run. A police car appeared, seemingly out of nowhere, with its sirens blaring. The officer jumped out of his car with his revolver ready.[48]

Bottles began raining down, showering the crowd with glass shards. People were now screaming, and more police cars were arriving. Someone fired a shot, halting the action for a few brief seconds. But then more shots cracked nearby, and the crowd began to panic. Within the hour, dozens of people had taken to the street and were moving in a mob. Police cars and two taxicabs were turned over. The looting began not too long after.[49] White stores were targeted; black stores were mostly left alone, as were white merchants who charged low prices.[50]

A brief moment of calm in the morning didn't last. People had heard a false rumor that Mayor Schmied was spending the day golfing, and a true account of his refusal to come to the West End to talk with black leaders, including A. D. King.[51] Nearly one thousand National Guardsmen were called up, and a curfew was put in place. But by 2 p.m., a new mob was running through the streets, smashing windows and throwing rocks.[52] The "disorder," as the newspapers called it, lasted another day. Police killed two teenage boys, one fourteen and the other nineteen.[53] Most of the rioters were young black men, and a fifth of those arrested were unemployed, although about fifty whites participated.[54]

Afterwards, Sims, Hawkins, and Cortez were arrested along with the black real estate agent who had been hit by the police officer and the middle class wife of a black doctor who had made contributions to BULK, all of them charged as co-conspirators in the riots.[55] The local newspapers, however, blamed black "frustration and anger." A *New York Times* reporter toured the Cotter Homes, the housing project next door to Riccardo's home in Southwick, in the aftermath of the riots. She found unemployed youth bored with the tedium of their days and outraged at the conditions they lived in. "They've got their little government reservation here," one boy told her.[56]

Riccardo had begun to see things the same way. He had watched his neighborhood burning around him, watched the racial integration at his high school dissolve before his eyes. He still wore his ROTC uniform and led the drill team—ROTC had promised him a college scholarship—but outside school he wore his leather jacket. In 1971, he headed off to college on an ROTC scholarship, but he told his mother that if his name was drawn for the draft, he would follow Ali's lead and refuse to go.

As he entered his freshmen year of college—later, he would decline to say which college he attended, refusing to acknowledge any association with a place he said taught him nothing—Riccardo started an extracurricular reading program. The first book on his list was the *Autobiography of Malcolm X*. Next he read Huey Newton's *To Die for the People*. He started out taking business classes, but he was inspired: "Here was a new way to struggle. No longer were black people begging whites for sympathy. They were going to take their justice," he told himself. He signed up for some political science classes, and decided he would get a teaching certificate so he could teach while going to law school. His plan was to be a criminal defense lawyer. In 1975, after finishing college, he moved to Newburg, one of only a handful of suburban neighborhoods outside of the Louisville city limits that was majority black, and took a job teaching history in the suburban Jefferson County schools.

Chapter 10

In 1954, Joyce Spond, a wide-eyed farm girl freshly graduated from Old Home High School in Bardstown, Kentucky, moved into her sister's newly constructed bungalow in Shively.[1] The house, already filled with young children, was a few doors down from the house that the white civil rights activists Anne and Carl Braden had bought on behalf of the Wades, an African American family, a year earlier. It now lay partly in rubble. As Joyce adjusted to her new neighborhood, she caught some of the rumors about the bombing passing over the backyard fences: People said the Wades and the Bradens had ulterior motives. The police, who had eventually settled into watching over the Wades' house from the yards of their white neighbors, leaked out what seemed to be incriminating details. Someone heard that the bomb had been planted indoors, meaning that it must have been an inside job. The theories of a Communist conspiracy printed in the *Shively Newsweek* met with nods of approval. The idea that a black family might see in Shively the same things that they did—a place where they could finally have a nice house, a good school, a safe place for their children to play—didn't occur to them.

The bombing had not halted Shively's development boom. The suburb's growth was the product of a major demographic shift occurring at the same time as the other major migrations of the first half of the twentieth century. After World War II, just about everyone was on the move:

The North became the cultural center of black life as the Great Migration emptied the South of millions of blacks; similar numbers of white urbanites responded to the influx of blacks to cities and the availability of cheap government loans by moving to new suburbs; and, less noted but just as dramatic, huge numbers of white people from the countryside abandoned their family farms and headed to urban centers to claim their share of the country's new prosperity.

In Kentucky, the population went from being 70 percent to only 50 percent rural between 1940 and 1960.[2] More than two hundred thousand people moved to Louisville in those two decades, and three-quarters of them moved to the suburbs. In Louisville, the suburbs grew as the city population dropped for the first time in the city's history.[3] In moving directly from farm to suburb, these people skipped the experience of "urbanization," holding onto the more conservative value systems they had brought with them from the countryside. The historian C. Vann Woodward called the process "rurbanization."[4]

Joyce Spond was part of this less-noticed migration of rural whites to the city. She had been born one of nine children raised on a farm in Nelson County, a Catholic stronghold in the center of Kentucky. Her father was a carpenter and her mother a homemaker. Life in rural Kentucky revolved around church and school. Joyce went to a one-room schoolhouse for elementary school, and then commuted to Old Kentucky Home High School, named for its proximity to the plantation commemorated in the state's official song. "My Old Kentucky Home" was about the idyllic countryside and the hard life for slaves on the plantation, and it was also about emigration. "A few more days till we totter on the road, then my old Kentucky home, good night," the lyrics went. The rolling hills around Bardstown, forty miles south of Louisville, were beautiful, but there was little work. High school graduates looking for a job outside of farming had only one choice: to move to the city.

Already, several of her siblings had left for Louisville, and Joyce saw no option but to follow. Many of her Shively neighbors had followed the same trajectory. Most were just a generation away from coal mining or subsistence farming. In the blocks around her lived other graduates from Old Home and schools like it across the state. They were strivers who saw the tracts of ranch houses and one-acre yards as the next step up the ladder. Once the Wades had moved away, it only took a few months for peace to return to the neighborhood. But underneath the surface calm, a deep anxiety was lurking.

The residents of Shively thought of themselves as ordinary Americans, patriotic and hardworking, and as the 1960s progressed, they wondered where the country was headed as they watched the news of the riots happening a few miles away in Parkland and in cities around the country. They worried that everything they had worked for could be taken away; the bombing in 1954 was enough proof that the violence of the radicals might intrude here. But for those who were paying attention, scarier even than the riots and the antiwar protesters tearing up black neighborhoods and college campuses were the nine black-robed men and the aggressive members of the Johnson administration who seemed determined to use their power to promote civil rights for blacks at the expense of whites. Moving to the suburbs was part of what was supposed to be a seamless journey from rural poverty to urban blue-collar endeavor to eventual white-collar success. The presence of blacks there threatened this path. If Shively became known as a black neighborhood, property values would decline, and, as important, so would the self-worth and social standing the whites who lived there were fighting so hard to attain.[5]

Joyce stayed with her sister for only a few months in the city while she gained her footing. She got a job at White Castle, and then enrolled in comptometer school to learn how to use an accounting machine. Her pale blue eyes and pretty face made marriage a likely prospect, however. Within a year, she had married and not long after was moving into her own Shively ranch house a couple of streets away from her sister's.

Joyce's husband was a Teamster who eventually took a good job working for the union. When Joyce became pregnant, she quit her own job to stay at home. She had a son, and a couple of years later, twin girls. Their house was a small bungalow with a front porch and a garage, but the most important feature, as far as Joyce was concerned, was Schaffner Elementary, two blocks away. To Joyce, the school's proximity was a luxurious amenity: from first to fourth grade, Joyce had walked two miles each way to the local one-room schoolhouse, and the trip to her high school had taken an hour and sometimes more on a school bus, one way.

Just as in the rural towns where the new suburbanites had come from, the school was the center of their lives. Joyce had been ambitious before her marriage, and now she poured her energy into the PTA, where she rose in the ranks to become the president. As the 1960s came to a close, her role expanded beyond organizing bake sales.

In 1964, Congress had passed and President Johnson had signed the Civil Rights Act. Among other major precedents in the law, it allowed the US attorney general to sue school districts that continued to segregate and to take away their federal funding.[6] The landmark law seemed to spark even more anger and violence: For five years running after the passage of the law, summer riots broke out in black ghettos.

Baffling to white suburbanites, the Johnson administration suggested that the violence and rage in the ghetto was their fault.[7] A study commissioned by the president, the Kerner Report, blamed the violence on "a destructive environment totally unknown to most white Americans" inside the "racial ghetto." Whites outside the ghetto had "prospered to a degree unparalleled in the history of civilization," while blacks were excluded even as "this affluence has been flaunted" before them. "What white Americans have never fully understood but what the Negro can never forget is that white society is deeply implicated in the ghetto. White institutions created it, white institutions maintain it, and white society condones it," the report said.[8]

Under Johnson's leadership, the US Department of Health, Education and Welfare (HEW) took on a more proactive role in the pursuit of school desegregation.[9] Until 1965, the NAACP, working mostly alone, had been slogging through court case after court case trying to force school districts to comply with the *Brown* ruling. With the passage of the Civil Rights Act, the federal government finally stepped in as an enforcer.

The new role was driven in part by another influential report commissioned by the president.[10] The Coleman Report, as it came to be known, was a sweeping survey of the state of education for minority children published in 1966. It found that white and black children, particularly in the South, still attended schools where segregation was "nearly complete." In schools where there was some integration, it was almost always a few blacks mixed in with whites, never a few whites in a black school. Looking at standardized tests, the report found a disturbing gap between black and white students. The gap started early, gradually widening as students reached the upper grades. Southern blacks, followed by Southern whites, did the worst on tests, but in the South, the gap between the two groups was largest.

The report's most important finding was that schools mattered less than what happened at home in the students' lives. Yet this was less true for minority students; for them, schools mattered much more in determining whether they would achieve: "It is for the most disadvantaged children that improvements in school quality will make the most difference in achievement." Facilities mattered, teachers mattered more, but most important was the family background of the child and of the other students the child was surrounded by, according to the Coleman Report. It concluded that if a student's classmates came from wealthier homes where parents had higher levels of education and where achievement was emphasized, the student would perform better in school. If the classmates were poor, with parents who had weaker educational backgrounds, the student would do worse in school.

The report gave the Johnson administration a mandate to push harder on desegregation. Just as important as its promise to cut funding for school districts that continued to segregate, in 1966, HEW created guidelines describing what a desegregated school district should look like.[11] No longer could school districts hide behind the vaguely worded *Brown* decision. The guidelines specifically targeted freedom of choice plans, like the one in Louisville, and required school districts to prove that these plans actually led to desegregated schools or risk losing federal funding.

The courts still had a big role to play. In the spring of 1968, an NAACP case contesting a freedom of choice plan in New Kent County, near Richmond, Virginia, reached the Supreme Court. The plaintiffs argued in *Green v. New Kent County* that the school district had created a complicated web of overlapping bus routes in order to ensure that the county's two high schools remained racially segregated.[12] Earl Warren, the chief justice who facilitated the passage of the unanimous *Brown* decision, was still on the bench. Also on the Court was a newcomer: Thurgood Marshall, the NAACP lawyer who had orchestrated the *Brown* strategy, had been nominated a year earlier. When the lawyers stood up to make their oral arguments to the Court, on April 5, it was less than twenty-four hours since Martin Luther King Jr. had been assassinated in Memphis.[13]

The Court's decision came swiftly. In May, the judges argued that merely telling families that their children could "freely" choose where they wanted to go was not enough to ensure equity.[14] School districts must take *affirmative* action in ensuring racial mixing and create "a system without a 'white' school and a 'Negro' school, but just schools."

For civil rights activists, the decision, although it was still vague about what school districts should actually do to end segregation in the schools, was something to celebrate during an otherwise traumatic year. Along with the death of Martin Luther King, Johnson was escalating the war in Vietnam, and that June Robert Kennedy, a favorite of many blacks because of his efforts to help African American communities and his association with Dr. King, was assassinated while running for the Democratic presidential nomination.[15] But for white Southerners in the suburbs, the court's decision was added to other ominous signs—the riots, the antiwar protests, the spread of drugs, sex, and crime—that the security of their place in the world was in danger.

That summer, a Republican presidential candidate responded to their fears. Richard Nixon, carefully positioning himself between the segregationist third-party candidate, Governor George Wallace of Alabama, and the liberal Governor Nelson Rockefeller of New York, pitched his campaign to voters living in places like Shively in what would later be called "The Southern Strategy."[16] It was these people—white suburbanites, many not too many years removed from the farm, living in cities under siege by the civil rights movement—who had almost won him the 1960 election against Kennedy.[17] He understood what they wanted to hear. He spoke about the need to restore "law and order." He sounded reasonable on Vietnam, vowing to end the war, but responsibly.[18] And, most important to his Southern constituents after the *Green* decision, he laid out a reassuring stance on school integration.

Brown, Nixon said, speaking during a television interview in Charlotte, North Carolina, "was a correct decision."[19] "But on the other hand," he added, "the proactive desegregation of the schools, as the justices had ordered in the *Green* decision, "should be very scrupulously examined and in many cases I think should be rescinded." The setting for the interview most likely wasn't an accident. Charlotte was the setting for one of the nearly two hundred cases questioning freedom of choice plans.

In 1965, encouraged by the new provisions in the Civil Rights Act, local NAACP lawyers in Charlotte had sued the school board on behalf of a black family whose son had been assigned to a black school farther from their home than the local neighborhood school.[20] In April 1971, the

Supreme Court handed down a unanimous decision in the case, *Swann v. Charlotte-Mecklenburg Board of Education.*

Green, which had focused on a small town, had not settled what large cities like Charlotte and Louisville—where there was significant residential segregation—should do to create racial balance in their schools. The *Swann* case was more precise: "We find no basis for holding that the local school authorities may not be required to employ bus transportation as one tool of school desegregation. Desegregation plans cannot be limited to the walk-in school."[21] In other words, the justices believed busing was a potential and even preferable tool for rooting out school segregation. The Court foresaw the potential arguments against this solution, but believed it was worth it, even if it was "administratively awkward, inconvenient, and even bizarre in some situations." They also argued that though it might be inconvenient, busing students across town certainly wasn't a novel idea. After all, students had been bused ever since the country began shifting away from one-room schoolhouses. About 40 percent of students traveled to school by bus in 1970, the Court noted.

The justices may have predicted there would be resistance to their ruling, but it's unlikely they could have predicted how much.

Chapter 11

In the fall of 1971, dozens of school districts started the school year with new student assignment plans, many of them involving busing.[1] Joyce Spond watched these developments with concern. The *Shively Newsweek*, which had floated the idea that the Wades and Bradens had been co-conspirators in the house bombing, followed the desegregation cases closely, and Joyce read it regularly. Louisville, where most schools were as segregated as they had been before 1954, was ripe for a court case.

In 1969, the NAACP had filed a complaint to the federal department of Health, Education and Welfare about the segregation in Louisville's schools. HEW inspected, and found that Central High School's all-black student population was in violation of federal law. The agency's recommendations focused on changing the student assignment system so that some white students would be zoned to attend Central. Other options were busing some black students to other schools in exchange for white students, pairing Central with a white vocational school and sharing students, or closing it.[2]

All of the options were bad ones. The superintendent of the Louisville schools, Newman Walker, complained that changing the zoning would just cause white students assigned to Central to move away, accelerating the already rapid decrease in the city's white population.[3] (By the end of the 1960s, almost half of Louisville's students were black.)[4] Surveys had found that "a considerable majority of whites and blacks" opposed busing, according to school administrators.[5] School officials worried that Central's academic program would be watered down if it were paired with a white vocational school and shop classes became the focus. And closing the school would be a public relations nightmare; as a local reporter noted, it was a "proud, closely-knit place with a long tradition."[6]

The school system did nothing.[7] By the following year, there was less pressure on the city from HEW: Nixon had pushed out the director, Leon Panetta, for being too enthusiastic about seeking out discrimination in the schools. As a result, the agency had essentially stopped trying to enforce the 1964 Civil Rights Act.[8] Although the students of Central had been instrumental in Louisville's civil rights movement, they were not necessarily impatient for change at their own school.[9] The fierce pride in Central had only grown since the first round of desegregation in 1956, in part because of the school's ascendance in that all-important arena of Kentucky culture: the basketball court.

The glory began in 1957.[10] In the Louisville invitational tournament that year—only a year after Central students had begun competing against white teams—the Central team took home the trophy after trouncing a strong team from Manual, a predominantly white school. In 1965, Central broke the record for longest winning streak in Kentucky high school basketball history, then lost by two points to a small-town team in the state semifinals. In 1968, the Yellowjackets' circumspect coach, Bob Graves, abandoned his usual caution and predicted his team would take the state championship. It lost that year, but the following year, Central won the Louisville tournament and went on to the state tournament again. It played a team from a coal-mining county in western Kentucky, and seventeen thousand people packed into the stadium to see the game. "These people have come here to see you lose," Coach Graves told his players before the game.[11]

Instead, the Central team broke records. One player scored 44 points, the highest number of individual points in Kentucky history. As a whole, the team broke the record for most points scored in a game, 101. And, most important, the Central players won, making them the first all-black team to win the Kentucky state championship. The team members came back heroes. The mayor threw them a banquet in Freedom Hall, a huge auditorium at the city's fairgrounds; the governor commissioned the whole team and Coach Graves as Kentucky Colonels; and the school administration hung a huge banner across the front of the school's now nearly twenty-year-old yellow-brick building.

But in 1970, at the prodding of the NAACP, the federal agency once again questioned Louisville about the situation at Central, warning the school district that it had until September to desegregate the school.[12] Central's student council president, Vernon Douglas, told the local newspaper that he was "shocked" at the NAACP's plan to try to desegregate the school. "It seemed like a plot to destroy Central," Douglas said. "It's a black institution. And I don't see anything wrong with the way it is."[13] In April of 1970, Douglas confronted the school board at a public meeting and asked what was going to happen to his school.

The superintendent hemmed and hawed, blaming the inaction of HEW, which had not given the school district any specific advice about which option it should choose. (A federal appeals court later found HEW guilty of blatantly ignoring its duty to enforce school desegregation.)[14] That month, the NAACP, which had filed the complaint in the first place, suggested its own plan: turn Central into a magnet school. The concept was a new one. The idea was to create programs "so innovative and desirable" that white students would choose to come to the school on their own. The local newspaper wondered in an editorial if this magnet idea wouldn't revive the city's old status as "a showcase for the nation" when it came to desegregation plans.[15]

But by 1971, when the *Swann* ruling was handed down, no action had been taken yet. The summer before, the Kentucky Civil Liberties Union (KCLU) had filed a lawsuit complaining that the Jefferson County Schools, a separate school system that encompassed the mostly white suburbs around Louisville, had purposely isolated black students living in Newburg, a factory village surrounding a GE plant not far from the Louisville city line, in their own, segregated schools.[16]

The following summer, the KCLU joined with the NAACP in filing a lawsuit that named as defendants the Louisville school district and the separate Jefferson County school district.[17] The plaintiffs were a group of "black citizens" of Louisville, according to the lawsuit. The top plaintiff on the case, John Haycraft, had no children.[18] He was a graduate of Central High School and a journalist who had marched in Washington, DC, with

Martin Luther King Jr. in 1963. The lawsuit demanded that the Louisville system incorporate some white suburbs along its fringe to aid in the desegregation of the city schools.

A group of civil rights activists, among them Lyman Johnson and the Kentucky teachers' union, didn't think the lawsuit went far enough. They joined the case as intervening plaintiffs, arguing that soon enough, the fringe suburbs would experience white flight, leaving the Louisville school district in the same boat.[19] In their complaint, they demanded that the Louisville and Jefferson County districts be merged, along with a tiny district within the Jefferson County system, Anchorage, which included a handful of all-white schools.

Although on its surface the merger demand seemed like a big step, in reality, the Louisville school system had been toying with the idea of dissolving itself and joining the county schools for a decade, mainly for financial reasons.[20] In 1969, the county and city school boards had met to discuss a merger, but the two sides could not agree. The county wanted simply to absorb the city district into its own system, but the city administrators hoped to retain some power and control in the transition. The matter was dropped. Once the desegregation cases were filed in court, however, the idea began to look more realistic.

In response to the Newburg lawsuit, Joyce Spond, along with three other mothers, founded Save Our Community Schools, also known as SOCS. They were not original—other groups had formed in other cities facing busing under the same name. The mothers believed the Newburg case was a harbinger of the busing schemes they were reading about elsewhere. In 1972, their concerns were validated when the civil rights lawyers proposed the merger. They invited their neighbors and church friends to join them, and more than four hundred people showed up at their first meeting in the Shively Heights Baptist Church.

Joyce told the standing room–only crowd there was an upcoming convention about busing in Washington, DC. She got a resounding response: "Go!" The participants passed a collection, and by the end of the night, they had enough to send three of the organizers, Joyce and two others, to Washington. Soon after, the three women drove to the airport with $270 in hand—most of it in $1 bills—to buy three plane tickets at $90 each.

At the convention, their fears were confirmed. Parents from districts where busing was under way reported that it had decimated local PTAs and that children spent hours being transported to faraway neighborhoods. Presenters railed against the disastrous effects that busing had on learning and school communities. The stated goal was improving education, but to Joyce's mind, it seemed clear that busing plans had nothing to do with that. She came back energized and empowered, ready to organize to keep busing from coming to Louisville. It helped that politicians in Washington finally seemed to be listening.

1972 was an election year, and as the campaign season started up, the spreading conflict over busing took center stage. "To many Americans, the most important journeys of election year 1972 are not the candidates' per-egrinations, or even President Nixon's visits to Moscow and Peking, but the trips that their children—black or white, Northern or Southern—take each day in school buses," wrote one *Time* magazine reporter that winter.[21] Nixon, getting ready to defend his presidency, clarified—and hardened—his stance on busing. "I am against busing as that term is commonly used in school desegregation cases. I have consistently opposed the busing of our nation's children to achieve racial balance, and I am opposed to the busing of children simply for the sake of busing," he said, adding that he had instructed HEW to make sure busing was kept to the "minimum required by law."[22]

Buoyed by the growing backlash against busing, Governor George Wallace, who had said he would defy any federal busing orders in Alabama, made his third try for the Democratic presidential nomination. In March of 1972, Wallace shocked the establishment by winning the Florida Democratic primary after promising voters that if they backed him, "they're going to stop busing little children to Kingdom Come."[23]

It was not only white voters—people like Joyce Spond—who got worked up over the idea of busing. During the same month that Wallace won the Florida primary, black groups from across the country and the political spectrum converged in Gary, Indiana, for a National Black Political Convention. The convention included pro-integration activists: The NAACP was there; Jesse Jackson was there; Shirley Chisholm was there. But the black nationalists in attendance were more vocal, and more numerous. As Roger Wilkins, the black journalist, wrote in a dispatch from the convention for the *Washington Post*, "Lately, speakers have taken to asking their black audiences, 'What time is it?' The powerful, black-throated response, 'Nation Time.'"[24]

Nation time meant a lot of things, Wilkins wrote, but for most, it meant independence from—not integration with—whites. In a loud voice vote, the Nation Time faction overwhelmed the integration supporters and adopted a resolution condemning busing as "racist" and "suicidal." The resolution argued that busing was based on the "false notion that black children are unable to learn unless they are in the same setting as white children."[25] Instead, they wanted equal funding to maintain and improve the traditional black schools that previous generations had built, often with little help from the white-controlled government at all.

In Louisville, the lawsuits against the school districts claimed to represent the majority of black citizens in Louisville, but a few years earlier, black parents in the West End had resisted a small-scale desegregation plan that would have mixed black and white students attending two elementary schools in nearby neighborhoods.[26] Nationally, polls had also tracked the resistance among blacks to busing. Although a majority of both blacks and whites favored desegregation and thought that methods like gerrymandering school zones or placing low-income housing in middle-class neighborhoods was okay, the vast majority opposed busing. A 1973 Gallup poll found that only 9 percent of blacks approved of sending black children out of their own neighborhoods in order to desegregate schools.[27]

The resistance to busing in Louisville and elsewhere ignored the academic gains that blacks had made since the beginning of school desegregation, however token it was. After 1956, the gap between white and blacks in Louisville narrowed, according to a study conducted by a local researcher at the University of Louisville.[28] Before desegregation, blacks in Louisville had scored about five months behind whites in reading. On some tests, they had scored as much as fourteen months behind. Five years later, the study found that they were only a month behind their white counterparts. Other research, including the nationally renowned Coleman Report, also suggested that academic achievement for black students—who were more often poor—was likely to be improved in integrated settings.

Why were so many blacks so against busing if it appeared to help their children do better in school and, as the NAACP argued, it was the moral and just thing to do? As one black father of three in Louisville's West End, who called himself only Phil, told the local newspaper, "It's a step backward for black people as far as understanding who we are." Busing felt like an effort to assimilate black people and erase their identity and culture, and, at the same time, seemed like a not-so-subtle way of reasserting white dominance over blacks. As the war over busing began to rage, there was a feeling that once again, black people had little control over their lives and their children. "It's the federal government pitting the people on the bottom of the economic ladder against one another. The real issue is, how come there ain't no black people out there in those neighborhoods?" Phil told the reporter.[29]

The Louisville lawsuits moved forward despite the negative opinions about busing, even among blacks, and in December of 1972, the civil rights attorneys faced off with the city and county attorneys in federal court.[30] The political climate had deteriorated even further for the busing proponents. A month earlier, Nixon had won reelection, helped along by his anti-busing platform. A movement was under way to introduce a constitutional amendment that would prohibit busing for school desegregation.[31] And several anti-busing bills, one of them written by the Nixon administration, were moving through Congress.

In Louisville, Joyce Spond's group, working out of church fellowship halls and living rooms, was in the process of collecting ten thousand telegrams to send to Congress opposing busing and supporting the amendment. Joyce was getting invitations from across the city to talk to other groups of concerned white parents. She now traveled to Washington and Frankfort, the capital of Kentucky, frequently, hobnobbing with senators and lobbying for her cause. Her group published voting guides on local candidates based on their stances on busing. For the most part, when she showed up for a visit, the politicians were happy to oblige her.

The one hope for those on the other side, the desegregation advocates, was the federal judge hearing the Louisville cases, James Gordon.[32] He was an imposing former army M.P. from a small tobacco town in western Kentucky. His mother, a cigarette-smoking suffragette, had been the first woman to pass the bar in Kentucky, and his father was a circuit court judge. In his own law practice after World War II, he represented the coal companies that had moved into western Kentucky following the war, but Gordon also had a history in politics; he had supported the Kentucky governor who had called for the state to abide by the *Brown* decision in 1954, and later helped run Lyndon Johnson's campaign in Kentucky. In 1965, Johnson rewarded him by appointing him to the federal bench. Gordon was gruff and cantankerous. Lawyers who argued before him joked that he was often in error, but never in doubt. He rarely took time to mull over a decision. Instead he often ruled the day after a trial, because otherwise he "would forget more and more of it."

Gordon took longer than usual to decide the two desegregation cases, however. Four months after the trial, in March of 1973, he released two long opinions in the Newburg case and the Haycraft case, dismissing both of them.[33] He believed busing would result only in more white flight, and that the evidence of segregation, while deplorable, was not the fault of the school districts. It was de facto decisions by individual citizens to live in racially segregated neighborhoods, not de jure policies by the government to deliberately separate the races, that had caused the racial imbalance in the city and suburban schools. The activists appealed the decision, but their chance of victory seemed slim.

Nixon, under scrutiny as the Watergate scandal began to heat up, had been at work fanning the anti-busing fervor even more vigorously than he had during his presidential campaigns. In March of 1972, he gave a speech saying that the idea to ban busing through a constitutional amendment had "a fatal flaw: It takes too long." What the country needed was "action now." He vowed to send a bill to Congress that would institute a moratorium on all new busing plans, effective immediately.[34]

At the same time, moving through the courts was a case from Detroit, where the courts had made the unprecedented decision of forcing three suburban districts to join as defendants in a lawsuit against the city schools.[35] The suburban districts had not been named as parties in the original complaint, but the local judges had reasoned—presciently— that if the suburbs were excluded from desegregation in Detroit, the city would quickly lose its white residents.[36] The decision was headed to the Supreme Court, which that year had gained two new, conservative Nixon appointees, William Rehnquist and Lewis Powell, to replace a pair of more moderate justices.[37]

In the Louisville case, a three-judge appellate court meanwhile reversed Judge Gordon's decision.[38] Louisville, Jefferson County, and Anchorage, the tiny all-white district in an outer suburb of the city, were ordered to merge their school districts and create a desegregation plan that would go into effect the following school year.

Joyce Spond was incensed; the telegrams, the meetings, the lobbying hadn't worked. The courts—which were not apolitical, just slower moving in their political shifts than the legislative and executive branches—were still filled with Kennedy and Johnson appointments from the civil rights era. But slow as they were to shift, the courts were indeed beginning to reflect the politics of the Silent Majority. The Louisville case, like Detroit's, was appealed to the Supreme Court to wait for a decision.

Gordon ordered the city and suburban district to come up with their own desegregation plans, including the merging of their two systems. Meanwhile, the judge received dozens of letters from the Ku Klux Klan, as local politicians railed against busing. Several newly formed anti-busing groups, along with Save Our Community Schools, tried to lobby the judge to see their point of view. The groups talked about combining forces, but they could never agree on the principles they were fighting for. The newcomers were more extreme than SOCS. Those in Joyce's group said their main concern was the quality of the schools; they even came up with their own suggestions for Judge Gordon to comply with the court of appeals order without implementing full-on busing. Students could do occasional interracial exchanges on field trips or for certain classes, for example. The other groups didn't want to compromise. They were against desegregation, whatever form it took.

In July 1974, it became clear the two districts would never agree on a compromise plan.[39] Instead, Gordon announced his own proposal on July 20, which he called Plan X. The specifics were vague, except for the requirement that schools have student populations that were between 12 and 30 percent black. The districts were given less than a week to go over the plan and work out the details. Jean Ruffra, one of the cofounders of SOCS, told the local paper that she was not surprised by Gordon's announcement, adding, "No plan was acceptable to us. . . . There is nothing we can do to appeal this decision."[40]

Less than a week later, before Gordon's court reconvened, the Supreme Court declared a decision in the Detroit case, *Milliken v. Bradley*.[41] This time the Court was split, and the conservatives won.[42] They scoffed at the lower court's reasoning that somehow the white suburban districts should be included in the case, arguing that "the inter-district remedy could extensively disrupt and alter the structure of public education." It was uncalled for and unconstitutional, they said. Shortly after, they sent the Louisville case back to the circuit court for review in light of the *Milliken* decision.[43] Desegregation in Louisville seemed to be dead.

People in Louisville were stunned, and, in the suburbs, many were re-lieved. In August, lawmakers in Washington, DC, shored up the subur-banites' sense of security. Twelve days after the Watergate scandal forced Nixon to resign from office, Gerald Ford signed into law a major educa-tion bill that included, for the first time, a section on busing.[44] The law outlawed busing a child beyond the second nearest school to his or her home.[45] It seemed like a great victory for anti-busing activists. But also for the first time in federal legislation, the law explicitly required previously segregated school districts to take affirmative action to undo racial separa-tion, and in practice, the law could not supersede court orders meant to remedy violations of the Constitution, meaning busing was still a viable option for districts.

And so the busing fight continued to rage in many places. In Boston, white parents had taken to the streets and were boycotting the schools to protest a new desegregation plan there. But in Louisville, the 1974 school year began calmly after a soggy, humid summer.[46] Despite some token integration, most suburban schools remained nearly all white.[47] Many of the inner-city schools in Louisville were still exclusively black, twenty years after the *Brown* decision and a decade after the passage of the Civil Rights Act. Joyce's children walked to Schaffner each day. Life was quiet without the organizing and protest work that had kept her busy for the past few years. In October, the circuit court heard rearguments in the case, but it seemed likely that it would follow the Supreme Court's lead in *Milliken* and reverse its previous order to merge the two districts in Louisville.[48]

Instead, the circuit court shocked everyone by ordering Louisville to move forward with the merger plan.[49] In April, the Louisville school board voted to dissolve itself, forcing the merger with the Jefferson County Pub-lic Schools. Judge Gordon announced the details of the finalized busing plan in July.[50] All schools in Jefferson County, including the tiny district of Anchorage, were required to have a ratio of black students that fell between 16 and 25 percent. Partly because of their larger numbers, and partly in an effort to minimize white flight, white students would be bused for only two to three years. Black students, in contrast, would be bused for eight to ten years. Five schools, all but one of them traditionally black schools located downtown and in the West End, would be closed.

A few days before school started that summer, lawyers representing Save Our Community Schools went to beg the Supreme Court for a last-minute stay, petitioning the only two judges who were in Washington, DC, for the summer, Powell and Blackmun.[51] They were denied. Joyce Spond had been busy all summer, and not only fighting against busing. She also volunteered for the school board, manning a hotline for parents confused about where their children would be assigned.[52] If busing was going to happen, she wanted it go smoothly. Among anti-busing advocates, she was mostly alone in that goal.

The anti-busing movement Joyce helped start had taken on a life of its own. Other mothers in Louisville, inspired by the civil resistance to busing in Boston that year, were planning street marches. Sue Connor, a plump, redheaded mother of four, founded a branch of Concerned Parents, a more extreme anti-busing group that had spread across the South, and began organizing an army of angry parents.[53] From the kitchen of her brand-new wood-shingle house in a quiet subdivision in Jeffersontown, a suburb situated between Louisville's tony eastern suburbs and the working-class south, Connor manned the phones, printed flyers, and strategized.

In Boston, the resistance had unself-consciously borrowed the tactics of the civil rights marchers, but it didn't always mimic their restraint.[54] White mobs had beaten dozens of blacks, stoned buses full of black children, vandalized school buildings, and attacked police cars.[55] (In several instances, blacks responded in kind.) In Louisville, Sue Connor and other anti-busing leaders called for peaceful protest, but they were mostly powerless to control their followers, many of them from poorer areas to the south: Pleasure Ridge Park, Okolona, Shively, and Fairdale.

Connor announced that her group would hold a protest in front of the federal building downtown on the first day of school. At the last minute, the Ku Klux Klan announced it would hold a demonstration there, too, complete with white hoods and a cross burning. Connor called off her protest. "Where the Klan goes, we don't go," she told reporters. Instead, she said her group would fan out to suburban churches, where protesters would hold an all-day candlelight vigil. Violence would be hard to avoid, however, she said: "I'd like for people who say there is no worry about violence to wake up. If there is violence, I am going to point my finger at the forced busing advocates and the NAACP."[56]

As the busing protests took off, Joyce retreated from the furor. She still opposed busing, but in the lead-up to the court decision, she had become friends with Bernard Minnis, a black official in the school district, and with the president of the NAACP, who occasionally invited her to parties. Years later, as the neighborhood around Schaffner shifted, Joyce stayed put. She remained active in the schools her grandchildren attended, and she got to know her new neighbors, all of them African American.

Chapter 12

Riccardo X's first day working for the Jefferson County Schools was in October of 1975, following a month of angry and sometimes violent protests against the new busing plan. For any brand-new teacher, the first day of school is terrifying. Everything you learned in classes and practiced as a student teacher can never quite prepare you for the moment when you stand in front of the two dozen children who will be yours to teach and to keep under control for the rest of the year. The fact that Riccardo was only a few years out of high school himself didn't help. The anxiety was only compounded when he learned where the district was sending him: Southern High School, in Okolona, the heart of the anti-busing protesters' home turf.[1]

On September 4, the first day of school, an estimated 2,500 people had attended the Klan rally downtown.[2] They confronted police in riot gear, throwing rocks and shoving, and ten demonstrators were arrested. In the schools, the only violence occurred at Fairdale High School, where protesters threw rocks at the buses carrying black students.[3] Among them was seventeen-year-old Jacquelyn Stoner, who would later move houses in order to ensure that her own children were sent to the wealthier—and less hostile—East End.

That night, in the parking lot of the Bittersweet Shopping Center, just across the street from Southern High School, the protests escalated.[4] Demonstrators, many of them high school students, set bonfires fueled with school bus tires. They broke store windows and battered parked cars. The riot lasted four hours before a beleaguered group of police officers beat the protesters back with riot shields and clubs. The Jefferson County executive, who functioned like a mayor, had been a vocal opponent of busing throughout the court case and could take at least some of the blame for the lack of peaceful compliance to the desegregation order. A day after the Bittersweet riot, he was forced to call in the National Guard.

Protests continued for weeks. A white teenager shot out the eye of a police officer with a slingshot.[5] Hundreds of white protesters were arrested. Black students were harassed in school, and one was arrested for carrying a .38 caliber pistol onto a school bus as self-protection. At Ballard High School, in the wealthiest section of the suburbs, twenty black students were suspended for "grabbing girls and hugging them" in the hallways.[6] At some schools, false rumors spread that black boys had raped white girls.[7]

On his first day of school a month after the chaos had begun, Riccardo braced himself as he packed his school materials in a briefcase and a pistol in his pocket, and made the fifteen-minute drive from his house in Newburg, across the enemy lines, and into Okolona. Judge Gordon, hoping to avoid the chaos that had overtaken other cities in the first few weeks of busing, came up with an idea to create fenced protest zones outside of every school. Protesters could have their free speech, but the children would—in theory—be protected in case things got out of control. At Southern, the protesters were gathered in the parking lot of the Bittersweet Shopping Center, still spitting distance away.

As Riccardo pulled up to school, protesters shouted epithets and spit at him, but they stayed behind their fence. Many white students and a few black students stayed home during the first days of school, but they were beginning to trickle back by October. After school let out, Riccardo drove home, relieved that the first day was over, and that he had survived.

Despite the onerous requirements of Judge Gordon's busing plan, which required black children to spend more time in buses and which closed down schools with a long legacy in the black community, African Americans, for the most part, didn't protest.[8] On the first day of school, three black protesters, led by a slender woman named Rachelle Edmonson, picketed against busing at Central.[9] But for the most part, black parents were resigned, and some were enthusiastic about the desegregation plan. "We don't like it, we hate it just as much and want to demonstrate over it, but it's too much of an opportunity to miss for our children," one mother told the local paper.[10]

Riccardo X hunkered down at Southern and taught his history classes. Eventually, white students started going to school again. By winter, the marches had ended. The city settled into an uneasy peace. For many black Louisvillians like Riccardo and Jacquelyn who traveled into the suburbs that year, there would be lasting scars. "To actually experience first-hand people who hate them because of the color of their skin is quite an emotional experience," John Whiting, the principal of Shawnee High School in the West End, told the *Courier-Journal*. Others said it was worth it. "You cannot achieve nothing without sacrifice," said one black father whose children were bused.[11]

At Central, the sacrifice was different: subtler, but, students said, just as upsetting. Seniors had been exempted from busing for the first year, and that spring, the last all-black class at Central graduated.[12] The year before busing, the basketball team had once again taken home the state championship trophy, beating Male High School, an old rival, in an especially sweet victory.[13] But Central's future in basketball looked bleak under Plan X.

The following year, Central High School, where only a handful of white students had attended since 1956, became majority white. Most white students would have to stay for only two years, however, meaning the school's student population would be in constant churn. There wouldn't be time to build a good team. The school was still able to win sports trophies, but they were for swimming, tennis, and fencing, individual sports that did little to rally school spirit.[14] Most of the newcomers wouldn't even bother to learn the school song. Central no longer felt like "our school." It felt like no one's school.

During the fall of the second year of busing, Central High School students held a contest for the best Afro. It was 1976. Over the summer, black Louisvillians had packed the pews and the street in front of a West End church to see Angela Davis. *Ebony* magazine ran advertisements for the Afro Styler, for "a bigger, fuller, softer Afro in minutes." Many of the black kids at Central, male and female, had grown out their hair to keep up with the trend and embrace black pride.

But the winners of the contest were two white students from the suburbs. Voting on senior superlatives that year had gone the same way. Most Successful, Best Dressed, and Most Popular were all white students. Out of thirty-six awards, only seven black seniors won. Their peers called them "Uncle Toms." A white teacher was assigned to teach the school's black literature course. None of the student government leaders were black. Rumors flew around the school that the district was planning to rename it "River Glen High School."

"It seems like black don't count," said one Central student. "With desegregation, we can't get recognition." Another student, who had previously served in student government before the white students arrived and voted her out, proposed organizing a separate black organization. "Its purpose would be to tell blacks about their own culture," she explained. "Right now, there's nothing in the school that we can hold on to."[15]

Central's black students found themselves facing the incredible irony at the heart of the fight for racial equality in America. For blacks, fighting for a color-blind society meant trying to kill off a piece of one's identity that was simultaneously a stigma and a symbol of pride, history, and community. W. E. B. Du Bois had described the dilemma three-quarters of a century years earlier: "One ever feels his twoness,—an American, a Negro; two souls, two thoughts, two unreconciled strivings; two warring ideals in one dark body."[16]

The doors of opportunity had opened up to a degree unprecedented for blacks in America by 1975. But the transformation of Central into a white school, and the resulting loss of power and influence by black students, tapped into this persistent anxiety about the loss of black culture and identity. Blacks had fought for decades to be able to live and eat and learn wherever they wanted. But the Black Power movement, the descendants of Marcus Garvey and Malcolm X, questioned whether the means—integration with whites—was worth the cost. Desegregation diluted black voices. It frayed black ties to one another. It also highlighted the differences among them.

In the years before busing, many black parents with more money and education had stopped sending their children to Central. They sent them to Male and, increasingly, Atherton, the formerly all-white high school in the white East End. In pursuit of better opportunities for themselves and their children, more black families moved away from downtown and the West End entirely, taking advantage of the slow but steady lifting of political and social obstacles.

Black doctors, lawyers, maids, and factory workers had once been contained all in one place by the brutalities of legalized segregation. Now, the barriers were lifting, giving those at the top the ability to move on. The federal Fair Housing Act in 1968 had reversed the federal government's former stance of aiding and abetting housing discrimination, and overt racism was becoming less socially acceptable.[17] In 1970, most of the suburbs around Louisville were less than 1 percent black.[18] By 1980, neighborhoods in the strongholds of anti-busing resistance, including Shively, Okolona, Valley Station, Jeffersontown, and even Fairdale, had seen their black populations rise to between 1 percent and 5 percent. The shift was subtle but significant. The image of suburbs as places of lily-white, *Leave It to Beaver* uniformity no longer fit the reality. This shift was what the civil rights movement had been fighting for all along. But the victory was only partial. Those at the bottom—the vast majority—stayed behind.[19]

Before busing began, Central increasingly educated the poorest of the poor in Louisville. As school desegregation was implemented, many feared the possibility of white flight. (And indeed, thousands of whites abandoned the public school system by moving to other counties and sending their children to private school.)[20] Few talked about busing as a way to combat the problems caused by black middle-class flight from the inner city. In a way, though, it was. The integration of the schools diluted the black community's power over its schools, but it was a calculated trade-off.

A 1980 poll by the University of Louisville found that racial attitudes—at least among the young—had changed since busing began five years earlier.[21] More than half of fifteen- to twenty-four-year-olds favored desegregation and thought there were few or no "important differences" between blacks and whites, up from about 40 percent. "We found out we have the same kind of problems, growing up, with parents, it comes out we're just the same, we're just different colors, just different parts of Louisville," said Krystal Dave, a black student bused to Fern Creek, a high school on the outer edge of the county.[22]

And the achievement gap was closing. Although scores for high school students on reading tests remained mostly flat, the scores for elementary-aged black children rose significantly as white scores stayed the same.[23] "The black community understood the dilemma of busing, how inconvenient it was and is for young people to be on the corner to catch a bus," said Robert Cunningham, black founder of a pro-busing group in Louisville, Parents for Quality Education, during a federal hearing of the US Commission on Civil Rights in 1976. "But we felt that it was worth the sacrifice. If that young child doesn't get on the bus . . . he may be on that corner the rest of his life."[24]

Riccardo X was among those who remained unconvinced the trade was worth it. After two years at Southern High School, he moved on, frustrated with the racism he still saw around him. For the next decade, he roamed the Jefferson County Schools, moving from school to school teaching world civilization—white history, as he saw it—while searching for a place where he could work with black students to teach them about their own culture and heritage. Busing, he believed, seemed like an effort to erase black students' sense of their history and self-worth, exactly what he thought they needed to overcome the limitations white society had placed on them.

IV

The Numbers Game

Chapter 13

On a late summer day in 1980, Louisville's school superintendent, Ernest Grayson, called the media to the school district's new headquarters near the city-county line. It was not the typical back-to-school press conference. Instead, Grayson mounted a podium and announced that he was suing the school board. The charges were conspiracy and racketeering. The lawsuit was a counterattack. For the past two years, the school board had been trying to push him out of the job. Grayson alleged that the school board was trying to bribe him—by offering him a different position in the administration if he would agree to step down.[1]

The bizarre battle between the board and the superintendent nearly overshadowed the five-year anniversary of busing that fall. Under Grayson's leadership, two major financial scandals had broken out, including allegations that Grayson allowed school bus drivers to be overpaid by a quarter of a million dollars.[2] Perhaps worst of all, a year earlier, Grayson had proposed that white students should spend more time outside of their home school zones.[3] Busing white students for longer than two years would be more fair, and would improve continuity and fix problems at high schools, in particular, Central, where school spirit had flagged and sports suffered as white students cycled in and out.

White parents were furious. The school board quickly rejected the plan, saying white parents "weren't ready" for more busing yet.[4] Not long after filing the lawsuit that summer, Grayson was fired.[5]

The school board had its own problems. Six months after Grayson left, the school board chairman told a group of reporters that he believed "poor kids, by and large, do not subscribe to the same set of standards" as wealthy and middle-class students—that essentially, they were less interested in learning.[6] As a result, he argued, separate schools with extra resources were needed for the "students we don't know what the hell to do with," so the system "could have some shot at teaching them." He spent the next few weeks trying to calm the outrage among Louisville's black leaders.[7]

To bring order and smooth the many ruffled feathers, the school board sought someone with fresh perspective to replace Grayson. (The concept of the outsider-as-savior would later become something of an obsession among education reformers, as they recruited business entrepreneurs and lawyers to lead failing school systems, and brought in droves of career-changers to take jobs as teachers and principals in order to shake up the profession.) In the early 1980s, the Louisville school board limited the list of candidates for the superintendent job to educators with experience in public education, but they traveled far from Louisville in their search and hired Don Wayne Ingwerson, a longtime superintendent in the Orange County Public Schools in California.

Ingwerson was tall, with light blue eyes and a year-round tan. He "exuded confidence, poise and an aura of command," one *Courier-Journal* reporter wrote.[8] But he had little experience with the racial conflicts that had roiled the South for the past three decades. He was born in the tiny town of Pawnee City in eastern Nebraska.[9] He met his wife in Kansas, and the couple spent their early years together in small-town Kansas and Denver, Colorado. His wife performed in local television commercials and wanted to be a serious actress, so the couple moved to Southern California, where they lived for more than a decade.

Orange County was vastly different than Louisville. The county was a loose network of wealthy suburbs without an urban center. It was politically conservative, but there was also religious diversity and a laid-back beach vibe. Evangelical Christians, along with a large contingent of Mormons and Buddhists, thrived there.[10] In Louisville, Democrats reigned, pulling votes from the black community downtown, the liberal upper-middle class of the East End, and the union members in the south. Religion was mainstream: most people identified as Baptist, Jewish, or Catholic. The culture was Southern, friendly but reserved. Most significant, a quarter of students in the Jefferson County schools were black, while Orange County was less than 2 percent black. (A third of the population was Asian or Hispanic.)[11]

No doubt the school board members hoped Ingwerson would bring some of the easy confidence of Southern California culture to Louisville as he took over the city's chaotic school system. For his part, Ingwerson was looking for a challenge. Louisville, one of the largest districts in the country after its merger between the city and suburbs, seemed an ideal place to test his mettle. Although he had been brought in to deal with the variety of scandals left behind by his predecessor, one of his first orders of business was to reexamine the school's busing system.

The schools had changed dramatically in five years. Despite the upheaval over busing and problems with the superintendent, test scores for black students were up.[12] Violence was down.[13] The dropout rate—which some black teachers worried would spike for black students shipped out to suburban schools—had stayed level.[14] One of the local newspapers reported a new sense of camaraderie that had replaced the hostility of 1975. There were still flare-ups of overt racism, but the reporters also found empathy and understanding among students. As one senior at Shawnee High School in the West End put it, "Whites found out that not all blacks walked around with rakes in their hair and .38s in their back pockets. And blacks found out that not all whites walk around with pencils behind their ears."[15]

The district still had problems, of course. The suspension rate for blacks was down, but still disproportionately high in comparison to their numbers in the system.[16] The recently inaugurated Advance Program, for "gifted and talented" children, was disproportionately white.[17] (Other school districts around the nation were also implementing gifted and talented programs at around the same time, which tended to attract mostly white, advantaged students.)[18] A teacher survey by the school district's Division of Community and Human Relations found that 90 percent of teachers believed poor families valued education less than wealthy families. "If we believe that, then we will make it come true," said Sara Jo Hooper, who directed the survey. She had hoped to run programs to counter these prejudices. But her office was dismantled before she could do so.[19]

Many white parents fled to private schools, which had been losing enrollment before busing, but saw an increase of more than a thousand students after 1975.[20] Others fled to the small towns on the other side of the

Jefferson County line. Those who stayed were less involved, just as Joyce Spond had predicted. Parent-Teacher Association membership dropped by fifteen thousand members.[21]

White parents weren't the only ones who were unhappy. A May 1981 article in the *Courier-Journal* surveyed several disgruntled black parents and leaders who complained that the busing system was unfair.[22] Black schools in the West End had been closed to facilitate desegregation, and the black community was beginning to worry that Central might be next.[23] Under the 1975 assignment plan, Central's white students had to stay at the school for only two years. But many whites didn't even want to come for that long. In 1983, nearly one in five white students selected for busing requested and received medical transfers, compared to 2 percent of blacks.[24] Ballard High School, which served the wealthy East End, was overcrowded thanks to students who claimed that asthma or other ailments prevented them from venturing downtown. Even as many white students shirked busing, most black students were still bused for the majority of their school career.

In newspaper articles, black parents voiced frustration about difficulties visiting their children's distant schools for meetings, and about a loss of community ties without neighborhood schools. One parent mourned the death of the old, majority-black city school system, where black children had experienced "a personal touch."[25]

Not everyone was unhappy. Carolyn, a fifth grader, told the newspaper that she thought the adults should just "bug off for a while." "It's not the kids who are disagreeing. It's the adults," she said.[26] Maria, a white student at Valley High School in a white working-class neighborhood near the army base, said, "It's like when you tear something down, you gotta give it time to build back up. And I think that's what we did—or whoever did—whenever busing started. We tore down the school and tried to rearrange it so it would be better. And it is getting better, I think—gradually."[27]

"Gradually" was not a time frame that was generally acceptable in public education reform, however. During his first year in Louisville, Ingwerson went on a listening tour to churches, PTA meetings, and living rooms, both black and white, to get his bearings and hear from people on the ground. Although polls had shown that Louisvillians mostly accepted desegregation as a work in progress, despite its shortcomings, Ingwerson came away with one conclusion: Louisville's busing system was broken.[28]

In early 1983, he appointed a committee of citizens to come up with a way to fix it.[29] Ingwerson wanted to reduce the amount of busing for all students and to shore up Central's ailing enrollment numbers. His preference was to revive the magnet school idea from the 1960s and turn the school into a "flagship" for the district, rather than trying to force white students to attend there against their will.[30] Above all, he told parents, his goal was to steer the district away from the numbers game of busing, and change the focus to quality and results.

Ingwerson was not alone in this goal. Around the same time Louisville welcomed the new superintendent from Southern California, a commission appointed by the Reagan administration published a scathing report in April 1983 about the status of the schools nationwide. Entitled *A Nation at Risk*, the report scandalized the country. SATs scores had dropped as much as fifty points since the 1960s, the report said. Two in five minority youths were "functionally illiterate." Although the commission acknowledged that the average American citizen was better educated than earlier generations, it nevertheless made the contrasting claim that for the first time in American history, "the educational skills of one generation will not surpass, will not equal, will not even approach those of their parents." Americans shouldn't have been surprised by these statistics, the report argued, "given the multitude of often conflicting demands we have placed on our Nation's schools and colleges." The implication was that while the United States had been dilly-dallying with "social" issues in schools, such as civil rights and busing, other countries had surged ahead in educating their youth.[31]

The report tapped into what the public already felt: a deep sense that the public schools were deteriorating fast. A 1981 Gallup poll had found that the public's faith in the schools had been shaken during the 1970s, the era of busing. The culprits behind the failing schools were, according to the people who were surveyed, a lack of discipline, an increase in drug use, poor standards, lack of money and, for 11 percent of all parents (and 18 percent of private school parents), integration.[32]

President Reagan trumpeted the report's findings. He had been on a mission to dismantle the Department of Education, and in *A Nation at Risk* he found support for his arguments. "I think you can make a case that it began to deteriorate when the federal government started interfering in education," he said.[33] It was a not-so-subtle signal to the white middle class that federal intervention in their schools—including court-ordered busing—was coming to an end. While this turned out to be a premature hope, the *Nation at Risk* report did mark a new philosophy in education reform that would pick up steam over the next three decades. American public education had begun its seismic shift from a focus on providing equal opportunities to a focus on producing equal outcomes. Raising expectations and standards, not ensuring equity and sufficient resources through integration, was becoming the new mantra.

The *Nation at Risk* report ignored some major developments in American education, however. During the 1970s and into the 1980s, something fundamentally good happened in American schools. Despite panic about widespread functional illiteracy, reading scores for all students rose on the National Assessment of Educational Progress, known as the Nation's Report Card.[34] And, even more significantly, the black-white achievement gap had shrunk rapidly.

A Nation at Risk studied high schools, not the young students who were entering school in the wake of busing. So the report missed out on the most significant gains for black students who had started school from 1978 until 1980. Black high school students had gone from scores that lagged fifty-three points behind those of whites in 1971 to a score gap of thirty-one in 1984 (over the next four years, the gap continued to close). In particular, black students in the South saw huge jumps in their performance. The increase was as much as it would have been if black students had attended school for an extra year and a half.[35]

Changes to the black family, including an increase in parental education levels, were only a small factor driving these huge leaps forward. Changes in the curriculum, such as more challenging requirements in math and reading, likewise only explained part of the story. School factors, like smaller class sizes and more funding, seemed to have played a bigger role. So did desegregation, along with social changes like affirmative action and the War on Poverty programs that accompanied it.[36] But these outcomes were largely ignored. As the Reagan administration, politicians, education experts, and school districts around the country fretted about a rise in school violence and the need to improve standards and excellence, the historic leaps on the National Assessment of Educational Progress's tests were swept aside, as were the policies behind them.

For those in the black community who had always viewed busing with skepticism, the new focus on outcomes and standards was greeted with enthusiasm. Here was an idea they could embrace: judging progress by how well black children performed in school, not by how many black children were seated next to white ones.

Chapter 14

Carman Weathers was born in 1935 and grew up in Beecher Terrace, a village of two-story housing projects built in the 1930s just west of downtown.[1] His mother had died in childbirth, so his great-grandmother raised him. Her mother, Carman's great-great-grandmother, had been a slave on a plantation in Jefferson County. Her portrait hung on their apartment wall, and Carman's childhood was steeped in stories of her strength and stubbornness in the face of hardship. She had fought her master to keep her children from being sold "down the river" in the lead-up to the Civil War, when the slave trade was slowing and enslaved children in the United States were commanding a higher price. She also taught herself to read and believed deeply in education as the way up and out for her children. Carman lived in awe of her, and also of his great-grandmother, who inherited her mother's steely personality. They were self-made women who, despite their poverty and lack of resources, seemed dignified and powerful in Carman's eyes.

During the day, his great-grandmother served as a maid to the family of a Jewish lawyer and his wife who had emigrated from Germany. The rest of the time, she reigned over Beecher Terrace, settling disputes, giving out advice and dispatching Carman to do chores for the needy. He mowed grass on the weekends for elderly neighbors and each day carried the extra bottle of milk his great-grandmother always ordered for the single mother next door, with her six boys, or for another struggling family on the block. Even the white ladies she worked for called on her often for advice.

Carman's interaction with white people, however, was limited to the few times a year that he was invited to play with the two children of his great-grandmother's employers. It was more integration than most of his friends in the neighborhood ever experienced. They attended Samuel Coleridge-Taylor Elementary School, named after a black English composer, in an old building near the projects. The school served whites when it opened in 1853 as the Tenth Ward School until the population in the West End shifted from white to black and the school was renamed. By the time white students returned to the school on buses, the old building had been torn down and replaced with more housing projects.

For high school, Carman's only choice was Central—Jim Crow was still in full force. During his tenure there in the early 1950s, the high school moved to its new building, just a few blocks from his home. Carman was leader of the jocks. He was short but stocky, strong and loud. He spent his school years chasing a football and, when he was off the field, girls. When he could get away with it, he avoided schoolwork, although he admired his teachers, including Lyman Johnson, who taught him civics. He didn't care much about academics, in spite of his great-grandmother's admonitions to study, but Carman was very bright and he did like to talk about politics and ideas with his best friend, Robert Douglas. The two were an odd pair, but Robert had picked out Carman from the crowd on the first day of school and decided they would be friends. Robert was tall and thin, and read a lot of books. He was introspective and a daydreamer. But both liked to talk, and when they got together, they spent hours discussing the bad situation of blacks in America and what to do about it.

They stayed in touch after they graduated and went to college, and then on to graduate school. Robert became an artist and immersed himself in civil rights activism, working as an open-housing organizer. At one point, he was involved with the activists who organized the rally that sparked the 1968 riots. Carman pursued his own version of protest.

Carman's first job was as an assistant football coach at his alma mater, Jackson State University, a historically black school in Mississippi. He loved the job. The team won often, and the school sent nearly fifty players to the pros in the 1960s and '70s.[2] But after four years, he became frustrated. As formerly white public and private universities dropped their ban on black students, they seemed to be drawing away some of the best black players. It was Carman's first taste of desegregation, and he didn't like it. He left for a new job at the all-black Crispus Attucks High School in Hopkinsville, a town south of Louisville with a relatively large black population for Kentucky.

Crispus Attucks took black students from two counties, and competed in football with black teams around the state. After five years as an assistant football coach at the school, Carman picked up the local paper one day and read the list of school salaries that reporters gathered and printed annually. The assistant coach at the white school, Hopkinsville High, was making about $3,000 a year more than he was. Carman knew the man. He didn't have a master's degree, as Carman did, and he had only been there three years. Carman made an appointment to see the superintendent.

As Carman tells the story, the superintendent agreed to meet with him, and then explained that while he was sorry about the discrepancy, white people needed bigger salaries because their cost of living was higher. "That's the same way I feel about my lawyer, because he needs more money," Carman replied. "And he's about to get more money." Shortly after, Carman got a raise.

His victory was short-lived. In 1968, the school board closed Crispus Attucks High School to comply with a federal order to desegregate the county's schools.[3] The black teachers and administrators scattered to the formerly white schools. Many went to Louisville to look for jobs. Carman's head coach was sent to Hopkinsville High School. Carman was offered an assistant coach job at Christian County High School, in a different district. He took it, although in moving out of his district, he lost his tenure status. Carman and a librarian also imported from Crispus Attucks were the only black teachers in the building.

Carman told the white Christian County administrators that he didn't want them to bring all the "black problems" to his door, but soon enough, he was flooded with requests to deal with disciplinary cases and political struggles, including a dispute over whether the football team—now nearly all black—should give up the preintegration tradition of choosing the homecoming queen. Carman refused to step in, and the football team selected a black girl as queen.

He didn't last long at Christian County. In the early 1970s, Carman returned to Louisville, gave up coaching, and took a job at Russell Junior High in the West End, working with students at risk of dropping out. Once again, all of his students were black. He loved the work, and the students responded well to his voluble pied-piper personality.

Then, in 1975, Carman discovered his job was once again on desegregation's chopping block. Judge Gordon announced the details of Plan X that fall; Russell Junior High was among the five schools that the judge planned to close.[4] Four were traditionally black. Carman was stunned. He joined protests to save the school, to no avail. Why should Russell be punished because white people won't come? Carman asked. The judges and school administrators and lawyers fighting for desegregation weren't interested. The black students at his school were needed to integrate the schools in the suburbs, and Russell was housed in an old building in one of the West End's rougher neighborhoods. In September 1975, the doors were unceremoniously shuttered and Carman once again had to find a new job.

He was not alone. In years following *Brown v. Board*, thirty-eight thousand black teachers lost their jobs.[5] Other staff—coaches, principals, counselors, cafeteria workers—were also let go.[6] One report at the time said what happened to black school staff was not integration, but *disintegration:* "the near total disintegration of Black authority in every area of the system of public education."[7] Some teachers were fired outright, but in later years, the decline in black teachers was in part due to a decline in hiring.[8] A 1972 report about Louisville argued the city was one of the worst culprits in the South.[9] About 600 teachers in the city system were black. The schools would have needed to hire an additional 450 to bring their numbers up so they matched the level of black students in the system. Another report found that while Kentucky had employed 350 black principals in 1954, there were only 36 black principals left by 1970.[10]

After Russell closed, Carman moved to Thomas Jefferson High School in Newburg. The school was exempt from busing because it was naturally desegregated with blacks from the Newburg enclave and low-income whites from nearby Okolona. To Carman, it was a beautiful school. The principal, Stanley Whitaker, was a dynamic leader and the atmosphere was mostly calm. Carman settled in and once again felt at home.

Other schools that were struggling to stay diverse shut down around them—a vocational high school downtown, Shawnee Junior High, and several elementary schools.[11] In 1980, a controversy erupted over a proposal to close several traditionally white high schools in the South End.[12] During the public hearings to discuss the plan, hundreds of parents and students turned out to protest, chanting, singing, and carrying signs, including one that read, "White People Wake Up!" The deputy superintendent, David DeRuzzo, acknowledged their frustration: "Closing a high school leaves a void in the community," he told the newspaper. "Communities look to their high schools not only as a place where their children will be educated, but also as a place that binds the community together."[13]

The school board scuttled the plan to close the formerly white schools. Instead, a year later, it turned to four other high schools.[14] Three traditionally white schools, including Fern Creek, in the suburbs on the outer edge of Jefferson County, and Thomas Jefferson were slated for closure. The middle-class parents who sent their children to Fern Creek protested against the closing of their school and won.[15] The other three, located in poor and working-class neighborhoods, were shut down; if there were parents, students, or teachers who were upset, they got little attention from school officials or the press. Thomas Jefferson was reopened as a middle school that drew from far beyond the borders of its previous boundaries. Its former students were split up and bused elsewhere. For the third time, Carman was left without a job after his school had been closed to accommodate desegregation.

In Carman's eyes, the closure of Thomas Jefferson tore the Newburg community apart, draining its unity and spirit. The promise that busing would help black children seemed ridiculous to him if it meant simultaneously undermining the strength of the communities they lived in. In the eyes of the school board, the closures were unavoidable: African Americans had demanded desegregation; to make it work, they would have to make sacrifices. But as black schools and teachers were discarded with little concern for how their loss might impact black communities, patience began to give way.

Chapter 15

Lyman Johnson stood at the podium in Central High School's auditorium. His gray hair was combed back from his lined forehead, and large, slightly tinted glasses hid his tired eyes. It had been more than a decade since he'd walked these halls as a teacher and, later, an administrator. He had served on and then retired from the school board, but he was unwilling to sit out the brewing fight over Ingwerson's plan to overhaul the desegregation system in Louisville.

It was March 19, 1984, and two hundred black activists and students, along with a handful of whites, had gathered at Central to protest the superintendent's alternative busing plan, finally released that winter after months of debate. "Young people, I've run out of gas," Lyman said. "I've done the best I could. Don't let the wagon roll back downhill." The crowd gave him a standing ovation as he made his way back to his seat. Audience members yelled that Ingwerson should go back to Orange County and leave Louisville alone.[1]

Superintendent Ingwerson's planned overhaul had quickly escalated into a major public controversy as his citizens' committee tried to hash out a deal. One of the biggest concerns was the fate of Central. The neighborhoods around Central were nearly 100 percent black. A newspaper reporter noted that it would make sense to bus in students from Ballard, the school that served much of the East End, which was overcrowded. But officials feared white flight if Central's zone was extended to include parts of the white, wealthy neighborhoods to the east.[2] "Any neighborhood that is assigned to Central will be perceived as a bad place to live," said one member of Ingwerson's committee.[3]

Thousands of black children had to leave their neighborhoods to attend high schools in white neighborhoods, but rather than force white children to do the same, officials proposed to end the busing of white high schoolers to the inner city altogether by making Central a magnet school. Black leaders called the hopes of desegregating the school using volunteers a "pipe dream." So the busing committee settled on a compromise. Central would get a temporary satellite district, which would be dismantled as soon as the magnet was up and running.[4]

Ingwerson's plan ignored the compromise.[5] Instead, he proposed turning a nearby school, Manual, into a magnet, and shuffling its students—many of them poor whites who lived on the southern edges of downtown—to Central.[6] No middle-class suburban students would have to come downtown. In addition, his proposal rearranged the desegregation plan so that substantially fewer whites would have to get on buses. He also increased the ratio of blacks to whites that would determine if a school would be integrated. And though the number of black students who would be bused was reduced, too, they still bore the burden of desegregation. During the high school years, only 250 white students would be bused out of their neighborhoods, compared to 2,500 black students. When asked how he thought black parents would feel about the plan, he told a newspaper reporter that, were he such a parent, he would be "very pleased," adding, "I would see someone caring for my child."[7]

Black parents themselves did not see it that way. Black leaders and ministers lobbed charges of "one-way" busing and accused the superintendent of wanting to kill Central.[8] "Blacks are still enslaved by whites by this plan," said one black parent during a hearing at the school.[9] Parents started a petition drive and promised mass demonstrations if Ingwerson didn't reconsider.[10] Business leaders and local politicians, including the mayor, pressured Ingwerson to compromise.[11] In April 1984, after the rally at Central and discussions with black leaders, Ingwerson announced a new plan that the school board quickly passed.[12]

He would assign of a desegregation czar in the school district administration.[13] Manual, down the road near the University of Louisville campus, was becoming a performing arts magnet with a special college prep track connected with the university. Central, located close to the courts, banks, and hospitals downtown, would stop drawing students from around the county and instead introduce magnet programs in law, business, and health. But in the coming fall, Central would still take some low-income white students from Manual, which was losing its attendance zone. Except for a handful of students living on the border with downtown, East End parents were still exempted from having to send their children to the inner city for high school.

The following year, some of the original plaintiffs in the desegregation lawsuit went back to court. They wanted the district judge to restore the desegregation case to the active docket. But the judge, Thomas Ballantine, was not sympathetic. He believed the school district had done an excellent job of complying with the court's orders. He refused to reopen the case.[14]

The results of the new plan were just what black leaders had feared. The overcrowding problems Central faced three decades earlier now seemed enviable. Since 1976, Central enrollment had been dropping, but in September 1984, Central's enrollment was even lower than school officials had anticipated—only one thousand students—and many of them were impoverished.[15]

By the spring, parents were volunteering to help overburdened guidance counselors call home to the dozens of students who skipped school each day.[16] Nearly two hundred students—a fifth of the school—were suspended in the first few months of school, more than double the number in the previous year.[17] The Advance Program had dwindled. The dropout rate was twice the county average. The statistics just got worse the following year, and the principal, along with two assistant principals and three out of four guidance counselors, requested transfers.[18] Twelve teachers also left. As Central's reputation suffered, the work of convincing white students to attend magnet programs at Central would become doubly hard.

Nevertheless, the following year, Jefferson County school officials announced that Central would finally begin its specialized programs.[19] The school was to get a countywide Advance and honors program, in the hopes of attracting high-performing white students, and a health careers program, which was to train nurses, nurses' aides, and technicians. But civil rights activists were furious.[20] "Why not train them to be doctors and medical researchers?" one black leader asked. Woodford Porter Sr., a black funeral home director who wanted black students to be spread throughout the county, saw the plan as a way to resegregate Central and eventually close it, "just like they did with DuValle and most of the elementary schools in the community."[21]

The specter of closing Central scared many in Louisville's African American community, but not everyone saw it as a bad thing that the school might draw more black students. In fact, for Carman Weathers, who was watching intently from the sidelines, this outcome would be ideal. An all-black high school that offered challenging coursework in the heart of the inner city was exactly what he thought Louisville's blacks needed to help them overcome continued racism and to reverse the deterioration of the inner city.

Chapter 16

The data showed that the trajectory of desegregation in Louisville and across the country had corresponded with improvements for both blacks and whites.[1] But it was easy to overlook improvements in test scores and other achievement measures amid other evidence suggesting that things were getting worse. By the mid-1980s, American cities were vastly different places than they had been three decades earlier, when the fight for school desegregation was first waged. White middle-class families were moving from inner suburbs to outer suburbs, and huge numbers of black middle-class families were following behind them. By 1990, more than a quarter of blacks lived in the suburbs.[2]

They left behind spiraling crime rates, rising teenage birth rates, and a crack epidemic. The trend coincided with the adoption of busing plans in cities across the country, but it was also repeated in cities that school desegregation never touched. Nonetheless, busing was blamed for white flight and the decline of urban school districts. Louisville residents were battling over how to make desegregation work, but in other cities the battle shifted to a debate over whether busing had run its course. In the mid-1980s, the Reagan administration shifted from defense to offence. Instead of discouraging the expansion of busing plans, it now began to encourage school districts to dismantle them.[3]

In 1985, the newly appointed attorney general, Edwin Meese III, said that busing had only a "marginal effect as far as improvement is concerned."[4]

That same year, the administration threw its support behind the city of Norfolk, Virginia, which was combating a lawsuit brought by twenty-one black parents after the school district ended its elementary school busing plan in 1983—the first in the nation to do so.[5]

Gene Carter, the Norfolk superintendent who put the brakes on the city's busing plan, was black. Carter believed that "a black youngster doesn't need to be seated next to a white youngster to learn."[6] Many blacks opposed Norfolk's move to limit busing, however. They remembered the city's anti-busing protests, which had been particularly intense; the district had shut down schools rather than desegregate them in the 1950s.[7] But Carter wasn't alone in questioning the wisdom of desegregation. Ten years after most busing plans had been implemented, many blacks around the country were impatient for larger gains for black students, and horrified by the rapid deterioration of inner-city black neighborhoods. Many also wondered whether busing weren't the culprit, or at least partially to blame. In Oklahoma City, a black school board member, Clyde Muse, led a push to dismantle that city's busing plan for elementary-age students at around the same time Norfolk ended its plan.[8]

In November 1986, the Supreme Court declined to hear the Norfolk case, letting stand the opinions of the lower judges that Norfolk's retreat from desegregation was permissible.[9]

In the *Swann* decision, the Court had said that ideally, all districts that had once maintained dual systems of education for whites and blacks would one day be declared "unitary," and no longer need the supervision of the courts in their daily affairs. They had not described how or when this declaration should be made in school districts, however. Like the Warren Court in the *Brown* decision, the Court under Chief Justice Burger was wary of getting involved in the details of running schools; the American conviction that schools should be controlled by localities, not the federal courts, remained deeply rooted.

The decision not to intervene in Norfolk was one of the last of the Burger Court, which, when Burger retired that year, was eulogized by critics as a wishy-washy reign.[10] The Court's character would soon change dramatically. In the fall of 1986, William Rehnquist took the mantle of the chief justice. He ruled with a much firmer hand.[11] His conservative credentials included a 1952 memo he had written as a Supreme Court law clerk, when the justices were mulling the *Brown* case. In the memo, he expressed support for *Plessy v. Ferguson*, the precedent the *Brown* plaintiffs were hoping to overturn.[12]

The Supreme Court's decision in the Norfolk case—or lack thereof—would have sweeping impact. The Reagan Justice Department kept up its attack on busing, suggesting to dozens of school boards that they reconsider their plans.[13]

In 1990, the Oklahoma case, *Board of Education of Oklahoma City v. Dowell*, which had slogged its way through the courts for years, finally reached the Supreme Court. Cases out of Denver, Atlanta, and Topeka soon followed.[14] Once again, the White House, now led by President George H. W. Bush, sided with the school districts.[15] This time, the Supreme Court agreed to take on the issue.

In Oklahoma, downtown neighborhoods had been nearly emptied of whites, and the school district was busing black students to schools further and further away from their homes to keep the schools integrated.[16] One of the underlying questions in the case was whether an all-black school should be considered a product of officially sanctioned segregation if less than fifteen years earlier the district had maintained segregated schools.

The Supreme Court handed down its decision on January 16, 1991. Five of the justices, led by Rehnquist, agreed that school districts that had eliminated the "vestiges" of segregation could end busing, even if it meant some schools would revert to having student populations that were all black or all white.[17] Justice Marshall dissented, asking whether thirteen years was enough to shed a legacy of legalized segregation spanning sixty-five years.[18]

The Oklahoma decision, much like *Brown*, was significant, but it was also vague. How would districts and courts know that the vestiges of segregation had been erased? Did all remnants of segregation—racially unbalanced faculties, different resource allocations—have to be removed at the same time? Or could school districts that were making incremental progress be partially released from court decrees? Rehnquist's opinion didn't say. A month later, on February 19, 1991, the court agreed to hear a case that addressed these questions out of DeKalb County, Georgia, which encompassed part of Atlanta.[19]

Unlike Oklahoma City, DeKalb did not have a busing plan in place; rather, the plaintiffs in the case—both white and black parents—had sued in the 1980s in an effort to force the city to adopt one.[20] More than twenty schools in the district were nearly all black, and these schools had fewer books, less experienced teachers, and less money.[21]

A court of appeals decision ordered the district to remove all the vestiges before it could be released from supervision. The county responded by trying voluntary methods to better mix black and white students, including magnet schools, but the court warned that if those tactics didn't work, busing loomed as a next step.[22] At that point, eighteen plaintiffs joined the case in protest. Most were black, and they opposed busing.[23] They wanted the DeKalb school district to focus on quality, not the numbers game of desegregation, which they saw as a ploy to further undermine the rights of black parents.

The Supreme Court set the date for arguments in the Georgia case for the following fall.[24] That summer, Thurgood Marshall, who had often vowed that he would never retire, hobbled into a conference room in the court building, leaning on a cane, to face a group of reporters. A day earlier, on June 27, at the age of eighty-two, he had announced his retirement, contingent on the appointment of a successor. Someone asked why he was going back on his vow. He pulled off his glasses and looked into the glaring camera lights. "This is it," he said. He, his wife, and his doctor had been discussing retirement for months. He was "old and coming apart." When asked if President Bush should appoint a minority justice in his place, he frowned: "I don't think it should be used as an excuse one way or the other . . . for doing wrong, for picking the wrong Negro and saying I'm picking him because he's a Negro."[25]

A few days later, President Bush nominated Clarence Thomas, a black judge born to illiterate parents in Georgia. Thomas, the *Washington Post* wrote at the time, was full of contradictions.[26] He was also on the opposite side of the political spectrum from Marshall. On nearly every issue that Marshall had fought for over his long career, the two men disagreed.

Thomas didn't believe in affirmative action, yet thought that "there is nothing you can do to get past a black skin."[27] He had flirted with the Black Panthers in college, and always been "partial" to Malcolm X, particularly his self-help teachings. He also believed that color blindness was the best way to dismantle racism: "Racial quotas and other race-conscious legal devices only further and deepen the original problem," he once wrote.[28] After a nasty confirmation fight following sexual harassment accusations by lawyer Anita Hill, Thomas was confirmed in October, thanks in part to seven Southern Democrats. The senators feared a backlash from black voters if they rejected the second African American justice ever to be nominated to the court.[29]

His appointment was too late for Thomas to hear arguments in the Georgia case, but the timing also excluded Marshall, who had officially left the bench a week before the court date.[30] Without Marshall's vote, the decision came back unanimous the following spring. DeKalb County would not have to implement a busing program. Justice Anthony Kennedy, a moderate Reagan appointee who leaned right but was also known for his ability to forge compromises, wrote the majority opinion. "In one sense of the term," he said, "vestiges of past segregation by state decree do remain in our society and in our schools. Past wrongs to the black race, wrongs committed by the State and in its name, are a stubborn fact of history. And stubborn facts of history linger and persist." But the long history of racial segregation was no reason to make desegregation the perpetual goal for school districts, Kennedy wrote. "Racial balance is not to be achieved for its own sake," he concluded.[31]

"A fatal karate chop has been placed to the neck of desegregation nationwide," the plaintiff's attorney, Roger Mills, said. "It looks very, very bleak for the future of black children."[32]

The racial mix in schools was becoming less pressing to many Americans, however. Polls showed blacks weren't that interested in desegregation. Although nearly 100 percent of both whites and blacks said they favored integration by 1986, only 55 percent of blacks surveyed in a 1986 *ABC/Washington Post* poll favored busing.[33] More striking was a 1984 poll reporting that 79 percent of blacks thought it was "more important to improve schools in black neighborhoods than to bus to achieve racial integration." Only 12 percent thought integration was more important.[34] In the wake of the *Nation at Risk* report, many black parents, along with the rest of the country, were beginning to pay attention to outcomes for black children, not just opportunities.

Standards and accountability were the pillars of a new movement that was supposed to revolutionize American education and improve the world standing of US students. International tests showed they were lagging behind countries like Italy and the Soviet Union, and in the early 1990s, anxiety about Japan—where students attended school 240 days a year compared to 180 in America—reached a fever pitch.[35] By making curriculum standards more challenging, and then testing schools on whether they were meeting those challenges, educators and policy makers believed they could ramp up achievement and close the stubborn achievement gap.

Central to the movement was the use of high-stakes standardized tests, which were seen as a quick, cheap, yet extremely motivating way to force change in schools. Between 1980 and 1992, the number of states with testing programs rose from twenty-nine to forty-six.[36] By the mid-1990s, forty states were using test scores to hold schools accountable for student performance.

Many modeled their testing programs on the one in Kentucky, which in 1990 became a pioneer in the standards and accountability movement when the state passed the Kentucky Education Reform Act.[37] The *New York Times* called Kentucky's law "the most sweeping education package ever conceived by a state government."[38] In short order, Kentucky's reforms would help change the face of American education.

As the new reforms were embraced, educational opportunities and outcomes were both on the decline. Poverty was becoming more concentrated in urban districts even as desegregation plans were abandoned. After years of gains, starting in 1990, black students began losing ground to whites on the National Assessment of Educational Progress, the only national exam that tracked student achievement over time.

Norfolk, Virginia, returned to neighborhood schools. Researchers examining the district several years after the case found that the white student population, which rose slightly in the last years of the busing program, dropped after the program was ended, from 42 percent to 37 percent.[39] On tests, black achievement declined in the first year after busing ended, and the gap with whites widened. In later years, test scores at most of the black schools worsened.

V

The Lawsuit

Chapter 17

After losing three jobs to school closings, Carman Weathers finally found a permanent home at Buechel Metropolitan High School in Louisville. There was little chance the district would close this school. In the mid-1970s, just as busing began, the school board had opened Buechel to serve students who needed "behavior modification."[1] The school was the only one in the district exempt from racial limits, and the vast majority of its students were black. In the mid-1990s, Buechel was split into two schools, a middle and high school.[2] Another alternative high school that accommodated mostly black students, named Liberty, opened in 1997.[3] The former school board chair had been widely condemned as racist in 1981 when he called for separate schools for the "students we don't know what the hell to do with," so the system "could have some shot at teaching them," but the alternative school idea fit his description quite well.[4]

At Buechel, Carman could do the work he loved with the students he cared most about. But he wasn't content. He was angry. He looked around him and he saw betrayal: The black people at the top of the pecking order decided that the best way for them to get where they needed to be was to be around white people, he thought. They were willing to sacrifice black people to integration, no matter what the consequences were. That was what had happened to the castaways at Buechel, and that was what he feared could eventually happen to Central if the white school officials and black civil rights activists who wanted to keep the school integrated got their way.

He believed that their single-minded focus on racial balance was Central's greatest threat. Carman had already lost three schools to desegregation. He was determined not to lose his alma mater as the fourth.

On December 17, 1991, the *Courier-Journal* published an op-ed Carman had written: "Our inclination has been to focus on the issue of busing; but the issue now, as it always has been, is the educational attainment of African-American children," Carman wrote. "The facts are that this creative social mutation called busing has not worked for the majority of African-American students over the last 16 years. . . . If we had consciously set out to design a system to encourage failure, the result would bear striking similarity to what we now have. Now is the time for change to come."[5]

The passage of the Kentucky Education Reform Act, or KERA, as the law was known, and the changes it was bringing about in the Louisville schools thrilled Carman. Here was an opportunity to finally bury busing and focus on what mattered: improving education for black children by improving the schools in their communities.

In 1989, Kentucky's Supreme Court issued a shocking ruling in a case brought on behalf of poor Appalachian school districts, declaring that Kentucky's "entire public school system" was unconstitutional. After a contentious political battle, legislation to change nearly every facet of Kentucky's education system passed in the spring of 1990.[6] The most notable piece of the legislation—and the one most imitated by school systems elsewhere—was the requirement that schools be tested to see if their students were making progress, and that the results be widely published. Schools that did well were rewarded financially; those that did not were sanctioned.[7]

The accountability measures and financial incentives were controversial and had mixed results. Kentucky's scores on the National Assessment of Educational Progress improved.[8] Yet one study found that while teachers did indeed change their teaching methods in response to bad test outcomes, they often did so by focusing more intently on test-taking skills and the relatively narrow set of knowledge and content covered by the test.[9]

In Louisville, another part of the law was just as contentious. KERA called for grades one through three to be merged into one group of students in a system similar to the Montessori model.[10] Elementary students would learn together before they joined age-based cohorts in fourth grade and started taking high-stakes standardized tests. In Louisville, this piece of the legislation had the potential to be a logistical nightmare.[11] Students

often moved around to different schools during their elementary years because of busing. They might attend first grade in one place, then move to
a new school for second and third grade before returning to the original
school. School officials reasoned that it would be unfair to hold schools accountable in fourth grade for students they hadn't taught. Superintendent
Ingwerson jumped into action, and by the fall, he made a proposal.

In elementary school, students would no longer be bused.[12] Instead,
students could volunteer to attend schools where they were in the racial
minority. Ingwerson offered a "scholarship" program to motivate parents:
$500 for every year a student spent away from his or her neighborhood
school. To maintain integrated elementary schools, around three thousand
students would have to volunteer. There was one problem: The school
system didn't yet have the money for the incentive program.

That September, most of Louisville's elementary schools maintained
ratios of black students between 25 and 40 percent. If the plan were adopted, it was estimated that a dozen elementary schools would immediately
have student bodies between 77 and 99 percent black, while twenty-nine
would have black populations of less than 5 percent. The KERA testing
problem wouldn't affect middle and high schools—students stayed put
during those years—but Ingwerson wanted to relax the racial limits in the
upper grade spans as well. At first, he seemed to have wide support.

A new group of black leaders had become influential in the city during the 1980s. They had risen up as discontent over the state of the inner
city and the burden of busing spread, and the new ideas about standards
and outcomes took hold. Their views clashed with those of the old guard
of civil rights leaders. They did not accept desegregation as a sacred goal,
and some saw it the way Carman did—as a hindrance to black achievement
and empowerment. These new leaders, including ministers, school board
members, and even the president of Louisville's NAACP, approved of
Ingwerson's plan.

Laken Cosby, the school board's only black member and a close associ-
ate of Ingwerson, was vocally supportive.[13] Cosby, once an avid civil rights
activist, was disillusioned with desegregation.[14] In the 1960s, he had moved
his family to the mostly white East End to put his belief in integration into
action. But in the predominantly white schools, his children had struggled,
and eventually Cosby lost faith. "We cannot say that because schools are
predominantly black that they are inferior to other schools. That's not

true," he told the newspaper after Ingwerson's plan to dismantle elementary school desegregation was announced.[15] Rather, he wanted to change the way blacks viewed education. High expectations for black students and higher standards would close the achievement gap, he argued, not sitting next to white children.

Other districts were beginning their retreat from desegregation in the aftermath of the Oklahoma City and DeKalb County Supreme Court cases. To many in Louisville, it looked like their city, which had some of the most racially integrated schools in the nation, would join soon them. Jean Ruffra, the Shively mother who had helped Joyce Spond in forming Save Our Community Schools, which had long since disbanded, was amazed at the news: "What goes around comes around, and it's 16 years later, and here we are right at square one."[16]

The peace didn't last long. On a Tuesday morning, a few days after the plan was announced, Kevin Cosby, the thirty-two-year-old son of Laken Cosby, the school board member, hosted a gathering of about a dozen black ministers and leaders who approved of Ingwerson's plan at the church in the California neighborhood where he was pastor.[17] Cosby was a dapper young man, with a neat mustache and serious eyes behind his large round glasses.[18] He had become an avid fan of Malcolm X after spending his teenage years trying and failing to fit in at the all-white, upper-middle-class Ballard High School in the East End, where his father had moved the family. His dissertation at the United Theological Seminary in Ohio was entitled, "The Development of an Afrocentric Lifestyle Ministry," and he had what some called a cult-like following at his growing church, where he preached African American self-determination. At a press conference, he said it was "time for blacks to take control of their own destiny."[19] Reporters took notes and then the small group disbanded.

That night, after the Reverend Cosby's press conference, the old guard of the civil rights movement mobilized, gathering three hundred people, mostly black, for a rousing meeting in a downtown church. Lyman Johnson, then eighty-five, needed strong arms to help him climb up to the podium. In speech after speech, the activists excoriated Ingwerson. Lyman, a member of the school board that had recruited Ingwerson from California a decade earlier, made one of the most pointed attacks. "I helped to bring him here and by God, I hope to help him pack his bags," he said, to a standing ovation.[20] Compared to Cosby's sparsely attended press con-

ference, the old guard seemed energized and powerful. But appearances
were deceptive.

The two sides of the black community were about to face off once
again to ask the questions that had stumped their predecessors for more
than a century: Was desegregation important for its own sake? Was racism
so infused in the system that without forced busing, black children could
never get their due? Was desegregation working because it helped dilute
poverty? Or was it a failure because it inhibited black self-sufficiency and
self-respect? Did busing teach black students that they were inferior,
and to assume they couldn't succeed without the proximity of whites? Did
it drain African Americans of their culture, pride, and community ties,
which had helped them survive the brutalities of racism for three hundred
years in America?

In the weeks that followed Ingwerson's announcement, the battle lines
became more entrenched.[21] The Reverend Cosby called another meeting to rally support for dismantling busing; this time, five hundred people
showed up. One supporter compared Cosby to Joshua, the apprentice of
Moses who led the Israelites when Moses died. "Moses is dead. Done a
good job and you can't take that from him. But [he's] dead and we're still in
the wilderness," the man said.[22]

The school board hired Barbara Sizemore, a consultant from the University of Pittsburgh, paying her $1,000 to spend the day talking to city
leaders about Ingwerson's proposal.[23] She told Cosby's rally that her city's
all-black schools were doing just fine. When the young preacher himself
got up at the end of the night, he shouted to his followers, "Why does
integration also happen at the expense of black institutions?"[24] The crowd
cheered.

Lyman Johnson attended Cosby's meeting. Afterward, he vowed to live
another fifteen years, to age one hundred, to fight against "resegregation"
of the city's schools. On his side of the fight, a group led by Georgia Powers, Kentucky's first black and first female state senator, and also a close
friend of Martin Luther King, created a new organization, Quality Education for All Students (or QUEST), to monitor the school system's moves
on the desegregation plan.[25] The group, which included NAACP members, ministers, and a white Republican lawyer named Steve Porter, gathered business leaders in the city to their side, and met with public officials,
including Ingwerson, in an effort to pressure them to reconsider the plan.

The divide cut across generational, class, and neighborhood lines. "I want mine at my home school," a black mother of two children—a daughter who attended school in the West End and a son who was bused to the suburbs—told the newspaper after a meeting hosted by the school board.[26] In contrast, another mother, who sent her children to the same two schools, said she didn't want busing to end: "The teachers won't teach the black kids as good, if the white kids aren't with them." Two polls conducted that fall found that the vast majority of parents agreed with her. One poll found that 70 percent of black parents were opposed to Ingwerson's plan, while another a few weeks later found 85 percent opposed.[27] Only 58 percent believed their children were benefiting from busing, however.[28]

Less than a month after he announced his plan, Ingwerson appeared to back down and put off a school board vote indefinitely.[29] But he hadn't given up. He believed that eventually, parents and community leaders would come around to his proposal to limit desegregation once they understood the plan better. He still believed busing wasn't the answer to closing the achievement gap: "If you wanted to close the gap on achievement scores, then the plan has accomplished a certain amount of that. If you wanted more, then it probably has failed," he told the newspaper.[30] In December, he put forward a new plan, which the school board voted on and approved immediately.[31]

Ingwerson's new idea was not as drastic a change. Elementary schools would be grouped into clusters that included several suburban schools and one downtown school. Together, schools in each cluster would work to maintain a racial balance by sharing students among themselves. Black students at each school would have to comprise 15 to 50 percent of each school's population, rather than the 0 to 60 that Ingwerson had originally proposed. Each cluster was given $150,000 to create new programs to entice students away from their neighborhood schools and into schools where they would boost diversity. If schools failed to draw enough volunteers, children would be forcibly bused to meet the required percentages. Ingwerson promised to appoint another citizens' committee to monitor the progress of the new system he dubbed "Project Renaissance."[32]

In February, the Jefferson County school district phone lines were clogged with anxious parents wondering where their children would attend school the following year.[33] The same month, Ingwerson won a national award for superintendent of the year, despite a letter-writing campaign by his critics.[34] By the end of the school year, all of the city's elementary schools had managed to attract enough transfers to meet the new standards, mainly by putting new magnets into place, including Advance classes and traditional programs modeled on discipline- and values-focused schools started in the 1970s.[35]

The superintendent's monitoring committee was meant to keep tabs on the new student assignment plan in order to tamp down frustration in the community. It included both integration supporters, including members of QUEST, and activists trying to end busing.[36] But it quickly began adding fuel to the fire.

On the committee were Carman Weathers and a University of Louisville education professor, Joseph McMillan. McMillan had graduated from Central in 1946, the same year as Fran Thomas.[37] In high school, when he was editor of the Central newspaper, he had campaigned to have the word *colored* removed from the school's name. McMillan had spent much of his teaching career in Michigan, but in the 1970s he returned to Louisville, where he launched a conference on the state of minority families. He straddled divergent poles of the civil rights movement. He had met Malcolm X in Michigan, and believed he was the most brilliant black mind of the century, but he also served on the NAACP and worked on Jesse Jackson's presidential campaign. Saving Central from the tyranny of the school district's racial quotas was, to him, the next step forward in the movement.

Weathers and McMillan created a group called Saving African-American Values and Economy, or SAVE. Joining them on the monitoring committee was Carman's old high school friend, Robert Douglas, who represented parents of public school children.

Another spot went to Anne Braden's group, the Kentucky Alliance Against Racist and Political Repression. The organization named its new director, a recent transplant from the South End to the West End: Fran Thomas. Fran had become active with the Alliance the previous year, when her daughter had been deployed to Iraq. She had spent most of her life as an army wife in the majority-white South End, where she had fought a realtor's racism to buy her house. Her career had been as a nurse at the local Veteran Administrations hospital. But at heart she was an activist. As a college student in the 1950s, she had worked on a black voting campaign. As a nurse, she became involved with the government workers' union. Her daughter's deployment reawoke the rebellious spirit in her. Fran didn't believe in President Bush's Gulf War. It seemed like a senseless waste of resources and possibly her daughter's life. She started marching in antiwar protests and moved on to demonstrations against police brutality and promoting educational equality. She convinced her husband to move back to the West End, where her activism wouldn't draw nasty comments from the neighbors. She got along well with Carman Weathers and Robert Douglas on the monitoring committee.

Just as the committee was getting to work, Ingwerson suddenly announced his resignation.[38] The school board begged him to stay, but by the end of the school year in 1993, he had packed his bags and was headed back to California. "I've had two difficult years—one was 1984 and one is this past year," he said. "And both of them deal with equity and quality issues. We didn't shirk from either one of them. Was it something I enjoyed? Heavens no. Was it something I wanted to wake up and keep going at year after year? No. But is it something that is necessary? Yes."[39]

The committee made little progress in the wake of his departure. Its members rarely agreed on anything as they rehashed the old arguments for and against busing. But it was a platform of relative power, and the members used it to push their separate agendas. They were able to peruse reams of data about the racial makeup of each school in the district, suspension and dropout rates, and academic achievement. No matter where they stood on issue of busing, they were displeased with what they found. QUEST activists put together a report in early 1993 showing that the city's schools were at their most segregated levels since 1974, and that within the schools, classrooms were often divided by race.[40]

To Carman and the others, the small number of black students in Advance Program classrooms, the disproportionate number of blacks suspended from school, and the stagnation of their achievement on tests confirmed that the integration plan wasn't working and had never worked. To counteract the problems they believed desegregation had brought about, they proposed an Afrocentric magnet school in Louisville, probably with Central in mind as the perfect location, but the other committee members quashed the idea.[41]

In August 1994, frustrated by the squabbling in the monitoring committee, Carman sent off another op-ed to the *Courier-Journal*. "From the very beginning of African-American culture in America, there have always been blacks who thought that the best way to survive in America would be to disappear completely, leaving no trace at all that there had even been an Africa, or slavery, or even, finally, a black man," Carman wrote. "Integration cannot work when the powerless conscious of blacks integrates with the consciousless power of whites."[42]

When the newspaper reported a month later that ten black students had been transferred out of Central so that the school could comply with the school system's racial guidelines, Carman, Fran, and Robert received the news like a slap in the face.[43] Two years earlier, the school had an enrollment of more than 1,400 students, thanks in part to a new dynamic principal, but during the fall of 1994, that number had dwindled to about 1,100. They knew a teacher inside the school who reported that people were nervous about the school board's intentions: Riccardo X.

Mr. X, as his students now called him, had moved around from school to school for a decade after his first traumatic year of teaching in 1975 near the heart of the city's busing protests in the Bittersweet Shopping Center. As a young boy in the projects he had dreamed of following his hero, Muhammad Ali, to Central, before he ended up attending Male High School instead. Now X was finally there, and he had reason to be content.

After years of battling principals to let him teach a black history course, he had found a principal, Harold Fenderson, who was thrilled to have a black history teacher, and at last he had students who were enthusiastic about the subject. He organized students to participate in a Liberation Bowl, a black history quick-recall contest in which they competed with teams from around the country. His team won six national championships. The local Liberation Bowl racked up $150,000 in scholarships for students. He also took students on "sojourns" to cities around the country to tour famous sites in black history. He was one of the most popular teachers at the school. But he was worried. If the number of students continued to drop, it would be easy for the district to close Central. He reached out to the members of CEASE and asked how he could help.

Over the next two years, they organized, attending board meetings and pushing for change from the pulpit of the monitoring committee. They also laid the groundwork for a lawsuit. Finding plaintiffs wasn't difficult. By 1996, many black parents were infuriated by Project Renaissance, the choice-focused student assignment plan that Ingwerson had introduced three years earlier.[44] Black students were more than five times more likely to be rejected from the new magnet programs that West End schools had implemented to entice white students downtown. Not enough white students took the bait, so even as many black students were blocked from attending their neighborhood schools, enrollments in the West End were dropping. Central's shrinking student population now seemed to be a problem trickling down to the younger grades.

Meanwhile, suburban schools were expanding—some were in such demand they opened portable classrooms to accommodate the growing student population.[45] The new superintendent, Stephen Daeschner, made some tweaks to the assignment plan in 1996 after a series of critical stories in the newspaper pointing out the distress in West End schools.[46] But not all black parents were placated.

CEASE demanded that the school district raise the ceiling for the percentage of black students allowed at each school and that more black children be included in the Advance Program. Gradually, new members were enticed to join. Deborah Stallworth, a nurse with a seven-year-old son, knew Carman Weathers from church and Fran Thomas from her activism in the neighborhood.[47] She wanted her son to attend the school down the street from her West End home, but it was oversubscribed with black students. Instead, he was assigned to a struggling school in the white, working-class neighborhood of Portland, two miles to the north. She was incensed. Stallworth campaigned relentlessly until the district finally agreed to move her son. Then she poured her energies into CEASE. Stallworth, organized and passionate, was soon appointed the group's coordinator.

Robert's niece Sandra Hampton signed up to be a plaintiff in CEASE's plan to sue the district.[48] Her son had applied to Central and been turned away—although she was pleased with his assignment to Butler, one of the discipline-focused traditional high schools, instead. Jacquelyn and Ja'Mekia Stoner, Gwen and Dionne Hopson, and three other disgruntled families also joined CEASE that fall and signed up to be plaintiffs in the lawsuit.

Finding black parents angry at the system was easy. The group's most difficult task was finding a lawyer. In 1998, two years after CEASE had held its protest outside Central's doors and recruited the Hopsons and Stoners, they were still looking. They knocked on the door of nearly every black lawyer in Louisville. Some suggested fees that were far beyond their meager budget—the lowest retainer they were offered was $10,000. Many black lawyers simply turned them away, horrified at the idea of bringing a case against desegregation. The prospects for their lawsuit seemed about as bleak as the plan to open an Afrocentric school in Louisville.

Chapter 18

The law offices of Teddy B. Gordon occupied a small, two-story brick building marooned among acres of parking lots and skyscrapers in downtown Louisville. The diminutive building was a remnant of earlier iterations of the city, when the street had been lined with retail stores and saloons, before business headed to the suburbs and wrecking balls transformed the streetscape. Somehow, the building had survived.

In the winter of 1998, the members of CEASE called Gordon, on a tip from a friend that he might be willing to take the Central case.[1] Inside the building, a small reception area was nestled under a staircase leading to the second floor. Instead of law books, the shelves in his office held a collection of dozens of teddy bears in every shape and size, each one labeled with a child's name. They were souvenirs from the many private adoption cases Gordon had handled over the course of his three-decade career.[2] In addition to adoptions, he did no-contest divorces, personal injury cases, and workers' compensation claims. In the early 1990s, he had made the local news for representing an overweight couple who injured themselves on a water slide at Louisville's amusement park, Kentucky Kingdom.[3]

On a few occasions, however, his cases had veered into civil rights law. In the early 1990s, he represented a white police officer who said he had been discriminated against because several black officers were promoted before him.[4] He also argued the case of a black police dispatcher who said his supervisor had used racial slurs.[5] When CEASE first contacted him, he

135

had been making headlines in a local election case. His client, an African American candidate for city alderman, sued her opponent for distributing chicken wings to poll workers on Election Day.[6] Gordon won the case and got his client's opponent removed from office, although voters reelected the man shortly after.[7]

A short man with a Kentucky twang, Gordon fit the stereotype of a small-town Southern lawyer, the last person one might expect to support an Afrocentric cause. His jowly face and expressive gray eyebrows called to mind the actor Charles Durning. He wore off-the-rack J.C. Penney suits and had a large American flag painted on the side of his office building. His style was folksy. He seemed like a conservative good old boy. But he wasn't really.

Gordon had deep liberal roots. His parents were Latvian Jewish immigrants and he had been raised in the East End, Louisville's left-leaning, upper-middle-class enclave. His father had fled the pogroms, and he related to his son the fate of several relatives left behind who had been murdered and hung from meat hooks. The family ran a grocery store in the West End, a few blocks southwest of Central High School. As a kid, Teddy commuted to the store after school and delivered groceries to the surrounding black neighborhoods.

His parents weren't particularly political, but Teddy recalled them repeating adages such as "Don't say anything so bad that you can't go talk to the person again," and instilling in him that their business depended on treating their black customers well. When he was in high school, he befriended a younger African American boy who worked at the store, Robert Jones, whom Teddy called Jonesy. In the 1960s, Teddy played football for Atherton, the traditionally white high school that served the old wealthy neighborhoods of the East End; Jonesy played basketball for Central. One winter, Teddy brought some of his football friends to watch a matchup of the Atherton and Central basketball teams. Jonesy was playing, and Teddy rooted heartily for him from the stands. But around him, he heard several Atherton students yelling out racial slurs, and saw them give him angry glances. He was shaken. He had watched the violent scenes of dogs and hoses aimed at civil rights protesters on television, but he had never witnessed overt racism in person before.

Still, as a teenager, Teddy was less concerned about the civil rights movement and more concerned about the Vietnam War and the possibil-

ity of getting drafted. He was against the war, and the antiwar protest politics of the 1960s stayed with him. In college, he majored in Russian—a
nod to his family heritage—but his goal was to go to law school and perhaps someday hold political office. After graduation, he got married and
eventually found a job teaching Russian in the Louisville public schools.
He juggled his teaching job with classes at the University of Louisville's
night law school. It wasn't a prestigious program. Standards for admission
were low, but it was cheap. After a few years, Teddy had his degree and
passed the bar, but he was never satisfied with the idea of becoming a lowly
ambulance chaser.

In 1971, Gordon ran for state representative as a far-left Democrat.[8]
He would almost certainly have lost badly, but on Election Day he was
disqualified, along with his rivals, because they had mistakenly signed up to
run in the wrong district.[9] It was the first of five unsuccessful local political
campaigns he launched over the next two decades.[10] This dogged persistence fueled his law practice, too. He savored the role of the underdog
and wore his lack of Ivy League credentials as a badge of honor. Losing
a case, or a campaign, just made him more determined to win the next
one. To gear up for a tough day in court, he blared the Tom Petty song
"I Won't Back Down" from his office computer. By the mid-1990s, after
winning a workers' compensation case in the Kentucky Supreme Court, he
thought he was ready to go after his life's goal, one that provoked laughter
when he confessed it to his friends: he wanted to argue a case in front of
the US Supreme Court.

When the members of CEASE—composed of Carman Weathers, Robert Douglas, Fran Thomas, and a half dozen other West End old-timers—
arrived on his doorstep that winter, Gordon was savoring his success in the
case of the chicken-wing-distributing alderman. He was shocked that they
wanted him to sue the Jefferson County Public Schools over the desegregation plan at Central. "Are you crazy?" he responded. "I voluntarily bused
my two kids." He thought of Jonesy, who had little choice but to attend
Central. "Isn't sending them back to Central a bad thing?"

The CEASE members patiently explained that, in their view, Central
had become one of the best schools in the district under the leadership
of a new principal, Harold Fenderson, who had rekindled and expanded
the school's magnet programs. The school offered nursing, law, and business courses, and internships at Pizza Hut and SuperAmerica convenience

stores.[11] It had high graduation rates. The school was in high demand among black parents. But desegregation's racial limits meant that most black students couldn't get in. High-achieving students like Dionne Hopson and Ja'Mekia Stoner were turned away. Instead of Central, they and many others attended schools in the southwest of the city, where some white families were just as poor as those living in the black West End. Dionne was at Pleasure Ridge Park, and Ja'Mekia was at Shawnee, where graduation rates were significantly lower than at Central. Meanwhile, the other good high schools in the city, Ballard, Male, and Manual, had tiny percentages of black students compared to their lower-performing counterparts.

Gordon listened. His sense of right and wrong was offended. He had never thought much about the desegregation plan; like many liberal East Enders, he accepted it as the moral thing to do. But listening to CEASE's view of the system, suddenly it just didn't seem right. He also saw a glimmer of potential. This could be his Supreme Court case. He had little experience in civil rights or education, but CEASE was desperate for a lawyer to take its case. What Gordon lacked in experience and credentials, he made up for in feistiness and ambition. He was also cheap. In the spring of 1998, Gordon told his new clients that he would charge them $1 as a retainer; he hoped they could recoup his fees in civil damages.

On April 22 that year, Teddy B. Gordon filed the Central case in federal district court.[12] He listed Sandra Hampton, Robert Douglas's niece, as the lead plaintiff, followed by Clara Hilliard, Gwen Hopson, Lisa Logan, Joan Shields Merritt, and Jacquelyn Stoner. By then, Central's enrollment had dropped to nine hundred students. "If the seats are open, why can't our children have them?" Jacquelyn Stoner asked a local newspaper reporter the day the case was filed.[13]

Six months earlier, Lyman Johnson had died at the age of ninety-one. He had been unable to keep his vow to stay alive until one hundred to fight the people who wanted to send "the wagon rolling back down the hill." Gordon and the members of CEASE were insistent that they wanted only to adjust, not end, the desegregation plan. "Integration can be defined as over 50 percent," Gordon told the press.[14] In his complaint, Teddy wrote that "only African American students are denied their first choice as to where to attend high school within the Jefferson County School System, based on their race, and only African American students are involuntarily bused to a high school other than their first choice." He also pointed out the racial disparities in the Advance Program, where only 11 percent of students were black. "Contrary to the admitted goals of integration and diversity of the Board, African-American students are denied an equal opportunity to gain entrance into the advanced program based on the systemic discrimination of the Defendant."[15] The complaint was short, only five pages, and it would also turn out to be rife with problems.

Judge John G. Heyburn seemed like a lucky draw for the plaintiffs. Heyburn had conservative credentials. He was the scion of an established legal family in Louisville.[16] His father and grandfather were both partners in one of Louisville's most prestigious law firms, and an office tower downtown bore his family's name. He had begun his career working on the campaign of Republican senator Mitch McConnell in 1977, when McConnell first ran for a local county position. President Bush appointed Heyburn to the federal bench in 1992, and Chief Justice Rehnquist picked him to work on budget issues for the Judicial Conference of the United States, a group that disseminated information to federal judges.

Growing up in Louisville, Heyburn attended Chenoweth, an East End public elementary school near several upper-middle-class enclaves. The school had opened in 1954, and was desegregated while Heyburn was there.[17] He could remember when the handful of African American students first appeared in his classroom. Later, however, his parents moved him to private school and then boarding school in New England. He graduated from Harvard and then the University of Kentucky Law School. His first job out of college was in the West End, working at the Park Duvalle Community Health Center. The medical center took up several buildings in the Cotter Homes, next door to the housing project where Riccardo X grew up, and had been founded after local activists agitated for better health services for the isolated project residents. During the summer, Heyburn started a tutoring program for the local kids, and got to know Lyman Johnson's son, who also worked there, and Lyman Johnson himself.

Heyburn sent his own children to one of the city's most exclusive private schools. Despite his early involvement with the Republican Party, it was difficult to decipher Heyburn's politics. In one of his most important cases, he had struck down a partial-birth abortion ban in Kentucky. He had also dismissed a corruption case against a shady national lottery company.

In May, the school district responded to the case. A large private firm with offices on the upper floors of a skyscraper in downtown Louisville and satellite offices in other cities around the country represented the Jefferson County Schools. Shelves of books, polished wood furniture, and rows of framed awards and degrees decorated the rooms. Frank Mellen, a lean, serious man with owlish glasses and a Harvard law degree, was the lead attorney.[18] Byron Leet, who would lead the questioning at the hearings, was more dapper, with fashionable clear-framed glasses, prematurely silver hair, and a more jovial disposition. He had graduated from Vanderbilt.[19]

Less than a decade earlier under Superintendent Don Ingwerson, the school district had fought a long campaign to loosen the racial limits on its desegregation plan and reduce the use of forced busing. But unlike many school districts elsewhere, which had been eager and even proactive in trying to end busing plans, the Jefferson County Public Schools had never tried to rid itself of desegregation entirely. The board paid attention to the polls showing that a majority of parents supported the plan. And the board members believed desegregation was actually an important educational goal. They also believed that if they gave in to Carman Weathers and his fellow activists and let Central exceed the racial limits, the entire plan would eventually collapse. A higher concentration of black students at one school would decrease the number available to attend schools in the predominantly white suburbs, thus increasing segregation everywhere, not just at Central. In addition, if Central were allowed to become primarily African American, it would set a precedent for schools and students elsewhere to clamor for exemptions from the desegregation rules.

The district's lawyers asked Heyburn to dismiss the case.[20] They rejected the allegations that black students were the only ones who didn't get their choice of high school and argued that the students lacked standing to bring a case. They also noted that the requests for remedies, such as monetary damages and placement in their first-choice school, were unconstitutional. The judge refused.

The lawyers spent the summer meeting in conferences with each other and Heyburn, and taking depositions from students and other witnesses. The civil rights leaders who had battled with Carman Weathers and his allies over integration and Afrocentric education throughout the early 1990s were not content to watch the lawsuit unfold from the sidelines. In the fall, QUEST, Georgia Powers' group that had formed in reaction to Ingwerson's attempts to dismantle forced busing in elementary schools, filed a petition with Judge Heyburn asking to join the lawsuit as a third party.[21]

The group added its own plaintiffs into the mix of people who would be fighting over the desegregation plan in court: five students attending Central, both white and black, who wanted to see the desegregation plan continue. Steve Porter, a white, Republican East End lawyer who had grown up down the block from Judge Heyburn and who had served on the monitoring committee with Carman and Robert, was the group's lawyer.[22] Rather than end busing, QUEST argued, the school district should go further, desegregating "all schools, programs, classrooms and faculty since the vestiges of de jure segregation remain."[23] The school district didn't want QUEST to join the legal fray, saying it would essentially be arguing the same thing as Jefferson County's lawyers. Teddy also protested the group's attempt to barge into his case.

Heyburn wanted to hear as many opinions as possible, however. He allowed QUEST to enter the case as a third party, and set a hearing date for the following spring.

Chapter 19

In the fall of 1998, Ja'Mekia Stoner entered her senior year at Fern Creek High School. After struggling for a year at Shawnee, the high school across the street from their house in the West End, where more than half the students were poor, Ja'Mekia and her mother had decided she needed to switch. She was bored, skipping classes, and on the verge of failing. They looked for a magnet program elsewhere that would better match her experiences in the affluent East End schools she had attended in elementary and middle school.

Ja'Mekia chose Fern Creek, a school on the outer edge of the county surrounded by white middle-class subdivisions. Parents, mainly white, had fought to protect the school from closure during the 1980s, leading the school system to close Carman Weathers's old school, Thomas Jefferson, and several other schools instead. Fern Creek was not the best in the county—in fact, student achievement was mediocre—but several of Ja'Mekia's cousins were students there, and they liked it.[1] The summer before her sophomore year, Ja'Mekia applied to join the school's communications magnet.

She was accepted, and at Fern Creek, she thrived once again: She joined the debate team and made friends. She stopped skipping classes and threw herself back into her schoolwork. The difference between Shawnee and Fern Creek was stark. At Fern Creek, Ja'Mekia believed, teachers cared about education. The work was more difficult, and she rose to the challenge. At Shawnee, she had assumed the teachers didn't care because they didn't ask her to try hard. But the fact that Fern Creek was a better school than Shawnee irked her. She didn't understand why she had to wake up at five in the morning to travel halfway across town to get a better education. She should have been able to travel across the street.

Ja'Mekia remained a plaintiff in the CEASE case, but in name only. Her mother, Jacquelyn, had never shied away from telling her children about her terrible experience of being bused to Fairdale, where violence and hatred ruined her last years of high school, but she was also wary of instilling in her children the belief that race and racism could define them and limit their options in life. In the spring of 1999, she decided that her daughter should not testify during the hearings. Ja'Mekia was content at Fern Creek and no longer interested in attending Central, and Jacquelyn worried that keeping the family involved in the case would only set her daughter back by reminding her of the obstacles she faced as a black woman. After meeting with CEASE members numerous times over the course of two years, Jacquelyn was tired of listening to the back-and-forth over race, and she didn't want her daughter to get caught up in the debate and lose her focus on school. She wanted her to move on.

Dionne Hopson's name also was still listed as a plaintiff. She had not been as fortunate as Ja'Mekia after her rejection from Central. A year younger than Ja'Mekia, in the 1998–99 school year, Dionne was seventeen and in her junior year at Pleasure Ridge Park in the South End. She hated it, but she had not applied elsewhere; she still had hopes of getting into Central if the lawsuit went well. In the fall, Gwen Hopson told the press that the family planned to stick with Teddy "to the end." Dionne had been "turned away because she was black . . . because no other whites wanted to come to the West End and go to Central High School, she could not go," Gwen said.[2] She and Dionne wanted justice. That spring, Dionne was assigned to be the first witness to take the stand.

On April 13, 1999, the lawyers filed into the courtroom.[3] Teddy took his place at a table on the far left, where he sat alone. On the other side of the aisle, half a dozen lawyers for the school board and the interveners rustled papers at their tables. The audience was filled with parents and members of CEASE. Some looked in dismay at their representative in the court. Compared to the debonair coterie of lawyers on the far right of the room, Riccardo X thought Teddy resembled the disheveled television detective Columbo.

Heyburn was a tall man, with a receding gray hairline and shrewd but friendly blue eyes behind large glasses. His courtroom was a relatively easy-going place, but the case before him that day was a complicated one. To win, the Central parents would have to prove that their rights to equal protection under the Fourteenth Amendment had been violated, that they were being denied something—an education at Central—that was unique and unavailable elsewhere in the system.

The school board's path to a win meant successfully arguing that its de-segregation system did not deserve the "strict scrutiny" of the court, a legal concept requiring judges to take a close look at any scenario that infringed on constitutional rights. If that argument failed and the judge decided to move forward, in order to win, the school board's lawyers would have to prove that the district had a "compelling interest" in using race for student assignment, a concept that had been laid out in detail in a 1978 Supreme Court case, *University of California v. Bakke.*[4]

Allan Bakke, a white man, had been denied admission to the University of California-Davis's medical school because of racial quotas that reserved a certain number of seats for minority applicants. The court ruled that Bakke's constitutional rights had indeed been violated and that the Constitution prohibited the use of rigid racial quotas. But the justices didn't go so far as to ban the use of race in admissions. Instead, they said government institutions—including public universities—might have a "compelling interest" to ensure racial diversity, and that in those cases, as long as rigid quotas weren't used, they could consider race for such things as college applications and student assignments.

Teddy opened the hearing. "Our purpose today is to allow more African American students in Central, regardless of any type of quota system," he began. He talked about the numbers who had been turned away from Central and refused their first choice. He mentioned dropout rates, sus-pensions, and self-esteem. But he did not mention the Fourteenth Amend-ment or equal protection. "The testimony we hope to show is that although there is diversity to some extent and the desegregation efforts by the school board have been a good attempt, what happened is that African-American students are no better off, in fact they're worse off, than they were 25 years ago. Test scores between the two races are still widely apart."

As Teddy wrapped up, Heyburn looked down at him: "Your central point, is it not, is that to the extent the pupil assignment plan denies black students admission to Central High School solely on the basis of race, that that is a denial of those students' equal protection under the 14th amendment?"

"That is correct," Teddy replied. "Constitutionally impermissible."

The judge went on to press Teddy on whether he understood that he couldn't make a legal case based on whether or not busing was bad for black children. His job was to argue that the system, regardless of whether it worked or not, denied their rights.

"That's correct," said Teddy, "although we believe that the student assignment plan as it exists should be thrown out as constitutionally impermissive."

Next up was Frank Mellen, the scholarly Harvard Law graduate who represented the school district. He began by warning the court that this case would likely reach far beyond Central if allowed to continue. "We think this case raises an issue that affects or impacts the entire plan." The school district had a compelling interest in using race to assign students to school because minority students benefited both academically and in more intangible ways from desegregation, he went on. They were more likely to live in interracial neighborhoods later on and "navigate in a diverse interracial society."

The lawyers sat down, and Dionne Hopson, the first witness, stood up. She had dreamed of being a lawyer since middle school five years earlier. But this was not how she had imagined she would first enter a courtroom. This was not a field trip with her fellow Central classmates. She was not an intern in an attorney's office. Instead, she sat down in the witness chair.

Teddy asked her to spell her name.

"Dionne," he said. "Did I pronounce your name right?"

She corrected him: "Dee-on."

He asked about her school background, and she told the story of being denied at Central.

"How have you done at Pleasure Ridge?" he asked.

"I slipped totally," Dionne said. "I mean, in the last two years, I just—
I lost my father, and it's like ever since I have been at Pleasure Ridge, my
grades have slipped drastically. It's like I went from an Honors student to
like C minuses and D's and U's, to barely passing, to barely making it."

"Why did you want to go to Central?" Teddy asked.

"Because it had the curriculum that I wanted," she replied.

"Are you offered the same curriculum at Pleasure Ridge?"

"No, I'm not."

"Obviously there's no way of telling, but if you had gotten the curriculum you wanted in the school you wanted, do you think you would be
a better student today?"

"Yes I do."

The school district lawyers objected, but the judge let it go. "It's not really legally significant, is it, how a particular student does, better or worse,"
Heyburn said. "But I'm going to let the testimony come in."

When the school system's attorneys cross-examined Dionne, they asked
her if, after being rejected at Central, she had applied to any other magnets.

"No, I didn't," Dionne said.

Then the judge turned to her. He asked gently where her parents went
to school, and when they had graduated. "Sixty-nine," Gwen yelled from
her seat. At that, Dionne was sent to join her.

Another student, Terrell Shields, who had already graduated from Fern
Creek, followed Hopson. Then Teddy called his third and final witness,
Joseph McMillan, who had formed the anti-busing group SAVE with Car-
man Weathers and Robert Douglas. McMillan, who often wore a round
African kufi cap over his close-cropped gray hair, walked up to the stand.
Teddy prompted him to talk about the alternative schools where the majority of students were black, Liberty and Buechel, where Carman taught.
He then asked about the rate of suspensions for black students. McMillan's
answer, that 41 percent of black students would be suspended at some point
in high school, caused gasps and shouts in the audience. After the judge
had quieted everyone down, Teddy finished his examination by asking if
desegregation had hurt the self-esteem of blacks.

It had, McMillan said: "The Supreme Court decision of *Brown v. Board
of Education* was based on an erroneous assumption in my mind." That is,
he believed that *Brown* had gone wrong by focusing on integrating black
students with whites, instead of trying to enforce equal outcomes for both

groups. Bringing the groups together physically mattered much less to him that bringing them together academically.

Satisfied, Teddy sat down.

The judge turned to the witness with a more esoteric line of questioning. "Blacks and whites have been arguing and discussing about this question of self-esteem for a hundred years at least?"

"Yes, sir," McMillan replied.

"Have you ever heard the term 'twoness'?" the judge asked.

McMillan nodded.

"And what do you think W. E. B. Du Bois meant when he used that term, 'twoness'?"

"I know what he meant. He meant that a black person has to have two sides. He's got to be in one instance black and in one instance white. That dual consciousness that Du Bois talked about still exists, that we have to be both/and instead of either/or," McMillan said.

"It's not just a fact that those two things exist; it's that there's constant tension between those two things?"

"Almost always constant tension between those two," McMillan replied. "It was in 1903 when he wrote that book, *Souls of Black Folk*, and it still exists today."

"So you would agree with his fundamental concept of this intellectual struggle, I guess, is an important thing that every African-American has to deal with?" Heyburn asked.

"Every African-American and every white American has to contend with that. We move toward the millennium, I hope that we will solve that, Judge."

The judge was quiet. It was clear that he had been reading before the hearing, and not just case law. In fact, he had read all of Taylor Branch's voluminous books on the civil rights movement, Richard Kluger's history of the *Brown* cases, *Simple Justice*, and the works of other sociologists and historians of black culture, including W. E. B. Du Bois, who had argued that the "history of the American Negro is the history of this strife, —this longing to attain self-conscious manhood, to merge his double self into a better and truer self" without losing either his black identity or his American one.[5]

Heyburn applied Du Bois's ideas to his very specific purpose. For the judge, the issue of self-esteem was important, but not because it might affect student achievement. He was trying to understand whether black students, after twenty years of proactive school desegregation, still felt the same sense of intimidation that had prevented freedom of choice plans from working. Was racial discrimination still pervasive enough and still felt so deeply in the black community that aggressive desegregation policies were necessary? Did black people still perceive themselves as separate, or did they perceive themselves as part of the whole? Had school desegregation done its job, or was there more work to be done?

Teddy stood up again to ask a few more questions, including "a real stupid" one: "We are a unified school system, right?"

"Yes, as of 1978," McMillan replied. "Unitary, they call it."

The lawyers in the room assumed that the question in the case was not whether Louisville was still under a court decree to desegregate its schools. No one realized that the judge was not so sure.

With that, before the lunch recess on the first day of the hearing, Teddy rested his case.

The school district lawyers set up easels with maps and charts. Their witnesses included Stephen Daeschner, the superintendent who had replaced Ingwerson in 1993, district administrators, the retired CEO of a Louisville bank, and a professor from Harvard, Gary Orfield. They moved through their questioning efficiently as they tried to establish that assigning students by race was beneficial both to the students and to the city as a whole. The school administrators explained the intricacies of the desegregation plan for the judge; the bank director said the diverse schools produced good employees and drew people to the city; the Harvard professor testified that studies showed minorities who attended integrated schools achieved better test scores and higher-paying jobs.

The superintendent, a Kansan, who, like Ingwerson, had been born in a small prairie town, talked about diversity.[6] He had worked in Alaska and also St. Louis, where desegregation had also been highly contentious and the fight over it ongoing. Daeschner had less swagger than his predecessor, perhaps having learned from Ingwerson's struggles and from his own dabbling with the Project Renaissance plan in 1996, that messing with desegregation meant risking his job. In his testimony he warned that changing just one element of the plan, including the fifteen to fifty ratio of blacks allowed at each school, could disrupt and perhaps overturn the whole system.

During his cross-examinations, Gordon's folksy, aw-shucks style was often barbed with sarcasm. In his first question to Gary Orfield, for example, a soft-spoken professor born in Minnesota, he pointed out that Harvard was spelled wrong on his résumé.

The sarcasm didn't always work. In his cross-examination of the superintendent, Gordon tried to establish that test scores had been falling for African Americans. "In fact, aren't the KERA results showing a five percentage point difference even in elementary schools over the last two years?" Gordon asked Daeschner.

"I don't understand," the superintendent replied.

"Lower for African Americans?"

"Difference in what? Please explain yourself."

"Once again, I apologize because I'm not familiar with the terminology, and obviously educators always have a brilliant way of stating things," Gordon replied.

Later, one of the school officials testified that test scores were actually up.

The judge frequently intervened to steer Gordon's questions toward the relevant legal issues. On more than one occasion, Gordon seemed to bolster the school board's cause. In one exchange, as he tried to establish that students barred from Central were denied a head start in a business or legal career, he led Orfield into a monologue about how magnets, though important draws in a desegregation scheme, didn't actually make a big difference in determining a student's career: "It is really silly to think that students know what they're going into in 8th grade," Orfield said. "I was going to be a dentist."

The school board finished its case on the second day, and closing arguments were scheduled for the following week. On Friday, the judge sent a message to the lawyers.[7] Based on what he had heard from Gordon and his witnesses, he was not convinced the plaintiffs had standing to bring a lawsuit. Most of the students had ended up at other schools or graduated, and none had ever reapplied to Central. Even if Gordon won the case, it would be both unconstitutional and logistically impossible for the judge to ensure that any of them got to attend Central. In addition, Gordon's complaint, written the previous spring, had ignored key issues. He had not asked for relief under the Fourteenth Amendment, the linchpin of his case. If it were appealed, it was almost certain that higher courts would throw it out. To move forward, Gordon would have to rewrite his complaint after the hearings ended if he wanted his case to be taken seriously.

The following Tuesday, April 20, 1999, two students walked into Columbine High School in Littleton, Colorado, and gunned down more than two dozen students and teachers. The next day, Gordon incorporated the shootings into his closing statement: "For the tragedy that happened yesterday, what must happen today is a school system of inclusion, not exclusion. We want the least possible number of estranged students possible. We want them near where they live. We want more parental involvement, and we want the $25 million that they bus our kids around from morning to night used for better school security. The end of racial guidelines occurs now. Thank you very much," Gordon said.

He turned to sit down, but the judge stopped him. He still had a few questions for Gordon, and his patience appeared to be cracking. They spent the next half hour going back and forth between Gordon's demands that Dionne—who, unlike the other students, still wanted to attend Central—be paid damages and allowed to go to Central the following fall, and Heyburn's insistence that neither of these requests were constitutional. Finally, Heyburn sent Gordon to his seat.

Heyburn wasn't gentle with the school board lawyers, either. As Leet began listing a series of court cases that were analogous to the Louisville scenario, the judge interrupted to grill him on more abstract points of the law. The school district was essentially arguing that "if the discrimination is benign, if it's for a good purpose, then it's okay, and if it's for a bad purpose, it's not okay, which is facially a very appealing argument," Heyburn said. "It's just that how do you as a constitutional doctrine go about determining when something is benign and when something is bad?" Where do you draw a line? he wanted to know. Were color-conscious policies necessary to identify and uproot racial discrimination, or did they perpetuate the old system of racial segregation and inequality?

The lawyers struggled to respond. There was no pat answer; historians, legal scholars, and sociologists had been grappling with those same questions for a century. The judge interrupted again to wonder about the odd situation in which the district found itself: "At some magic moment, when the school system becomes unitary, not only are they not ordered to [assign students by race], but in fact, what they had been ordered a moment ago to do is now impermissible? Is that possible?"

Leet said no; Gordon said absolutely.

Steve Porter, the lawyer for the third party in the case, stood up last to make his own plaintiffs' case. He argued that Central probably owed most of its success to the very student assignment plan the plaintiffs were trying to dismantle, and closed by invoking Lyman Johnson. "Lyman could tell us what unequal treatment is. He knew it," Porter said. "Then he spent the last 10 years or so of his life imploring us in that famous phrase, which you might have heard, not to let the wagon roll back down the hill. . . . That wagon could roll back down the hill if the plaintiffs are allowed their remedies."

The hearing ended, leaving some CEASE members feeling confident. Others were uneasy. As Teddy gathered his things, Riccardo X exchanged looks with the others. "Shit, we lost this," he thought. "He doesn't really know what he's doing."

CEASE's coordinator Deborah Stallworth, the nurse with the seven-year-old son, was also disheartened. Watching the white lawyers, the white school officials, the white experts, and a white judge decide the fate of her child and other black children had been draining. "There's nobody up there representing me for real," she told a newspaper reporter. "They have made this system so complex, so ridiculously hard to navigate that you don't know whether you're getting screwed or not."[8]

Chapter 20

Teddy spent the afternoon after the hearing rewriting his complaint to focus on Dionne Hopson and her bad experience at Pleasure Ridge Park.[1] He finished in a few hours, although the judge had given him five days to work on it. Over the next two weeks, CEASE members tracked down four ninth graders who had been denied entrance into Central the previous fall, and Teddy added their names to the list of plaintiffs.[2]

In June, the judge handed down what he admitted was a "surprising" ruling.[3] To the lawyers, activists, experts, and the reporters following the case, this was an understatement. In his opinion, Heyburn declared that in fact, after a careful review of the long history of Louisville's desegregation plan, the city had never actually been officially declared unitary. It was, as far as Heyburn was concerned, still under the 1975 court order to desegregate, so its student assignment plan could stay intact. Gordon and his clients would have to prove that the vestiges of segregation were erased from the school system if they wanted to go forward with their case. Only afterward could they turn to the matter of whether racial limits should be applied to Central or not.

The decision, nearly thirty pages long, methodically detailed the twists and turns in Louisville's desegregation story from 1954 on. It also addressed the deeper, underlying American dilemma the arguments in the case raised: the responsibility of the Constitution to be both color-conscious and color-blind at the same time. "While this case illustrates the tension between these two seemingly parallel sides of the same right, it will not decide which is more essential. Each is fundamental," Heyburn said. "Understanding and reconciling the two parallel, but sometimes contradictory, elements of equal protection may be the Court's ultimate challenge."

The long memorandum was evidence of Heyburn's investment in the case. It was eloquent and detailed and had gone through many drafts. If the plaintiffs pressed on, the case would likely be the biggest of Heyburn's career as a federal district court judge. And yet the ruling was also an obstacle thrown in the path of Teddy and the members of CEASE. In his decision, the judge was clear that the Central case could potentially open the door to dismantling the entire Louisville student assignment plan. If the plaintiffs appealed, they might set a national precedent that could upend desegregation programs in other cities, too. He wanted to make sure they understood the potential consequences of their lawsuit, and, if an end to desegregation made them uncomfortable, to perhaps reconsider.

Going forward would also force Teddy into odd contortions as he attempted to make his case. If the school system were declared unitary, then Gordon would be on much firmer ground in arguing that the racial limits on the schools should be lifted. Yet to get there, Gordon, who had spent much of the spring hearings describing the ways in which the school system was "arbitrary, capricious and discriminatory" and arguing that black students were purposefully sent to the worst schools in the system, would have to argue that racial discrimination in the schools was a problem of the past.

His clients, of course, were convinced of the opposite. They wanted to end busing, but that didn't mean they believed the vestiges of segregation were gone. In their eyes, things had only gotten worse: Blacks were still as powerless over their schools and their children's education as they had ever been under segregation. White people still ran the show. "I would like for someone, anyone to prove that 22 years of busing have relieved racial tension in this community," Carman Weathers had written in his most recent *Courier-Journal* op-ed.[4] His friend Robert Douglas put it more bluntly: The way desegregation had been carried out—with the closure of black schools, the firing of black teachers, and the one-way system of busing black children—was nothing more than a "neo-slavery method of dealing with black people."[5]

The new turn in the case wasn't any more comfortable for the school board's lawyers. If the judge found vestiges of desegregation in the school system, then the school board's case to keep the student assignment plan intact was easily justified. Yet it would be impossible for Mellen and Leet to stand up and argue that their clients still practiced racial segregation in their schools. Fortunately for them, QUEST was a part of the case. The school lawyers had protested the interference of the group as the second set of plaintiffs. But now, this third party could be helpful. QUEST disagreed fundamentally with Gordon and his clients, believing that desegregation had not gone far enough, and they were happy to make the argument the school board couldn't: racial discrimination was still alive and thriving in the Jefferson County Public Schools. Like the school district, the QUEST members wanted to save desegregation, but they wanted the student assignment plan to become more expansive, so that it addressed the racial disparities inside schools, not just between them.

Teddy and CEASE eagerly embraced Judge Heyburn's challenge. In fact, Teddy saw the ruling as an invitation for him to move forward. He also embraced the irony of the case, joking that he was now standing in the shoes of the Topeka Board of Education in the 1950s, fighting against desegregation; the Louisville schools were like Linda Brown and the NAACP, fighting for it. His clients were a little more circumspect. They had never actually argued for the desegregation plan to end, they just wanted the racial limits expanded so that Central might have more black students. If the school board agreed to lift the limit to 85 percent, they would walk away. As Deborah Stallworth put it, "We keep trying to tell people we don't want segregation. We just feel like it can be defined in a different direction."[6]

Teddy filed a new complaint, arguing that the school system should be declared unitary and racial limits lifted. A hearing was set for the following January. Even if Heyburn's order wasn't encouraging, the national climate was. Across the country, parents were taking school districts to court over their desegregation plans and winning. Cities that had devised elaborate busing systems and networks of magnet schools under pressure from judges two decades earlier were now being ordered by those same courts to dismantle them.

In the 1990s, circuit court judges struck down a ban in Montgomery County, Maryland, on any school transfer that increased racial segregation, and Richmond, Virginia, judges did the same regarding a weighted lottery system that gave preference to minority students.[7] A case out of Charlotte, North Carolina, where the concept of busing had emerged from the *Swann* ruling in 1971, was also on appeal.

A white father there was contesting a quota system used in the district's magnet schools, which had been set up in Charlotte's black neighborhoods in 1992 as a way to shift from forced busing to voluntary desegregation. The magnets seemed to be working. The schools had long waiting lists for white children, who were limited to 60 percent of enrollment. But the district court declared that Charlotte's school system was unified, and that the racial quotas used in the magnets were unconstitutional. Later, a Fourth Circuit judge, William Byrd Traxler Jr. from Greenville, South Carolina, would uphold the district judge's opinion, writing that "unfortunately, the end result of the challenged magnet schools admissions policy is placement of racial quotas ahead of educating students—an inappropriate result nowhere countenanced in the district court's orders or in the Supreme Court's desegregation decisions."[8]

Magnet schools were the target of other cases, too. The prestigious Boston Latin School, a highly selective public high school that in the 1970s had been ordered to maintain a minority enrollment of at least 35 percent, was told this quota was unconstitutional in 1996.[9] In 1997, a group of Chinese parents in San Francisco lost a case trying to end the city's desegregation court decree, but they succeeded in changing the admissions system at one of the city's top magnet schools, Lowell High School.[10] Black and Hispanic enrollments dropped significantly at both the San Francisco and the Boston school.[11]

Magnet schools, developed as a way to promote diversity, were now helping to undermine it. In many places, they had met the goal of encouraging white parents to become more invested in urban public school systems, but in doing so, they had fueled a sense of entitlement to a choice of schools. They also fed the perception that certain schools were unique and better than their counterparts, and that being denied entrance left one at a disadvantage. Just as the old "freedom of choice" plans had demonstrated in the 1960s, the concept of school choice and racial integration were once again turning out to be incompatible. A Columbia University law professor, Samuel Issacharoff, called the inability of school systems to find a way to reconcile the two a "tragedy."[12]

Many didn't see it that way. As the era of school desegregation was beginning to wane in the 1990s, a growing education reform movement based on the promotion of more school choice was following closely on the heels of the standards and accountability movement.[13] The two were, in fact, closely intertwined. Proponents of school choice believed that if schools, both private and public, were pitted against each other to compete for students, they would be forced to improve. The same market-based concept formed the argument behind the standards and accountability movement: Schools forced to compete with each other on the basis of student achievement would get better. And accountability systems were supposed to create a more informed marketplace of parents, who could compare the performance of their child's school with that of others and make better choices.

While many school choice supporters liked the idea of private school vouchers, others saw choice as a way for educators inside the public school system to innovate and break free from a status quo that clearly wasn't working as minority test scores stagnated. Despite opposition from teachers' unions and some education researchers, both liberal and conservative policy makers increasingly embraced school choice as the 1990s drew to a close. There was more evidence showing that integration improved student achievement than choice. But school choice won out based on politics and convenience.

The philosophical underpinnings of the two education reforms were diametrically opposed: Fundamental to a market-based system of choice-based education was Darwinian competition that created winners and losers; desegregation was meant to equalize all schools, lift all boats. But mixing students by race had never been implemented in many cities, while the courts and demographic changes were weakening or dismantling entirely the dwindling number of desegregation plans still in existence.

President Bush made open enrollment and vouchers a major plank in his education plan in 1991, and five years later, Bob Dole and Bill Clinton both embraced school choice when they faced off in the 1996 presidential election campaign.[14] Dole praised vouchers, calling school choice the "civil rights movement of the 1990s."[15] Clinton preferred charter schools, an idea born in Minnesota in 1991 to create autonomous, privately run but still publicly funded schools that could act as laboratories for testing education reforms.[16]

Despite the apparent incompatibility of the two education models, a popular argument for school choice rested on some of the same principles as the desegregation argument: Choice, like desegregation, would give students a way out of failing inner-city schools filled with high concentrations of black and Hispanic students living in poverty. But one sociologist, Peter Cookson, pointed out that school choice fit better with the American ethos, with its focus on individual freedom and market competition.[17] Desegregation, which had to rely on state coercion and cooperation among citizens, did not.

While some choice programs focused on giving students the option to transfer out of their neighborhoods (or to private schools), the school choice movement increasingly focused on creating good schools for inner-city students near their homes, avoiding the difficult political problems created by inconveniencing white suburbanites. If they succeeded, they would no longer have to fight battles over forcing middle-class parents to mingle their children and share their resources with poor black and Hispanic children.

Like other districts caught up in desegregation court battles that decade, Louisville, with its Project Renaissance plan, had attempted the difficult juggling act of mixing integration with choice. But as the decade ended, they were going against the grain. A 1999 Public Agenda poll had found that 79 percent of American parents strongly believed they should have a right to choose their children's school.[18] Another poll a year later found that while 80 percent of black parents believed that sending their children to an integrated school was important, 82 percent said raising academic standards was more important.[19] The choices the Louisville school board was trying to create under its desegregation plan were inevitably geared toward drawing white parents into the city, not creating a myriad of new programs for black parents to choose from. In Louisville, as the CEASE activists saw it, white people got choice, black people got integration. They preferred choice.

Chapter 21

January 30, 2000, was Super Bowl Sunday: Rams versus the Titans.[1] Teddy Gordon woke up early and pulled out his papers for the *Hampton* case. The following day was the first of the new trial. But Teddy was an avid football fan. In high school, he had played in spite of his small size, and he believed the game had taught him how to take a hit and keep running.

The Rams-Titans matchup promised to be a good one. Both teams were underdogs, and Teddy loved an underdog. He stacked up his files in front of the television. It was a low-scoring, defensive game, with the Rams only slightly in the lead throughout. With six seconds left, the Titans nearly tied it, but linebacker Mike Jones came out of nowhere and tackled their receiver just short of the line. The Rams won. The game's Most Valuable Player was an obscure quarterback, Kurt Warner, who just five years earlier was stocking grocery shelves after being passed over by the pros in his early career.[2] By midnight, after watching these unknown players suddenly become stars, Teddy felt exhilarated and prepared.

The next morning, Teddy wheeled a suitcase full of files into the courtroom. The tables were more crowded than they had been the following spring.[3] In addition to the school district lawyers and Steve Porter, the QUEST lawyer fighting to save the desegregation plan, the US Department of Justice and the American Civil Liberties Union had joined the trial.

A third set of plaintiffs, representing the Kentucky Alliance against Racist and Political Repression, also asked to join the fray with its own

lawyer and its own set of arguments. Fran Thomas was still the director there, but other members of the group, including its founder, Anne
Braden, who a half century earlier had helped an African American family
buy a house in Shively that was eventually bombed, had differences with
CEASE.

The Alliance agreed with CEASE members that the district's ban on
black-majority schools was inherently racist—that it supported the idea
that blacks were inferior to whites. Also like CEASE, the Alliance believed
that the school system was far from rooting out the institutional racism of
its pre-desegregation days. Its strategy was different, however. Rather than
try to do away with the desegregation plan so that Central could accept
more black students, the Alliance planned to argue that the school should
remain under court order until the achievement gap was closed.

Representing them was an African American lawyer from rural eastern Kentucky named Aubrey Williams who was studying to become
a preacher. Williams had followed Lyman Johnson as president of the
Louisville NAACP in the 1970s, and then served as a state representative
for southern Louisville.[4] Later, he was fired from a state job overseeing
a fund for workers' compensation. A state official called his management
style "erratic." Williams responded by saying it was unfortunate that "racism is alive and well."[5] Anne Braden, now a thin old woman, but with the
same deep-set brown eyes and jaunty bob of her youth, sat behind him
throughout the trial.

Teddy once again started the proceedings. His goal was to prove that
the vestiges of segregation in the school system were gone, and though his
syntax occasionally got tangled up, he stuck to his argument: "It is our position that there are no vestiges of prior de jure segregation, that an African
American majority in the school cannot be considered in any way, shape or
form a revestige or a prior vestige."[6]

Leet was more poetic. The word *vestiges* came from the Latin word for
footprints, he said, and though the school district had tried in "good faith"
to eliminate all of the footprints left behind by segregation, they would
quickly reappear if the judge ruled that the system must discard its racial
guidelines.

Just as the school district lawyers had envisioned, the additional plaintiffs, QUEST and the Kentucky Alliance, fervently attacked those "good
faith" efforts. "The Jefferson County Schools have always done just enough

to look good, but never enough to accomplish the mandates of *Brown*," Porter said in his opening. Aubrey Williams, with his preacher cadence, was even more forceful: "The Jefferson County Public Schools failed to realize, failed to understand and failed to address what it truly means to attempt integration. It means more than just placing kids in the same environment. It is about more than a numerical scheme or racial balances. . . . It's about educational opportunity. It's about seriously addressing those things that cripple a child."

But as eloquent as the arguments of the district and intervening lawyers were in comparison with Teddy's, the case law was against them. Most people in the room agreed that high suspension rates, low test scores, and the high numbers of whites in advanced classes compared to the high number of blacks in disciplinary schools were evidence of segregation's long reach. The question was whether the courts should or could force school districts to do something about those in-school discrepancies. No court examining whether a school district should be released from a decree had ever ruled that they should.

Teddy called his first and only witness, John Whiting, a former principal at Shawnee High School. Whiting was a large, imposing man with a neatly combed Afro.[7] He had graduated from Central in 1954, the year of the *Brown* decision, when hopes for desegregation were high. Two decades later, on the morning of the first day of busing in 1975, he found a black cat hanging from Shawnee's flagpole, and a card on his desk that read, "The KKK is watching you." In the afternoon, he helped sobbing black students returning from Fairdale High School climb out of buses with shattered windows.

Afterward, as he watched black schools shuttered and black administrators demoted, he began calling the merger between the county and city "a takeover." Yet throughout the 1980s, he had worked hard to make desegregation work. He believed that getting resources into inner-city schools depended largely on putting white children in them: "Green follows white," he liked to say. But, like many of the CEASE activists, he was deeply disappointed in how desegregation had been carried out.

Whiting's nuanced views did not make him ideal as the plaintiff's sole witness. Teddy's main task was to convince the judge that racial balance had been maintained at every district school over two decades, and so therefore the vestiges of segregation were gone. But when Teddy asked Whiting to affirm that no Louisville schools had an African American majority (ignoring the point he had made in the last hearing that the alternative schools, Buechel and Liberty, both did), Whiting veered from the script.

"I would like to expand the definition of desegregation," Whiting said. Outcomes mattered, too, he argued, and outcomes certainly reflected that racial inequality still existed. Later, asked whether the schools maintained "any type of dual or separate system for blacks and whites," Whiting suggested that the small number of blacks in the Advance Program and the large number in special education raised "some questions." He added, "I think we could debate whether it's institutionalized or whether it's blatant."

Soon after, Teddy let him sit down and once again rested his case before lunch on the first day of the trial. His questioning had lasted about fifteen minutes.

During the cross-examinations, Whiting delved further into his belief that tracking and achievement gaps were indeed markers of the city's century of school segregation. Afterward, one by one, the lawyers at the other tables stood up to ask Heyburn to dismiss Teddy's case. It was too monumental of an issue to move forward on such paltry evidence, they argued. "We do not think the plaintiffs have made their case, Your Honor," Porter said. "They have not carried their burden at all."

Judge Heyburn, however, believed it was too important an issue not to hear everything that each side had to say. The following day, the Harvard professor, Gary Orfield, appeared again, as the first witness for the defendants. His testimony repeated much of what he had told the court the previous spring: that minorities reaped benefits from desegregated schools, and that school systems that ended desegregation decrees saw their schools quickly resegregate and minority test scores drop. When it was Teddy's turn, he once again jabbed at the professor, trying to get him to admit that adding more blacks to Central would make little impact on the rest of the schools. Then he changed tactics.

"Let me ask you point blank," Teddy said. "What approach can we take in Jefferson County, Kentucky, to make both sides happy?"

"Well," Orfield replied. "Making everybody happy completely is usually . . ."

"Impossible?"

"You don't have a lawsuit if there's an easy answer to that," Orfield said. "If this goes to the extent of eliminating the desegregation plan, everybody is going to be unhappy in the long run and your clients are going to lose very badly."

That fall, at Heyburn's urging, the two sides had in fact tried to hash out a compromise that would allow Central to pull more students from its neighborhood while maintaining diversity.[8] CEASE offered to drop the suit if the school district allowed 150 additional black students to enroll at Central and created law and medicine magnets elsewhere to accommodate additional applicants. They also asked that 200 more black students be admitted at the district's best-performing schools, including Ballard and Manual. The school board refused the proposal. CEASE reduced its request to 75 additional black students at Central.[9] The school board again refused, arguing that letting one school go out of balance would open the door to requests from every school in the district. The judge had hoped that over several days of hearings, the opponents might be convinced to sit down to talk again. But, as the hearings went on, that looked increasingly unlikely.

Pat Todd, a spry blonde who favored cowboy boots and long skirts, ran the school district's student assignment program. She had grown up in a conservative family in Oklahoma, but had moved to Louisville in the 1970s to teach at an all-black school in the inner city.[10] From there, she had ascended the ranks of administration and become deeply involved with the monitoring committee, taking charge of the district's desegregation plan in 1996. She usually had the cheery demeanor of a kindergarten teacher, but with Teddy, her warmth faded.

Throughout the hearings, he had attacked the school district over statistics that showed black students were more represented in South End schools like Fairdale, where poverty among whites was high and outcomes were low. At Manual, Male, and Ballard, where blacks were only a fifth of the population or smaller, the college-bound rates were more than 80 percent. And at Central, 86 percent of students went on to college.

"Are there certain high schools in Jefferson County where African American kids have a better chance to go to a four-year college than other high schools?" Gordon asked.

"No, I do not accept your premise," Todd replied.

"You don't?" Teddy shot back. "Haven't we eliminated 65 percent chance of having an equal opportunity to go to college because you make the choice rather than these parents?"

"No, sir," Todd replied calmly.

Leet jumped up. "Your honor, I object to that, whatever it is," he said.

"She can answer," the judge replied.

"And I said no, sir," Todd repeated.

Teddy sat down.

To the lawyers and witnesses in the room, it seemed that Gordon was twisting himself into a knot as he tried to argue simultaneously that black students were being discriminated against by the school system but that the vestiges of racial segregation were gone. The lawyers from the two third-party groups, QUEST and the Kentucky Alliance, took advantage of the awkward position CEASE was in as they tried to convince the judge that racial inequality was still pervasive throughout the district and that the desegregation system should stay intact. Steve Porter sent subpoenas to the members of CEASE, and on February 18, the fourth day of the trial, he called Deborah Stallworth, Fran Thomas, Robert Douglas, and Carman Weathers to the stand. Gordon complained that they were "harassment witnesses," but the judge ignored him.

Stallworth, a middle-aged woman with soft features, was first up. Porter asked if there were other problems besides the quotas at Central for African American children in the school system.

"There's a lot of problems in the treatment of African American students in the Jefferson County Public School system," she replied. "The suspension rates are there, the high drop-out rates. The achievement gap that you have been talking quite a bit about here."

But she didn't have a problem with Central becoming 100 percent black?

"What I send my child to school for . . . is to get an education. I do not send him to be socialized."

Fran Thomas was called next. Her hair was white and short-cropped, but with her smooth skin and bright eyes she looked much younger than her seventy-two years.

"Would it bother you if Central High School were a hundred percent black?" Porter asked her.

"Mr. Porter, I have no qualms about being black, being with blacks, associating with blacks," she replied. "I have no qualms."

"Would it be good for the black community?" he asked.

"I think it would present a positive force in the African American community," she replied.

He asked her about her perceptions of the top-performing high schools in the county, Male, Ballard, and Manual, which had the fewest numbers of African Americans.

They are "elitist," she said. "You have to already be where you are in order to get there." Fairdale, in contrast, the high school in the South End where some of the worst violence had occurred during the days of busing, was still "racially-motivated against African Americans," she said.

"There's a history there, isn't there?"

"There is a history there," she replied.

"Why can't you forget?"

"I think I could forget if somehow or another that the Jefferson County public school system could erase race from their minds and take on the dream of Martin Luther King that one day we will be accepted for the contents of our minds and not by the color of our skin."

Did she believe racism still existed?

"Yes I do," Fran said. She stood up, and returned to her seat in the audience.

Carman stood up next. He still looked the part of a coach, with his rounded-out linebacker physique and bushy mustache.

When Porter asked why he didn't mind if Central became an all-black school, he was blunt. "One of the stresses that impacts on the cognitive ability of black children is racism. More black kids in a school, less racism. You don't have to be a brain surgeon to figure that one out," he said.

"You think white children are already taken care of—"

"Always," Carman said.

"—because the system is white-controlled, white dominated?"

"Always in this country," he said.

"And white racism pretty much controls it?"

"Always in this country," he said.

"In the Jefferson County public school system?"

"I think white racism is a predominant factor anywhere you see white people," Carman replied.

Teddy stood up to try to salvage the day: "As far as you are aware, is the system unitary under the rulings of the court?"

"If by unitary, you mean Jefferson county has gotten rid of all its policies that lend themselves to a dual system, yes," Carman replied.

"Do you see any vestiges of by-law segregated schools?"

"No."

Chapter 22

Judge Heyburn was not interested in Carman's, Fran's, or Deborah Stall-worth's testimony. After they stepped down, he told the lawyers he didn't want to hear people's opinions about racism, or about the school system's failures to eliminate the remnants of segregation. He wanted to see evidence.

Steve Porter and Aubrey Williams, representing the two groups who wanted to push desegregation even farther, tried to provide it for him. They brought data showing that more than half of the high school classrooms did not meet the racial guidelines. In hundreds of classrooms in the Jefferson County schools, only one or two black students were enrolled. In dozens, there were none.

At the same time, not only were black children less represented in the district's gifted and talented program, they were much less likely to be recommended to take the entrance test. And those who did take the test were much less likely to be recommended to join the program than white children, even if they scored in the top percentile. In fact, more than two-thirds of black middle and high school students who did well on the Advance Program tests were refused entrance to the program by the teachers and counselors who made the final determinations, compared to one-third of white kids. Wasn't this a stigma of inferiority? Telling black children as a group that they belonged in the lower academic classes, even when they tested high enough to qualify for the higher ones?

"Your honor, this is not just a little program. This is not an advanced placement course that kids get to choose and not choose," Steve Porter said. "This is not discipline and a kid acts up and it doesn't matter whether he's black or white, the teacher is going to do something about it. This is every class in the system. . . . It's bad."

The lawyers also hammered on the differences in test scores and grades that still persisted twenty-five years after the advent of busing, showing that the implicit promise of *Brown*—that black children would be brought onto equal footing with whites—had not yet been kept. "The court's goal [in *Brown*] was to repair the damage to the hearts and minds of the children," Orfield had said during his testimony. "That can't be done by letting the kids in the front door and then treating them unfairly inside the building."

Ultimately, however, the judge was not convinced that the "numbers spoke for themselves." The judge's roots were conservative, and he was trying to keep his opinion as limited as possible. He didn't want to make new law, or set a new precedent. The Supreme Court's only explicit order in 1954 was that the segregation between schools be dismantled. *Brown* might have inspired hope that children would be integrated inside classrooms and that their academic outcomes would be equalized, but it had never made those steps a legal requirement. Judge Heyburn was focused on the simpler question of whether any schools in Jefferson County were still racially identifiable: Had the school system complied with the letter of the law and ensured that no school went out of bounds from the racial limits? Was racial intimidation still a factor that kept black people from making free choices in where they sent their children to school?

The lawyers tried to get him to see these questions from a different angle. The superintendent, Daeschner, argued that the very problem that had prompted the lawsuit in the first place was evidence that the district had been unsuccessful in rooting out racially identifiable schools: "If we were doing the job that we should be doing and trying to do, we would be able to recruit, if you will, a proportional number of whites to blacks" at Central High School, he argued. The school might have a majority of white students, but both blacks and whites in Louisville still identified it as a black school, and for white students, that meant inferior.

When Harold Fenderson, the Central principal, was called to take the stand, he admitted the same thing. Why didn't white kids want to attend?

"It's geography. It's history. It's the perception of Central being an all-black school, which it's not," the principal said. "We've worked desperately to change, modify attitudes, paradigms, but we still have work to do."

The judge wasn't convinced. "I think there's a difference between our society now and our society then. I think we can draw somewhat different conclusions for why the numbers are the way they are," he said at one point in the hearings. For Heyburn, the case was also about "who should have the right to decide" how children in Louisville were educated, a judge or a school board. In other cases around the country, federal judges were giving back control to school boards. Despite the brevity and incoherence of Teddy Gordon's case, and even though the school board didn't want the court's control to end, as the judge closed the eight days of hearings it seemed Teddy and CEASE would prevail.

Around lunchtime on June 20, 2000, Fran Thomas, Robert Douglas, and several other members of CEASE gathered in the living room of Carman Weathers's ranch house on a corner lot in the West End to wait. That morning, Heyburn had handed down another long opinion, and Deborah Stallworth was on her way from the courthouse with copies. When she arrived, she passed them around the room, and everyone settled in quietly to read. Outside, a reporter was waiting for their reaction. After an hour, Carman emerged, smiling, and invited the reporter inside. "The decision was an affirmation of my DNA," he announced. "This says black people are not inherently inferior."[1]

In the opinion, Judge Heyburn began by noting that the case brought before him was "truly exceptional."[2] Only once before had individual citizens tried to remove a desegregation decree against the will of a school board, and never had such a case been brought by African Americans, for "whose supposed benefit such decrees were entered."

The legal problem, "so closely interwoven with social and moral threads, seems to defy an absolute solution," the judge continued. Yet he must make a decision. Since 1975, he wrote, the Louisville schools had "succeeded admirably in meeting the original objectives of the 1975 desegregation decree." The school district had been recognized as one of the most successfully integrated schools in the nation, and black achievement had risen substantially since the beginning of the busing program, if not to the level of whites. The arguments of the third-party plaintiffs about internal segregation and unequal outcomes were "thought-provoking" but constitutionally insignificant, the judge wrote, because they couldn't prove that those differences were related to the school board's former acts of de jure segregation. The Advance Program had not even existed in the city in 1975, he noted. It had been created just after.

Heyburn ruled that the court order set down in 1975 requiring Louisville to desegregate its schools should be lifted. The Jefferson County School system was now officially a unitary school district. He also ordered that black students who had been prevented from attending Central because of their race be admitted. "Central has two admissions tracks: one exclusively for blacks, and another for everyone else," Heyburn wrote, and that was a violation of the equal protection clause. Ironically, the special courses provided by magnet programs, devised as a way to promote desegregation through school choice, had become the potential downfall of the district's busing plan: In his decision, the judge hinted strongly that it might be advisable to lift quotas at other magnet schools, too.

Yet the judge left the rest of the desegregation plan intact. Now that the court decree was lifted, he used "strict scrutiny," the concept used by judges examining scenarios in which constitutional rights were abridged, to examine whether it was justifiable for the district to use race in assigning students. He found that it was. Diversity in schools could be a "compelling interest" under the strict scrutiny standard, he wrote. The judge's copy of Gary Orfield's book *Dismantling Desegregation*, about the all-black schools and falling test scores in other districts that had returned to neighborhood schools, had emerged from the trial dog-eared and covered in notes. Desegregation's history and purposes would be "ill-served if courts make the concept of local control a one-way street to neighborhood schools," Heyburn concluded.

Frank Mellen, the school district lawyer, later hypothesized that the judge had tried to save Central from closure, realizing what it meant to the black community, while trying to make as little impact on the rest of the system as possible.

The following day, CEASE held a formal press conference outside of Central High School.[3] Its members emphasized that their intent had never been to "resegregate" the system. But they were also unapologetic about their victory. Fran Thomas took the microphone. "This is the first time in history that black people have sued to get away from white people," Fran said. "We want to be in control of our own destiny." Gwendolyn Hopson stepped up next, booming out in her church-choir voice: "The days of quotas must end. I feel like this is a new era."[4]

But for the Hopson family, things remained the same. Dionne didn't end up attending Central. She was entering her senior year at Pleasure Ridge Park in the working-class South End and it was too late for her to join the law magnet even if she had attended Central. It had been four years since she had received her letter of rejection from Central; back then, she had believed that once they entered the court case, justice would be swift. Instead, the case had dragged on for years. Her hopes for her high school education and eventual career as a lawyer were deflated. At Pleasure Ridge Park, she loved reading Shakespeare and running track, but these were not enough to hold her there. She was still mourning her father's death, and the As and Bs she earned in middle school had dropped to Ds. She would try to hold on for another year at Pleasure Ridge Park, and then look for a job.

For the other students in the Louisville schools, it was still unclear what the fallout would be. The school board hoped it would be minimal. The board members voted and decided not to appeal Heyburn's decision.[5] In the higher courts, it was more likely the plan could be completely over-turned. In the meantime, the district began adjusting its magnet school admissions policies at four schools, including Central, to eliminate race as the deciding factor in admission. They hoped that the victory had been as satisfactory to Teddy Gordon as it had been for his clients.

Central's predicament under the racial quotas had received the most at-tention, but white students were turned away from their top-choice schools much more frequently than blacks. White families were the ones who called the district most often to complain, the school district representatives had explained during the hearings. Superintendent Daeschner predicted that if the plaintiffs won, "we will be sitting back in this courtroom I hope with this judge, but it may be another judge, with white plaintiffs asking the very question from the other side." A few beats later, Gordon had interjected: "Did you just state under oath that whites are turned away from Male be-cause of their race?"

VI

To the Supreme Court

Chapter 23

The woman sitting across the desk from Teddy Gordon was pretty—beautiful, even, he thought. Her long red-gold hair swished past her shoulders. She was tall and had a light spray of freckles across her cheeks. She seemed very smart, if a little shy.

The Central High School victory made Teddy well known around Louisville. In the three years since the judge's ruling, he had become the first stop for angry parents wanting to take on the school district with various complaints. He was in the midst of a case at that very moment to challenge the school district's entire desegregation plan, in fact. But he still had to pay his bills. Divorces, personal injury cases, and even traffic tickets were his bread and butter. Crystal Meredith had come to see him about a custody dispute with the father of her five-year-old son. Teddy's ears perked up when she said the heart of the conflict was the elementary school where the boy had been assigned.

Crystal had moved to Louisville from a more rural neighboring county in the summer of 2002, as her son was about to start kindergarten, so that he could enroll in the Jefferson County Schools.[1] Her moving day was in August, and the school district wouldn't let her register until she was settled into her new home. It was a small but neatly appointed shotgun house on a quiet street near the border of the Highlands, a middle-class East End neighborhood, and Smoketown, a black neighborhood bordering downtown. As a result of their late registration, her son had been among the last in line to choose a school. Crystal had hoped he could attend Bloom Elementary, two miles from their house. Instead, he was assigned to Whitney Young Elementary on Muhammad Ali Boulevard in the far West End, about fifteen minutes away.

He was one of only a couple of white children in his kindergarten class; most of his classmates were black or Hispanic, but that wasn't the issue. Crystal didn't want him taking the school bus—the stop was on a busy street—but it was also inconvenient to pick him up and drop him off. She wrote to the school district asking for a transfer to the school near their home, Bloom. She was rejected.

After she told the story to Teddy, he asked if she still had the letter from the school board. She did. The letter said that her request had been turned down because of the district's racial guidelines. Whitney Young Elementary needed a certain number of white students to maintain its racial guidelines, and losing Crystal's son would have tipped the balance. Under the district rules, kindergartners were exempt from the racial guidelines, but in this case, someone made a mistake. They should have checked the box saying that space was the reason for the rejection of the transfer request, not race. The mistake opened up an opportunity for Teddy, however. He was now less interested in the custody issue. He wanted to know if Crystal would join his lawsuit against the school board's desegregation plan as a plaintiff.

In October 2002, Teddy had filed a new complaint in federal court on behalf of David McFarland, a father of three boys who lived in Fern Creek, on the outer edge of the county.[2] McFarland was tall, with buzzed hair, wide shoulders, and the straight-backed bearing of a Marine, but he had a gentle, low-key personality.[3] He sold air-conditioning and heating systems for a living, and had graduated from Southern High School in 1977, just after riots had torn apart the South End in the aftermath of busing.

As a teenager, McFarland was embarrassed by the protests, and made friends with the black students who joined the high school basketball team. He didn't give the issues of desegregation or education in general much thought beyond feeling some sympathy for the players who had to wait for rides downtown after practice. Once his sons were born, however, he did look back with some nostalgia on the schools he had attended as a child, where discipline, respect, and the basics were emphasized.

In the 1970s, white activists like Joyce Spond had channeled their frustration with busing into an effort to preserve those values, and the traditional schools had been born. By the 1990s, a network of traditional elementary schools that fed into traditional middle schools and then to the district's two traditional high schools, Male and Butler, was firmly established. Students complied with a dress code, and teachers were treated as the voice of authority. The Advance Program and honors tracks that many East End parents fixated on getting their children into were eschewed. Everyone at a traditional school was expected to learn the same thing, at the same pace. Discipline and patriotism were prized. The schools were wildly popular among the white middle- and working-class parents of Louisville's central and southeastern suburbs. For whites, the waiting lists to get in, which started as early as kindergarten, were long. For blacks, however, getting in usually wasn't a problem.

After the Central High School case, the school system had lifted the racial limits on four of the city's magnet schools. But the district left the caps on the traditional schools. The traditional schools, by definition, were meant to be just plain schools.

David believed the traditional program was perfect for shaping his boys into respectful, well-behaved young men, but when he applied, one of his sons was rejected. David was not a confrontational person, but he was frustrated. It didn't make sense to him that siblings would be divided into different schools. He wrote a letter to Pat Todd, the school assignment director. He received a form letter in return. He wrote another, and made some calls, but was rebuffed again. Next, he sat down at the computer. The Central High School case popped up after a quick Internet search, along with Teddy Gordon's name. Not long after, he trekked down to Teddy's downtown office building. In a matter of weeks they had filed a complaint in federal court.

Teddy also wanted a client who would represent the students in the regular schools in the rest of the district, ideally an African American plaintiff; all of the other parents were white, and he still saw his mission as representing the interests of black students. But he didn't have much time, and he didn't expect Crystal Meredith to be the center of the case anyway. Neither did she. On May 2, 2003, Teddy added her to the list of parents in his complaint.[4]

Two weeks later, a black woman with twin sons denied placement in their neighborhood elementary school showed up at his office, angry and ready to go to court. But by then it was too late. The judge denied Teddy's request to add her, leaving Crystal as his sole client representing the children of the regular schools.

The school district's lawyers petitioned for Judge Heyburn to handle the case, and the trial was set for December 2003, with Heyburn once again presiding.[5] Many of the same characters were scheduled to testify: Superintendent Daeschner and Pat Todd would speak for the school system; the Harvard professor would return to speak about the benefits of desegregation. This time, Teddy offered no expert witnesses—he had asked Ward Connerly, an anti–affirmative action activist from California to testify, but Connerly couldn't make it.

Still, Teddy was energized. The case was even bigger than the Central High School case that had come before. The black plaintiffs and activists, Carman Weathers, Fran Thomas, Dionne Hopson, and Ja'Mekia Stoner, and the anger and disillusionment that fed their cause, were quickly fading from the public memory as attention turned to the group of white families taking on Louisville's desegregation system.

Teddy took his courtroom theatrics to a new height, dropping his notebook several times and bending to tie his shoe in order to throw off the soft-spoken Harvard professor, Gary Orfield. Later, he would describe these moments as some of his proudest during the trial.

The hearings lasted five days, and most of the time was spent arguing over whether the traditional schools offered a special benefit to students or not. David McFarland took the stand for about twenty minutes to tell his story. By then, all of his sons had been admitted to traditional programs, but he had decided to continue with the case on principle. Crystal spoke for less than five minutes. No one mentioned the clerical error at the center of her case: that her son had really been denied because there was a lack of space, not because he was white.

The following summer, on June 29, 2004, Judge Heyburn issued his decision. This time, the school district won. The racial guidelines could remain intact.

Heyburn cited a Supreme Court ruling of a year earlier to justify his decision. On June 23, 2003, the Rehnquist court had thrown out the University of Michigan's affirmative action plan for its undergraduate college. Under the system, underrepresented minorities who applied were given a certain number of points that tipped the scale in favor of their admittance. In *Gratz v. Bollinger*, the Court ruled 6 to 3 that the system wasn't "narrowly tailored."[6] In other words, it was focused too heavily on race for its own sake.

But in a related case also brought against the University of Michigan, *Grutter v. Bollinger*, Justice Sandra Day O'Connor joined the liberal side of the Court.[7] The majority found that the university's law school could keep race as one of its admissions factors, because it was part of a system that was much more fluid than the one in the undergraduate school. Admissions officials kept race in mind as they looked at a candidate's application and tried to create a "critical mass" of minorities in each entering class of law students, but it wasn't so blatant as awarding points for being black or Hispanic. Diversity was also a useful part of a law school education, the justices argued. It "promotes learning outcomes and better prepares students for an increasingly diverse workforce, for society, and for the legal profession."

Likewise, Heyburn argued that the Louisville school district had good reasons for maintaining integrated schools. In Louisville, the school board had a reasonable belief that "school integration benefits the system as a whole by creating a system of roughly equal components, not one urban system and another suburban system, not one rich and another poor, not one Black and another White," the judge wrote. Once again, Heyburn also brought up the irony of a court forcing a school district to stop doing what it had been ordered to do only a quarter century earlier.

And yet, by 2004, Louisville was largely alone in its pursuit of integrated schools.[8] Under the law, the judge argued that the end of desegregation court decrees shouldn't force school districts to abandon integration, but on the ground, that's exactly what most were doing. In many places, middle-class flight to suburban districts outside of the city core had made trying to desegregate schools extremely difficult. Desegregation was both out of reach and out of favor in most places, yet concerns about minority achievement had reached a fever pitch. Black and Hispanic children were more isolated than ever in poor, failing schools, and local governments were struggling to come up with a response.[9] Many districts and states followed the will of the majority, and the majority preferred choice.

States across the country embraced charter schools. Their numbers increased from zero in the early nineties to more than three thousand by 2003.[10] Although many opened in white, suburban neighborhoods, supporters mainly saw the schools as a way to improve education in failing inner-city districts where schools were losing the battle against poverty.

At the same time, the Bill & Melinda Gates Foundation began pouring millions of dollars into a new "small schools" movement, which was based on research showing that vulnerable students could thrive in smaller learning environments.[11] The small schools idea was also built on choice: Often, the schools were built around themes, much like magnet schools, which were supposed to draw in students. But unlike magnets, integration wasn't the goal.

In 2000, George W. Bush was elected president, and in January 2002, he signed the No Child Left Behind Act (NCLB) into law.[12] The purpose of the law was to force states, school districts, and schools to pay attention to the performance of minority students. It bore a striking resemblance to Kentucky's own education reform law of the 1990s, and many suggested KERA had been a model for NCLB, along with similar reforms in Texas. Schools that received federal dollars for low-income students were to separate out and report the performance of minorities on state tests. Schools that didn't improve at a set rate were to be punished, potentially with closure. Central to the law was the concept of school choice. If schools stayed stagnant or didn't improve fast enough, students could request a transfer to a "successful" school. The competition was supposed to spur schools to get better.

Teddy Gordon had used the new No Child Left Behind law to attack the school district throughout the second trial. The first round of school scores had been released before the hearings, and only half of the Jefferson County schools were meeting their test score goals—meaning, in most cases, that black students weren't keeping up as well as they were expected to. Teddy used the numbers as a weapon to undercut the argument that desegregation helped minorities do better in school.

Yet, during the following year, the National Assessment of Educational Progress found a smaller achievement gap between white and black students in Kentucky—who were largely concentrated in Louisville—than in nearly every other state in the country.[13] On eighth grade math and reading tests, Kentucky had the second-smallest gap between whites and blacks in the nation, after Washington State.

It was possible that Kentucky's relatively small gap was due to the state's high number of poor, white students. But Kentucky's performance on reading tests for all students was about average. Black students in Kentucky posted smaller gains on reading tests in 2005 than the nation as a whole, but the state's black students started out ahead. And the graduation rate among African American students was 2 percentage points higher in Kentucky than the rest of the country.

Some of Kentucky's relative success was possibly linked to the statewide education reforms introduced in 1991, but its relatively narrow achievement gap also fit with the evidence the school district had presented at the trial, that integration was linked to smaller disparities in achievement. In Heyburn's decision, the judge noted that Gordon had not presented any evidence to the contrary.

Teddy Gordon was not dissuaded by his district court defeat in the *McFarland* case. That summer he ran for a position on the Jefferson County school board, on an anti-busing platform, telling the newspaper that it was time he "put his money where his mouth was."[14] He lost badly. But he was more determined than ever to press his new cause. He was reading about charter schools in a book called *No Excuses*, by Abigail and Stephan Thernstrom, about all-black schools in the inner city that were successful despite the odds. He had paid attention to the widening impact of the new No Child Left Behind law. He followed the successes of the movement to end affirmative action in California and watched it spread to other states. He felt the wind at his back.

Chapter 24

Central was a different place by the fall of 2002, when Teddy filed his second case. Following Judge Heyburn's decision to lift the racial guidelines at Central High School, the percentage of black students was climbing to 80 percent.[1] The number continued to creep upward, along with enrollment.[2]

Riccardo X should have been happy. Finally, he was working at a school where his black history classes were not only appreciated, there was a large pool of African American students eager to sign up. On the walls of the Black Cultural Center in his second-floor classroom, he taped up news clippings about CEASE's battle with the school board alongside posters about African history and famous black leaders. He wanted to make sure his students remembered that this black-majority school did not become that way without a struggle. But instead of rejoicing as a majority-black freshman class began its first year at Central, Riccardo had spent the fall leading his students in protests on the circular driveway in front of the school.

Less than two years after the victory in the *Hampton* case, the school district had fired Harold Fenderson, Central's principal.[3] The district cited a litany of problems, some minor, some less so, including a school employee who had been cashing bad checks from the school's accounts and more than a dozen students who had graduated without the minimum number of credits.[4] Some of those students had taken Riccardo X's black history class, which Fenderson had allowed to count for a geography requirement.

Riccardo believed the firing was payback for Fenderson's poorly hidden empathy for CEASE's cause during the Hampton trial. Asked if a school with a large African American population would be a problem, he had replied that pre-*Brown* "there were many successful African Americans who attended all African-American schools."[5] Looking back, Riccardo thought those comments helped seal his fate.

In the black community, Fenderson's firing was a uniting force. CEASE members joined the student demonstrations outside the school, and then held a rally at the church where Lyman Johnson had once stood in the pulpit and railed about dangers of resegregating the schools.[6] Fenderson, who was also an evangelical preacher, had been widely regarded as a strong leader who was lifting up the expectations and achievement of young African Americans, in the mold of predecessors like Lyman and Maude Brown Porter.[7] He had set up partnerships with the University of Kentucky, law firms, and businesses like SuperAmerica, the gas and convenience store chain. During his tenure, Central finally got its own football stadium. It seemed white school administrators were ignoring once again what the black community wanted for its schools. In the wake of the firing, people worried that the district might eventually try to close down Central after all.

Standing in the pulpit where Lyman had once stood, Riccardo X announced to the crowd at West Chestnut Street Baptist Church that the "war was on" to save Fenderson and Central, "the pride of the black community."[8] But the war did not last long.

Fenderson hired Teddy Gordon to defend him. They submitted an appeal of more than one hundred pages to the school district, disputing the accusations point by point.[9] Fenderson also sued the district, arguing that his due process rights had been violated. In the end, however, Fenderson settled and soon after left the district for a job at the University of Kentucky. Daniel Withers, an African American assistant principal, was appointed to take his place.

By the summer of 2004, the controversy had faded away. Central was a majority-black school with a black principal, yet it was clear to Riccardo that the black community had not really won control of the school. They were just as powerless over what happened there as they had ever been. Except for a handful of teachers who shared his politics and missed Fenderson, too, X felt alone. As Teddy Gordon prepared to appeal his case with the white parents, Riccardo X watched from a distance. He regarded Teddy's new mission to dismantle the school district's student assignment plan as he had the Vietnam War. As far as he was concerned, he didn't have a dog in this fight.

The three parents who had fought the admission system for the traditional schools, including David McFarland, dropped out of the case after Judge Heyburn's decision. To go forward, Teddy would have to rely only on Crystal Meredith—if he could convince her to appeal. But by the summer of 2004, Crystal's son was headed to second grade at Bloom, the school in her neighborhood, after she had made another request for a transfer. Teddy hoped she would be willing to fight the system anyway, but she was nowhere to be found. He called her repeatedly, but she didn't pick up. He hired a private investigator, and after weeks of searching, he finally found her.

Meredith was fiercely protective of her son, and the media attention would likely be intense if they kept going. But Teddy had never been one to quit. The Supreme Court was now in sight. He convinced her, reminding her that she had promised to stick with it when he first took on her case three years earlier. In June 2005, they appealed to the Sixth Circuit Court of Appeals. In July, a panel of judges handed down a brief decision affirming Judge Heyburn's ruling. Shortly after, Teddy got to work on his appeal to the Supreme Court.

To the supporters of the desegregation plan, Teddy's case seemed like a long shot. In his request for the Sixth Circuit hearing, Gordon had submitted a short brief full of muddled arguments. In his conclusion, he argued that American society had finally become color-blind, pointing to the "rainbow composition" of the workplace, "emphasized by the color-blind appearance of our local television networks."[10]

His appeal to the Supreme Court, which he filed in January, was not much better. Michael Dorf, a Columbia law professor who had clerked for Supreme Court Justice Anthony Kennedy, called the brief "extraordinarily weak."[11] He told the *Courier-Journal* that Gordon was "out of his league," saying his writing was "something you'd expect from a prisoner" who was representing himself. In addition, despite the tilt of the country away from desegregation, the Supreme Court's University of Michigan decisions seemed to bode well for Louisville. Sandra Day O'Connor, the moderate swing vote on the Court, was tolerant of schools that used race as a factor in admission. The decision didn't apply to elementary and secondary schools, and the circuit courts had clashed on the issue, but the Supreme Court had already turned down more than a dozen similar cases. It seemed highly likely the Jefferson County case would be batted down, too.

In 2005, the same summer the Sixth Circuit denied his appeal, Gordon got lucky. O'Connor announced she was stepping down.[12] President Bush nominated John Roberts, a reserved fifty year old with a firmly conservative track record, to take her place. In September, Chief Justice William Rehnquist died in office after a battle with cancer, leaving another vacancy. The Bush administration elevated Roberts to the chief justice position and named Samuel Alito, a former Reagan Justice Department lawyer, to take O'Connor's place. In just a few months, the Court swung sharply to the right, leaving Justice David Kennedy, previously counted among the conservatives, as the Court's swing vote. The changes came just before Teddy filed his appeal.

Yet victory for Teddy wasn't a sure thing. In the University of Michigan Law School case, Kennedy disagreed with O'Connor and signed onto the conservative wing's minority dissent written by Chief Justice Rehnquist, which argued that the school's use of race was unconstitutional. But Kennedy also took the trouble to write his own separate opinion. In it, he distanced himself from the conservative judges, arguing that race might play a role as a "modest factor among many others." He was frustrated that the liberal wing of the Court refused to scrutinize the law school's use of what he saw as a racial quota, however. A racial quota, Kennedy wrote, "can be the most divisive of all policies, containing within it the potential to destroy confidence in the Constitution and in the idea of equality."

At the time of the university cases, Kennedy's separate opinion was largely irrelevant. But three years later, he was the tiebreaker. Gordon's prose may have been clumsy, but his appeal hit the same points about racial quotas that Kennedy had argued in his Michigan dissent. In the summer of 2006, Gordon's appeal was granted. The oral argument was set for December.

Another desegregation case reached the Court at the same time. The second lawsuit was based in Seattle, where parents were also disputing racial caps in the city's schools. Seattle had never been under court order to desegregate. The city had voluntarily implemented a plan to boost racial diversity in the schools after the NAACP sued in the early 1960s.[13] Seattle's system was more limited in scope than Louisville's, and the city had never implemented forced busing. Instead the district used race as a tiebreaker at high schools with waiting lists, giving preference to minority students if the majority of students at the school was white. In 2000, a group of white parents whose children were unable to get into the school of their choice sued the Seattle school district.

The Seattle plaintiffs, organized by a group called Parents Involved in Community Schools, were visibly enthusiastic, in contrast to Teddy's one rather reluctant plaintiff.[14] A large law firm, Davis Wright Tremaine, with international offices and more than five hundred attorneys, took on their case pro bono.[15] After the case was appealed, the Seattle district stopped enforcing the plan to wait for a final judgment from the Supreme Court.[16]

Once the Supreme Court agreed to hear his case, Teddy was bombarded with offers of help. A right-leaning think tank in California, the Pacific Legal Foundation, flew him out to practice in a moot court. His new conservative allies suggested replacing him with a more experienced lawyer with conservative credentials. But Teddy, still a staunch Democrat, was determined to argue the case himself.

In an amicus brief submitted to the Supreme Court on behalf of the Louisville and Seattle school districts, 553 social scientists argued that racial diversity was better for students of all races when it came to instilling democratic values and improving academic performance—slightly more than the number of researchers who signed a similar brief in support of the 1954 *Brown* case.[17] They cited a huge body of evidence in favor of desegregation compiled since the famous "doll studies," which the NAACP had used in *Brown* to show how segregation damaged the self-esteem of black children. The research showed that racial diversity improved critical thinking skills, increased the academic performance and graduation rates of African American and Hispanic students, and improved their chances for success later in life. Research by Eric Hanushek, a Stanford professor whose views leaned to the right in education policy, found that decreasing the ratio of black students in a school was correlated to improved test scores for black students.[18] A survey of eleventh graders in Louisville suggested that racial diversity had a positive impact on aspirations and critical thinking for both blacks and whites.[19]

The Pacific Legal Foundation, which had helped coach Teddy over the summer and fall, argued in its own amicus brief—much longer than Teddy's own—that the social science research was disputed, and that it rested on "uncertain footing."[20]

In the fall, Teddy bought himself a new suit at J. C. Penney and packed his lucky red underwear. The first weekend of December, he drove to Washington, DC, with members of his family. Crystal did not accompany him. He believed she would be overwhelmed by the media attention and had suggested she stay home.

Early on the morning of December 4, people lined up outside the Supreme Court.[21] The temperature was below freezing, but people had spent the night in hopes of getting a seat. Some were there to protest. They worried that a ruling ending Louisville's and Seattle's desegregation plans would reverse the gains achieved since *Brown v. Board of Education*. Others were excited, hoping that an opinion in favor of color-blind government would help heal America's racial divide. As the spectators were seated, Teddy strode past them to the podium in the Court's chamber carrying a single sheet of paper.[22] On it was a typed outline of the constitutional concepts he wanted to cover. A list of court cases was jotted in pen in the margins. He quickly scrawled the names of the justices, in the order they were seated, on the back. The room felt small. Mellen stood just a few feet away, and the faces of the justices loomed above.

Teddy went first. He started off strong: "Crystal Meredith wanted to do what most moms and dads do all across this country. She wanted to put her son's hand in hers and walk around the corner and enroll her son in school," he said, his voice rising and falling in a steady rhythm.[23] But then he seemed to lose the thread of his argument. "But the enrollment, there was a barrier, and the pickaxe, that barrier was personified as a quota. It wasn't near any one of the percentages or tipping percentages that the quota system in Jefferson County public schools applied. But she was not allowed in."

Ruth Bader Ginsburg jumped in before he could go further. One of her first questions was why Crystal hadn't enrolled earlier. She had moved from Florida, Teddy said. It was unclear if he had forgotten that she had grown up in Louisville and merely moved across the county line, or whether he made it up on the spur of the moment to make the case sound better. From there, he got in few words as the liberal wing of the Court pounced on the irony of the case: Wasn't it an anomaly, Ginsburg asked, that "what's constitutionally required one day gets constitutionally prohibited the next day?" Teddy rebutted that desegregation "hasn't worked," and finally hit his stride as his argument came to a close.

"Educational outcome is the only key to unlock the chains of poverty," he said, reading from the page in front of him. "African Americans in Jefferson County, Kentucky, the largest percent go to the worst performing schools. The lowest percent go to the better performing schools. That can't be constitutional."

Frank Mellen faced an onslaught of questions from the right-leaning justices, Alito, Roberts, Scalia, and Kennedy. Thomas, as he usually did during oral arguments, kept quiet. Mellen's focus, however, was on winning over Justice Kennedy.

Earlier that morning during the arguments in the Seattle case, Kennedy had suggested that the limitations on choice bothered him. "The question is whether or not you can get into the school that you really prefer," he said. "And that in some cases depends solely on skin color. You know, it's like saying that everybody can have a meal but only people with separate skin can get the dessert."[24]

For both lawyers, the hour seemed to last only a few minutes. Before it ran out entirely, Teddy stood up again. He had reserved two minutes of his time, and now he had the last word. He used it to read the last paragraph typed on his piece of paper: "All I can say is that, may this day be the embryonic beginning of Dr. King's dream, as paraphrased, that all children are now judged by the content of their character and their education, not by the color of their skin."

Chapter 25

Teddy Gordon was going about his usual business, handling a traffic ticket for an old client, when the Supreme Court handed down its ruling in the Louisville and Seattle cases on June 28, 2007, the last day of the Court's session that year. Within a few hours, he was presiding over a press conference, flanked by Crystal Meredith and Deborah Stallworth.[1] They had won.

In the majority opinion, Chief Justice Roberts condemned the Seattle and Louisville desegregation plans as "extreme," suggesting that they were in fact vestiges of the discrimination they were intended to uproot.[2] "The way to stop discrimination on the basis of race is to stop discriminating on the basis of race," Roberts wrote. In a concurring opinion, Justice Thomas was also sharply critical, comparing Seattle and Louisville to the five segregationist school districts in the *Brown* case. As to the school districts' arguments that racial integration promoted academic achievement and long-term career outcomes, Thomas wrote, "If our history has taught us anything, it has taught us to beware of elites bearing racial theories."

Justice Kennedy agreed with the majority's decision, but only in part. He wrote his own concurring opinion, and because he was the swing vote, it was his opinion that mattered most. He did not approve of the Louisville and Seattle plans, but wrote that racial integration was still a compelling government goal. "That the school districts consider these plans to be necessary should remind us that our highest aspirations are yet unfulfilled," he wrote. "But the solutions mandated by these school districts must themselves be lawful. To make race matter now so that it might not matter later may entrench the very prejudices we seek to overcome." While Justice Harlan's call for color blindness in his *Plessy v. Ferguson* dissent was a noble aspiration, he wrote, in the "real world" it was not a "universal constitutional principle."

School districts that wanted to reduce the achievement gap could not ignore race, his argument suggested. But Kennedy believed Louisville's racial guidelines were too "broad and imprecise," basing this belief mainly on the unexplained clerical error that had prevented Meredith's son from attending his elementary school of choice.

Teddy was triumphant at the press conference. "All the schools are equal," he told reporters. "We will no longer accept that an African-American majority within a school is unacceptable."[3]

Crystal stood up and read a short statement in shaky voice. "The day my wonderful son was born, I promised I would do everything I could to do what's best for him," she said. "Going to the US Supreme Court is not really what I had in mind." But it was "exactly where I had to go to keep my promise," she added.[4] Afterward, Deborah Stallworth, the only member of CEASE who attended the press conference, gave her a hug.

The other members of CEASE didn't show up. They felt similarly to Riccardo X: the *Meredith* case wasn't their fight. By that time, Central appeared to have regained some of its former glory: once again, it functioned much like a prep school for the black community's most promising students. Its students tended to come from lower-income families, but the school selected them based on grades and recommendations, and even after the departure of its beloved principal, Harold Fenderson, Central's graduation rate had held steady.[5] Carman Weathers, Fran Thomas, Robert Douglas, and the other members of CEASE were pleased at their victory and saw CEASE's work as done.

After the Central High School case, Fran Thomas left her position as director of Anne Braden's group, the Kentucky Alliance against Racist and Political Repression. The case had highlighted their differences: Fran was fighting for black self-determination; Anne had fought on the side of the desegregationists. Fran couldn't bring herself to retire from activism, however. Instead, she joined the board of the NAACP, where she occasionally clashed with members over support of integration, but was otherwise satisfied that she was still in the thick of the fight against racism.

Anne Braden, who remained in the same West End house she had lived in fifty years earlier, died in 2006. Not long after, Fran and her husband moved from their West End home overlooking the Ohio River, where CEASE had first formed, to an immaculate new colonial-style house with a large porch and lawn. This time, the house was not deep in the suburbs, but on the same land that had once been stripped during urban renewal and turned into the housing projects where Riccardo X grew up. The government had come back to the neighborhood, this time to build attractive, single-family housing that would draw a mix of incomes back into the city. It seemed to work. Middle-income families moved into a pocket of the city once known as a haven for gangs, and a few white families even moved in, too. Fran picked a house on a quiet block named after her former teacher and adversary, Lyman T. Johnson.

Carman Weathers stopped writing letters to the *Courier-Journal*. The newspaper no longer printed his essays. After retiring from his job at Buechel, the majority-black school for students with discipline problems, he decided to start up his own school, inspired by the home- and church-based schools run by Southern blacks in the aftermath of Reconstruction, and later by the civil rights activists during the height of the desegregation fight. He called it the Freedom School. The first year, five students met for seven weeks during the summer on the deck in his backyard.

The idea was to combat the summer learning loss that was a key factor in the achievement gap: Poor children might be able to keep up with their middle-class counterparts during the school year, but they often fell far behind in the summertime, when wealthier children traveled with their families, went to camp, or participated in other educational activities.[6] Carman's students studied math, reading, and other basic subjects. He also tried to instill a sense of self-esteem and purpose. After four years, the group of students had grown from five to seventy, and he had recruited a dedicated group of volunteer teachers. The school had to move to a church basement to accommodate them all.

Meanwhile, Central's success began to teeter. In 2004, the school was placed on notice under the new rules of the No Child Left Behind law that it was falling behind in student achievement. In subsequent years, it underwent "restructuring," but performance in mathematics in particular still lagged. In 2010, only a quarter of students passed state math tests. Nearly two-thirds passed reading tests, but the percentage was dropping from year to year. The graduation rate dropped slightly, from nearly 94 percent to about 92 percent.[7]

Riccardo X was increasingly disappointed in the caliber of students who signed up for his black history courses. He was also disappointed in the school's administration and his fellow teachers. He stopped running the Liberation Bowl because he couldn't get funding. He holed himself up in his classroom, the Black Cultural Center, but was suspended twice for arguing with white teachers in the school. In February 2010, Black History Month, he played a song about reparations during the morning announcements, angering a white teacher who believed the song was divisive and offensive. In 2012, he announced he was quitting after thirty-five years in the school system and eighteen years as a history teacher at Central. As he put it, he was "leaving the plantation."

Despite its decline, Central's performance still outstripped some schools in the district. Many black students, usually the ones lacking the wherewithal to get into Central or the better schools in the East End, were still confined to even lower-achieving schools in the southern part of the city. As was the case with many highly regarded and beloved segregated high schools under Jim Crow, Central served only a small sector of the black community. The racial achievement divide still gaped wide. One unique example of a relatively successful black-majority school didn't necessarily solve the wider problems of how to reach Du Bois's dual goals for black America: integrating with and finding success in the larger society while keeping its sense of identity, pride, and community intact.

Louisville's school administrators and black leaders who had fought for desegregation were dismayed at the Supreme Court ruling. Writing for the liberal wing of the Court, Justice Stephen Breyer, a Clinton appointee, wrote that the *Meredith* decision undermined *Brown*'s promise of racially integrated schooling—a tool that had demonstrated effectiveness in narrowing the gap. Democratic candidates on the presidential campaign trail that summer, including Senator Barack Obama, lambasted the ruling.[8] But despite their dismay at Gordon's partial victory, district officials in Louisville still saw a door left open in Kennedy's opinion. He had argued that districts could still be "race conscious," using factors that correlated with race, like income, geography, and parental education to assign students,

as long as they didn't use race as the deciding factor in assigning a child
to school.

As Teddy crowed, the school district began adjusting its plan to incorporate these new criteria.[9] School officials in Louisville were not about to
throw out desegregation entirely if they didn't have to. Poll numbers favored diversity, and the school board still believed that desegregation raised
test scores, helped students adjust to a diverse world, and boosted the city's
image. The district followed in the footsteps of a handful of cities, including Cambridge, Massachusetts, and Raleigh, North Carolina, which had
already begun to create student assignment plans that relied on income
instead of race.[10]

Socioeconomic status was an imperfect measure. The income of students was often derived from whether they applied for free- or reduced-
price school lunch. Especially at the high school level, students who needed
it did not always apply. At the same time, black children were, on average,
more likely to live in long-term poverty than white students.[11] And income
alone did not encompass the deep divide in wealth between whites and
blacks, including home ownership, assets, and other measures of economic
well-being.[12] Where should the limit be set? Was a child with a family
making a few hundred dollars more than the poverty level less needy than
one who fell just below the cutoff?

Yet high concentrations of poverty were correlated with low student
achievement, and the racial achievement gap among whites and blacks at
the same socioeconomic level was generally small.[13] Students who were
poor were more likely to experience unstable family situations, including
parents with low levels of education, domestic violence, homelessness, and
abuse. All of these things tended made it harder for them to learn than their
wealthier peers. Race was a socially constructed concept; income was more
material and concrete, and much less controversial.

The following year, Jefferson County Public School officials divided
the city and suburbs into two regions, A and B, defined by the concentration of poverty, parent education levels, and race.[14] Region A encompassed
most of the city's black neighborhoods, while B encompassed most of its
white areas. Schools were required to draw between 15 and 50 percent of
their students from Region A.

The new system closely resembled the old one. Teddy was furious at
what he saw as the school district's intransigence. He promised lawsuits,

and soon was receiving a steady stream of parents—mostly from the white suburbs—who were unhappy with their children's school assignments and ready to file complaints against Louisville's new plan.

Teddy filed another federal lawsuit, but he was defeated in district court. Judge Heyburn sided with the school district, as he largely had in the earlier cases. Teddy tried the state courts instead, arguing that Kentucky law required that students be allowed to attend the school nearest their home. As Teddy's case moved to the Kentucky Supreme Court in the spring of 2012, a federal lawsuit was filed in Texas challenging a university affirmative action program there. The Supreme Court accepted the case on appeal. The University of Michigan decision upholding the use of race in higher education admissions—which Judge Heyburn had once relied on to preserve Louisville's desegregation plan—was now also under threat.

The era of desegregation had been fading for nearly two decades: The Supreme Court cases simply marked the end. Louisville was one of the few cities in the country that still aimed to create diversity in its schools.[15] Most other American cities had long before given up. Even Seattle let its plan sunset rather than try to find another way to increase racial diversity in its schools. Soon, many of its schools were racially homogenous.[16]

Was Louisville's fight to keep its desegregation plan intact worth it? Integration may have helped Kentucky shrink its achievement gap between whites and blacks, but by 2009, the gap was still wide on the National Assessment of Educational Progress, and only average in comparison with other states. What had the district gained? More specifically, what had black students and the black community gained? Had white Louisvillians learned to share their resources equally? Had black Louisvillians been empowered to be equal members of society? Were the old divisions and inequities based on race being dissolved?

Under desegregation, the achievement gap closed as it had never before. Black and white students got to know one another, and became more prepared for a diverse world. Well-off families were forced—at least in theory—to redistribute not only tax money but the best teachers, the best principals, the attention of the best colleges and universities, and the high expectations for their schools. But some of these families had used their clout to undermine this exchange of resources, demanding gifted and talented programs that tended to favor their children and other special programs within schools that ended up with tiny percentages of minorities.

Desegregation plans had been geared toward placating whites, so that they wouldn't flee the system and take the money and the good teachers with them. In the name of preventing white flight, black communities lost schools, teachers, and principals, while black children spent hours on buses and years of their life attending schools outside of their neighborhoods. Many black students ended up in schools where the white children were just as poor as they were, like Fairdale, or in disciplinary alternatives, like Buechel. Even as the test scores and college enrollments for black students skyrocketed during the era of desegregation, they did not catch up with whites.

Ja'Mekia Stoner, ten years after the Central court case ended, still found the experience infuriating. "We got lucky because we did get the opportunity to go to better schools, but why did I have to get up at five in the morning and travel halfway across town to get a better education?" she would ask as a poised, confident twenty-five year old. The Central experience had been "hurtful," but the lesson she took from it was that as a black woman, she would have to work harder for the things she wanted. So she did. She went on to college and then graduate school to become a social worker and a therapist. Despite the fear of public speaking that had kept her from pursuing law, she spoke with the passion and precision of an experienced debater. Once, however, her confident façade had broken, during an interview for a state job. The interviewer asked if she had ever been discriminated against, and she broke down in tears.

Dionne Hopson was more ambivalent about desegregation, even though she had stuck with the Central High School case to the end. She was able to see both the upsides and the downsides of a system that, though flawed, tried to bring students of different backgrounds together to learn from each other.

In high school in the South End, Dionne stayed close to black friends from her neighborhood and tried to avoid the racial fights that occasionally broke out in the hallways. But there, it was harder to be the bright, motivated student that the teachers and principal at Coral Ridge Elementary once had high hopes for. In her last years of high school, she lost interest in academics, hurting still from the loss of her father and the disappointment of the Central case. She started cutting classes, and then dropped out. But in 2000, a counselor convinced her to earn her GED. Dionne still believed she might return to school someday to become a lawyer, and eventually, she began taking classes at the local community college with that goal in mind. When people asked her about the Central case, she told them she never intended for the school to become all black. "Desegregation was a good thing," she said, because it led to open-mindedness. She just wanted students to have a choice.

EPILOGUE

In 2009, I sat in Carman Weathers's darkened living room as he leaned into his blue leather couch and reached back into his memory. "There have been two main black struggles over how best to repatriate these ex-slaves," he said. "Some people said the best way to do it is to put them around their slave masters, and they'll catch on. And other people said we need to retreat. We need to build up strength so that we can do things for ourselves. We were never allowed to assimilate on our terms. We were assimilated on somebody else's terms."

His ideas could come off as anachronistic, but he also had a point: Desegregation should have been a two-way street.

I began research for this book frustrated that desegregation—a system I had participated in and benefited from as a child—was being discarded in favor of alternatives with little track record in improving student outcomes, which simultaneously tended to encourage school segregation. But the experiences of Weathers and others made it clear that the forced integration of black and white students had not realized all the promises of *Brown*. In some cases, it even hurt communities.

Nevertheless, under the choice and accountability movements that replaced desegregation, which have logged about as much time as busing did in many systems, the closing of the achievement gap stagnated. Desegregation, in conjunction with the anti-poverty programs of the 1960s, appeared to be one of the most successful interventions for black students in the history of public education. Black achievement on standardized tests rose at a rapid and unprecedented rate during the 1970s, when aggressive desegregation plans were in full force in a large number of cities. They never again reached the same pace of growth.[1] Study after study found that for black children, integration had modest positive effects on their short-term achievement, and more significant impacts on their long-term outcomes, launching them into better colleges and careers.[2] In the end, I was frustrated not only that desegregation was being dismantled without salvaging its undeniable benefits, but that the mistakes—which might inform current education reformers—were also being ignored.

When busing programs began to end in the 1990s, desegregation was shrugged off as an education reform that didn't work.[3] Could school districts learn something from desegregation's successes? Could something be learned from its failures? Few asked.

Charter schools, which on average perform about the same as regular public schools, haven't necessarily empowered black parents.[4] In some cases, charters have promoted grassroots activism and participation, but at the same time, they are also remote from the democratic process.[5] Charters are typically run by private organizations, and usually exempt from rules and oversight that regular public schools have to follow. (As of 2012, Kentucky—where parent and community involvement in school governance had been a major piece of the KERA reforms—was one of the few holdouts that still banned charters.)

As the first decade of the twenty-first century came to a close, education reformers went from looking at whole-school achievement to crafting accountability systems for individual teachers. A large body of research showed that teacher quality has a strong effect on student achievement.[6] The Obama administration embraced these findings, and launched a $4 billion "Race to the Top" competition in 2009 to drive states to create new teacher-evaluation systems based in part on test scores, so that good teachers could be rewarded and bad ones weeded out. Yet in many cases, the reforms focused in particular on cities with high percentages of minority teachers, putting their jobs, once again, on the line.

In New Orleans, where charter schools replaced much of the public education system in the wake of Hurricane Katrina, the percentage of black teachers dropped from 75 percent of the workforce before the storm to 57 percent in 2009.[7] Similar shifts in faculty demographics happened elsewhere. In New York, where Mayor Michael Bloomberg and his schools chancellor, Joel Klein, were implementing a slate of similar accountability-focused reforms, the percentage of minorities among new teacher hires dropped precipitously. In 1990, less than half of new teachers were white; in 2007, white teachers made up two-thirds of the city's new hires.[8] In Washington, DC, more than two hundred teachers and administrators lost their jobs under the reforms of former schools chancellor Michelle Rhee. Rhee cast herself as a hard-nosed reformer and said she was ridding the system of deadwood. A group of black and Hispanic principals sued the district, saying it was discrimination.[9] In Chicago, the teachers' union filed a federal complaint in 2012 after the district let go a disproportionate number of black teachers. They argued that the layoffs were a "systematic effort" to rid the school system of black teachers.[10]

Accountability reforms have also led to more school closings. The Obama administration awarded more than $1 billion to reform failing schools, most of them in inner cities, most of them dominated by black and Hispanic students and teachers. The federal Department of Education laid out four options for reform that districts could choose from if they wanted the money. Two of the options called for closing down a school completely. A third required firing the principal and half of the teaching staff.

In 2009, districts closed more than 1,515 schools, compared to 149 the year before, according to a report published by the Harvard Graduate School of Education.[11] Districts cited different reasons for closing schools: falling enrollments, security problems, poor performance, to save money. Angry parents launched protests just as passionate as the fight for Central High School in Louisville.[12] In a few cases, they sued to save their schools. District administrators were flummoxed. Thomas Payzant, who ran the Boston public schools for a decade, was shocked by the outcry when he suggested closing a traditionally black school in Roxbury because of a falling student population: "I thought my logic was impeccable," he said. "I realized it was a mistake."[13]

In the era of choice and accountability, the dominant narrative is still one of escape, just as it was during desegregation: Minority children are "trapped in failing schools," according to the rhetoric of reformers.[14] The mission is to get the students out. Once again, it seems that those in power are treating black schools as they did black neighborhoods during urban renewal—with an imperious sense of what is good for the community, regardless of what the people who lived there want. The focus is on tearing out dysfunction and blight, instead of finding existing strengths and building on what people value and what is working well.

For many black community members, helping black children "escape" is not the outcome they have been fighting for all these years. It's essential that black youth achieve high test scores and other markers of success on par with white students, but it is not the only goal.

The achievement of black children leapt upward in the wake of desegregation, and more slightly as the accountability and school choice movements took over. And yet along the way, activists like Carman Weathers argued, black communities lost something precious. The all-black schools that communities built and nurtured under segregation were about more than climbing the rungs of American society and fitting in at white-dominated colleges and white workplaces. They were about nurturing identity, pride, and a sense of history in black children. No one wanted Jim Crow to return, but it seemed shortsighted to summarily discard the efforts that had driven many of the students and teachers in those schools to beat enormous odds.

Is there another way forward that does not rely on escape, but that instead acknowledges and values both sides of black consciousness and, as Du Bois had written a century earlier, allows for "a man to be both a Negro and an American . . . without having the doors of Opportunity closed roughly in his face"?

Finding a way to create harmony between separate and often conflicting identities has not been just a black problem. The struggle with twoness that Du Bois described as tearing apart the African American soul has also pulled at the seams of the nation.[15] Is America a white, Christian nation, where individuals either succeed against any odds stacked against them or are allowed to fail? Or is it a melting pot, where anyone is welcome and where opportunities are made available to all—especially those who start out behind? The explosive and rancorous partisan politics that erupted after Barack Obama's election to the presidency suggest that this question still deeply divides the nation. The racial and socioeconomic disparities in the nation's schools make it unlikely that the country will become more prepared to work together and value its differences anytime soon.

Soon, America's Silent Majority will no longer be middle class and white. Demographers have predicted that by 2050 or earlier, whites will for the first time shrink to less than 50 percent of the American population.[16] As the country has grown more diverse, the nation's schools have become more segregated. The number of schools with a minority student population of more than 90 percent doubled in the 1990s, according to the Pew Research Center.[17] "Racial isolation remains far too common in America's classrooms today and it is increasing," Arne Duncan, the US education secretary, declared in a 2011 press release urging school districts to push for racial integration in schools. Rising segregation "breeds educational inequity, which is inconsistent with America's core values," he said.[18]

Reviving forced busing is unrealistic. But other ideas have emerged about how to take advantage of the country's increasing diversity. Suburban districts are being transformed by an influx of minorities even as gentrification brings wealthy whites back to the inner cities.[19] Some researchers have pointed to provisions in No Child Left Behind that could be expanded to encourage wealthy white districts to open their doors to poor, minority students.[20] Others educators have reimagined the role of charter schools, which have generally fed racial separation, as sites that could bring students from different socioeconomic and racial backgrounds together.[21] And efforts focused on integrating housing in order to create diverse communities and schools have made headway in a handful of cities, including Atlanta and Indianapolis.[22]

During the first years of his administration, President Obama spent billions of federal taxpayer dollars to improve schools and to lift the performance of poor, minority children. School districts across the country funneled money into new accountability and data systems to track student performance in the hopes that measuring student achievement would help improve it. They dismantled bureaucracies in efforts to jump-start academic achievement. They opened more and more charter schools and other experimental models, spurred on by No Child Left Behind and the very real threat that future generations of Americans will lag far behind students in other countries. The Obama administration promised an army of new teachers and new standards.

All of these steps may help improve test scores. But American schools are about more than test scores, and the protests against school closures are not just sentimental gestures. Just as many black activists have seen schools as more than a place where black children should learn to fill in the right bubbles and apply to college, America's schools have always had a larger mission. As Justice Kennedy wrote in his opinion in the Louisville-Seattle case, the nation's schools have a "historic commitment" to creating an integrated society. They are responsible for "teaching that our strength comes from people of different races, creeds, and cultures uniting in a commitment to the freedom of all."

The fights against the increased importance of tests and the closure of schools in minority neighborhoods are about preserving the other mission of public schooling: to build and sustain community, a concept that encompasses more than the local neighborhood. Public schools are the place where American society is constructed and rejuvenated.[23] Their success must be judged not only by academic achievement, but on how well the system teaches students to adapt to the values of pluralism and inclusiveness that undergird American society, and by how much their graduates are able to expand the notion of community and identity beyond the limits of neighborhood and caste, to the diverse group of people that make up the nation.

ACKNOWLEDGMENTS

The Hopson and Stoner families graciously opened their doors and allowed me into their lives. I thank them for their time and willingness to tell me their stories, even when the memories were difficult. I could not have written this book without the participation of Fran Thomas, Robert Douglas, Carman Weathers, Joyce Spond, Judge John Heyburn, and Riccardo X, who spent hours with me, sharing their stories and making sure I got the facts straight.

Thank you also to Teddy Gordon, Don Ingwerson, Pat Todd, Loueva Moss, Deborah Stallworth, John Whiting, Aubrey Williams, David McFarland, June Embers, Bernard Minnis, Raul Cunningham, Susie Guess, Sandra Hampton, Norbert Logsdon, Beverly Goodwin, Byron Leet, Frank Mellen, Steve Porter, Blaine Hudson, Georgia Powers, Steve Daeschner, Sheldon Berman, Daniel Withers, Mike Daniels, Hiram and Barbara Moss, Suzy Post, Yolanda Green, Anita Smith, the Hilliard family, Daryll Owens, Joseph McMillan, David Johnson, Carol Haddad, Nelson Fitts, the Easton family, Joe Hardesty, Ken Stites, Houston Barber, Amy Cubbage, Dan McCubbin, Traci Foster, and Gary Orfield. All were generous with their time, sharing stories and ideas that were critical in shaping my reporting. A special thank you to Walter and Imar Hutchins, who helped me fill out the story of Lyman Johnson.

This project would not have been possible without the vision, support, and enthusiasm of Samuel Freedman. My year as a Spencer Foundation fellow in education journalism at the Columbia University Graduate School of Journalism was indispensable. It gave me the time, resources and, especially, access to people and ideas that reshaped my thinking and approach to this project. Thank you especially to Bette Weneck, Amy Stuart Wells, LynNell Hancock, Elizabeth Green, Peg Tyre, and Nicholas Lemann.

Robert Rodosky and the research and archives staff in the Jefferson County Public Schools provided a wealth of documents. I am also very grateful to everyone at the University of Louisville archives, in particular Carrie Daniels and Tom Owens; to Mark Taflinger of the *Louisville Courier-Journal*; to Alan Wernecke and the staff at the Western District, who helped me access a suitcase full of court transcripts; and to Khristopher Brooks, who tracked down the last elusive facts. For many parts of the book, I relied extensively on the outstanding reporting of journalists at the *Courier-Journal*.

Thanks to my agent, Robert Guinsler, for believing in this book and finding it the right home. I'm incredibly grateful for the enthusiasm and guidance of my editor, Gayatri Patnaik, and to Rachael Marks and Robin DuBlanc.

My grandmother Dorsie Richmond shared her own experiences of desegregation, and helped spark my interest in its history. I am very lucky to have as a model her curiosity about the world and her dedication to making it a better place. Thanks to my parents, for teaching me the discipline and love of writing as a child, and for cheering me on as an adult. Margaret and David Graves have always provided me a second home in Louisville, and I am so thankful for them. They listened and encouraged me throughout the years I spent researching this book, and their experiences and insights were invaluable.

I am grateful every day for the love, patience, and tough editing of my husband, Matthew Sweeney.

NOTES

In some citations of newspaper articles the author's name is absent because some archives and collections did not include reporter bylines.

Preface

1. Meredith v. Jefferson County Board of Education, 548 U.S. 938 (2006); Parents Involved in Community Schools v. Seattle School District No. 1, 551 U.S. 701 (2007).
2. Sandra Hampton v. Jefferson County Board of Education, 102 F. Supp. 2d (W.D. Ky. 2000), decision of Judge John Heyburn.
3. *Hampton*, transcripts, US District Court-Western District of Kentucky, volume 7, 103.

Chapter 1

1. Hopson story from author interviews with Dionne Hopson, November 2, 2009, and January 15, 2010, and with Gwendolyn Hopson, November 1, 2009, January 15, 2010, and February 15, 2010.
2. Harold Fenderson (Central principal) to Dionne Hopson, May 17, 1996, Hopson private collection.
3. Ibid.
4. Jefferson County Public Schools to Gwendolyn Hopson, August 14, 1996, Hopson private collection.
5. Coral Ridge: Author interview with Beverly Goodwin, January 12, 2010.
6. "Fairdale," in *The Encyclopedia of Louisville*, John E. Kleber, ed. (Lexington: University Press of Kentucky, 2000), 279.
7. School Report Card Archive, Kentucky Department of Education, http://applications .education.ky.gov/.
8. Fifth-grade report card for Dionne Hopson, signed by Beverly Goodwin, 1993, Hopson private collection.
9. School Report Card Archive.
10. Mark McKinney, "Parkland: A Ghost Town?" *Louisville Courier-Journal*, September 28, 1969; Clarence Matthews, "Parkland's Leaders Endorse Development Plan," *Louisville Courier-Journal*, September 15, 1993.

11. John C. Pillow, "Parkland: Homestead Saw Rise of Little Africa," *Louisville Courier-Journal*, 1989.
12. "Maupin, Milburn Taylor," in Kleber, *Encyclopedia of Louisville*, 594.
13. Author interview with Harold Fenderson, January 14, 2010; Chris Kenning, "The Firing of a Popular High School Principal," *Louisville Courier-Journal*, November 27, 2002.
14. "Racial Imbalance Forces 10 Blacks to Leave Central," *Louisville Courier-Journal*, September 23, 1994.
15. Gwendolyn Hopson to Joan Chambers, January 11, 1996, Hopson private collection.
16. Pleasure Ridge Park High School to Gwendolyn Hopson, undated, Hopson private collection.
17. Veda Morgan, "Group Steps Up School-Integration Fight," *Louisville Courier-Journal*, August 16, 1996.

Chapter 2

1. Stoner story from author interviews with Ja'Mekia Stoner, April 13, 2010, and with Jacquelyn Stoner, January 19, and April 13, 2010.
2. Robert W. Peebles, *Evaluation of the Jefferson County Public Schools Desegregation Plan*, report commissioned by the Jefferson County School Board, October 24, 1994, appendix 2.
3. Ibid., 9.
4. "Neighborhood Identity," in *Portland Long-Range Plan*, Louisville Metro Planning and Design Services Division, http://www.louisvilleky.gov/.
5. Linda Stahl, "Absenteeism High as Jefferson Schools Open," *Louisville Courier-Journal*, September 5, 1975.
6. Author interview with Jacquelyn Stoner; "Protesters Delay Buses at Fairdale," *Louisville Times*, September 5, 1975.
7. Chris Kenning, "The Firing of a Popular High School Principal," *Louisville Courier-Journal*, November 27, 2002.
8. No Advance Program: Hampton v. Jefferson County, 72 F. Supp. 2d 753 (1999), transcripts, volume 7, 130, US District Court-Western District of Kentucky.
9. Veda Morgan, "Group Steps Up School-Integration Fight," *Louisville Courier-Journal*, August 16, 1996.

Chapter 3

1. "Time Blurs His Words, but King's Influence on Region Endures," *Louisville Courier-Journal*, May 4, 1993.
2. Kentucky State Legislature website, "State Song," http://www.lrc.ky.gov/.
3. "African Americans," in *The Encyclopedia of Louisville*, John E. Kleber, ed. (Lexington: University Press of Kentucky, 2000); see also, J. Blaine Hudson and Bonetta M. Hines-Hudson, "A Study of the Contemporary Racial Attitudes of Whites and African Americans," *Western Journal of Black Studies* 23 (1999).
4. Author interview with Robert Douglas, June 15, 2009.
5. Based in part on author interviews with Darryl Owens, November 3, 2009; John Whiting, January 13, 2010; Mattie Jones, January 16, 2010; Georgia Powers, January 18, 2010; Raoul Cunningham, April 3, 2009.
6. "Powers, Ingwerson Cover No New Ground at Meeting on Plan to End Busing," *Louisville Courier-Journal*, November 2, 1991.
7. Details of Carman Weathers's life from author interviews with Carman Weathers, June 17 and August 19, 2009.
8. Details of Robert Douglas's life from author interviews with Robert Douglas, June 15, June 16, and August 19, 2009.

9. Details of Fran Thomas's life from author interview with Fran Thomas and Loueva Moss, October 31, 2009, and author interview with Fran Thomas, January 2012.

10. "Proposal for Police Review Board Stirs Debate," *Louisville Courier-Journal*, July 30, 1993.

11. "Racism Alleged in Hiring of Schools Chief," *Louisville Courier-Journal*, August 21, 1993.

12. "Call in Enrollment," Jefferson County Public Schools, September 9, 1994, Robert Douglas private collection.

13. Details of Riccardo X's life from author interviews with Riccardo X, November 2, 2009, April 15, 2010, and January 2012.

14. "Racial Imbalance Forces 10 Blacks to Leave Central," *Louisville Courier-Journal*, September 23, 1994.

15. "Central Racial Limits Spur Emotional Debate," *Louisville Courier-Journal*, October 25, 1994.

16. Wade Hall, *The Rest of the Dream: The Black Odyssey of Lyman Johnson* (Lexington: University Press of Kentucky, 1988), 83.

17. Ibid., 162.

18. Richard Wilson, "Year-long Battle in 1949 Paved Way for Integration of Kentucky's Universities," *Louisville Courier-Journal*, February 2, 1977.

19. Hall, *Rest of the Dream*, 72.

20. "Central Racial Limits."

21. Ibid.

22. Don Terry, "The March on Washington: The Organizer; In the End, Farrakhan Has His Day in the Sun," *New York Times*, October 17, 1995.

23. Ibid.

24. Don Terry, "Family Values; Marching to the Beat of a Million Drummers," *New York Times*, October 15, 1995.

25. Lee Sigelman and Susan Welch, *Black Americans' Views of Racial Inequality: The Dream Deferred* (NY: Cambridge University Press, 1991), 24–26, 35.

26. Katherine Magnuson and Jane Waldfogel, eds., *Steady Gains and Stalled Progress* (New York: Russell Sage Foundation, 2008), 1–11.

27. US Census Bureau, *Black Americans: A Profile* (Washington, DC: US Department of Commerce, 1993), http://www.census.gov/.

28. Melanye T. Price, *Dreaming Blackness: Black Nationalism and African American Public Opinion* (New York: New York University Press, 2009), 105.

29. Ibid., 185.

30. Rosemary L. Bray, "The Way We Live: An African-American Life; Claiming a Culture," *New York Times*, April 23, 1989.

31. Barbara Kantrowitz, "A Is for Ashanti, B Is for Black," *Newsweek*, September 23, 1991, 45; Yvonne Shinhoster Lamb, "Black Private Schools: Academics with a Twist; Christian, African Curriculums Taught in Small Classes," *Washington Post*, August 29, 1991.

32. Shaun Hill, "Schools Urged to Adopt Afro-centric Curriculum," *Washington Post*, February 2, 1989.

33. Kantrowitz, "A Is for Ashanti."

34. Author interviews with Robert Douglas, Carman Weathers, Fran Thomas, and Riccardo X; meeting agendas and memos from the private collection of Robert Douglas.

35. Veda Morgan, "Group Steps Up School-Integration Fight," *Louisville Courier-Journal*, August 16, 1996.

36. Author interviews with Douglas, Weathers, Thomas, and X; Douglas meeting agendas and memos.

37. "Petition for an Equitable Utilization of Central and Shawnee High Schools," undated, Robert Douglas private collection.

38. "Request for Enrollment," undated, Douglas private collection.

Chapter 4

1.   Hall, *Rest of the Dream*, 7–10, 22–25, 29, 28.
2.   Trip to the white school: ibid., 30–31.
3.   Ibid., 30.
4.   Ibid., 32, 42, 54.
5.   C. Vann Woodward, *Origins of the New South* (Baton Rouge: Louisiana State University Press, 1951); John W. Cell, *The Highest Stage of White Supremacy: The Origins of Segregation in South Africa and the American South* (Cambridge, UK: Cambridge University Press, 1982); Nicholas Lemann, *The Promised Land: The Great Black Migration and How It Changed America* (New York: Knopf, 1991).
6.   C. Vann Woodward, *Reunion and Reaction: The Compromise of 1977 and the End of Reconstruction* (New York: Oxford University Press, 1966).
7.   James D. Anderson, *The Education of Blacks in the South, 1860–1935* (Chapel Hill: University of North Carolina Press, 1988), 25–26.
8.   Ibid., 5, 31; Vanessa Siddle Walker, *Their Highest Potential: An African American School Community in the Segregated South* (Chapel Hill: University of North Carolina Press, 1996), 37–38.
9.   Anderson, *Education of Blacks*, 30; Thelma Cayne Tilford-Weathers, *A History of Louisville Central High School, 1882–1982* (Louisville, KY: Central High School Alumni Association, 1982), 12; Vanessa Siddle Walker, "Valued Segregated Schools for African American Children in the South, 1935–1969: A Review of Common Themes and Characteristics," *Review of Educational Research* 70, no. 3 (2000): 253–85.
10. Walker, *Highest Potential*, 3.
11. Adam Fairclough, *A Class of Their Own: Black Teachers in the Segregated South* (Cambridge, MA: Harvard University Press, 2007), 4.
12. Walker, *Highest Potential*, 205; Fairclough, *Class of Their Own*, 100.
13. Teacher qualifications: Fairclough, *Class of Their Own*, 224.
14. Plessy v. Ferguson, 163 US 537 (1896).
15. Booker T. Washington, *Up from Slavery* (New York: Dover, 1995), 102–12.
16. Fairclough, *Class of Their Own*, 92–95.
17. Hall, *Rest of the Dream*, 44, 150.
18. Ibid., 37, 47, 35.
19. Ibid., 42, 54.
20. For more about the Great Migration, see Lemann, *The Promised Land*.
21. George C. Wright, *A History of Blacks in Kentucky*, vol. 2, *In Pursuit of Equality, 1890–1980* (Frankfort, KY: Kentucky Historical Society, 1992), 1–3.

Chapter 5

1.   Louisville history: George H. Yater, "Louisville: A Historical Overview," in *Encyclopedia of Louisville*, John E. Kleber, ed. (Lexington: University Press of Kentucky, 2000).
2.   Aaron D. Purcell, "Flood of 1937," in Kleber, *Encyclopedia of Louisville*, 297.
3.   Richard Kluger, *Simple Justice: The History of* Brown v. Board of Education *and Black America's Struggle for Equality* (New York: Vintage Books, 2004), 108–9; "Buchanan v. Warley," in Kleber, *Encyclopedia of Louisville*, 139.
4.   Ben F. Rogers, "William E. B. Du Bois, Marcus Garvey, and Pan-Africa," *Journal of Negro History* 40, no. 2 (1955): 158.
5.   Lee Sigelman and Susan Welch, *Black Americans' Views of Racial Inequality: The Dream Deferred* (NY: Cambridge University Press, 1991), 19; Campbell Gibson and Kay Jung, *Historical Census Statistics on Population Totals by Race, 1790 to 1990, and by Hispanic Origin, 1970 to 1990, for the United States, Regions, Divisions, and States* (Washington, DC: US Census Bureau, September 2002), table 1, http://www.census.gov/. There were an estimated 10 million blacks in the United States in 1920.

6. Rogers, "William E. B. Du Bois," 158–59.

7. "African Americans," in Kleber, *Encyclopedia of Louisville*, 16.

8. "Great Depression," in Kleber, *Encyclopedia of Louisville*, 354.

9. Thomas remembers Roosevelt coming to her school. Also see Eleanor Roosevelt, "My Day: First Lady Visits Projects in Louisville," *Atlanta Constitution*, October 6, 1938.

10. Central's early years: Thelma Cayne Tilford-Weathers, *A History of Louisville Central High School, 1882–1982* (Louisville, KY: Central High School Alumni Association, 1982), 5–10.

11. Maude Brown Porter: author interviews with Central alumni from that era; Everett J. Mitchel II, "The Enforcer: Diminutive Teacher Was a Strict, No-Nonsense Disciplinarian," *Louisville Courier-Journal*, February 10, 1987.

12. Central sports: Tilford-Weathers, *A History of Louisville Central High School*, 27–39.

13. Thanksgiving games from interviews with alumni; Central song lyrics: Tilford-Weathers, *A History of Louisville Central High School*, 58–59.

14. Municipal College: "African American Education," in Kleber, *Encyclopedia of Louisville*, 13.

15. Jessie Halladay, "1965 Louisville Murder Solved without Arrest: Cold Case of Alberta Jones Finally Has a Suspect, but No Trial," *Louisville Courier-Journal*, May 4, 2010; "Alberta O. Jones," Notable African Americans Database, University of Kentucky, http://www.uky.edu/.

Chapter 6

1. Johnson in college: Wade Hall, *The Rest of the Dream: The Black Odyssey of Lyman Johnson* (Lexington: University Press of Kentucky, 1988), 55–56.

2. Ibid., 59.

3. Adam Fairclough, *A Class of Their Own: Black Teachers in the Segregated South* (Cambridge, MA: Harvard University Press, 2007), 311; "Living Legend" lectures at University of Louisville, January 22, 1990, Lyman Johnson Papers, University of Louisville Library.

4. Fairclough, *Class of Their Own*, 309.

5. Ibid., 310, 226.

6. Richard Kluger, *Simple Justice: The History of* Brown v. Board of Education *and Black America's Struggle for Equality* (New York: Vintage Books, 2004), 91.

7. Ibid., 108–9.

8. Ibid., 100, 194–215.

9. Ibid., 258, 274, 290–97.

10. Hall, *Rest of the Dream*, 154–55; Richard Wilson, "Year-long Battle in 1949 Paved Way for Integration of Kentucky's Universities," *Louisville Courier-Journal*, February 2, 1977.

11. Catherine Fosl, *Subversive Southerner: Anne Braden and the Struggle for Racial Justice in the Cold War South* (New York: Palgrave Macmillan, 2002), 86.

12. Ibid., 4, 13, 57–80.

13. George C. Wright, *A History of Blacks in Kentucky*, vol. 2, *In Pursuit of Equality, 1890–1980* (Frankfort, KY: Kentucky Historical Society, 1992), 158.

14. Fosl, *Subversive Southerner*, 103–33.

15. Ibid., 136–37.

16. Tracy E. K'Meyer, *Civil Rights in the Gateway to the South* (Lexington: University Press of Kentucky, 2009), 62–63, 137.

17. Ibid., 64; Fosl, *Subversive Southerner*, 139.

18. Fosl, *Subversive Southerner*, 139–41.

Chapter 7

1. Tracy E. K'Meyer, *Civil Rights in the Gateway to the South* (Lexington: University Press of Kentucky, 2009), 35.

2. Wade Hall, *The Rest of the Dream: The Black Odyssey of Lyman Johnson* (Lexington: University Press of Kentucky, 1988), 154.

3. Richard Kluger, *Simple Justice: The History of* Brown v. Board of Education *and Black America's Struggle for Equality* (New York: Vintage Books, 2004), 293–94.

4. For more detail on the five cases, see Kluger, *Simple Justice*.

5. Ibid., 574.

6. For details on *Brown II*, see ibid., 585–619.

7. Ibid., 659.

8. Charles Wollenberg, "*Mendez v. Westminster*: Race, Nationality and Segregation in California Schools," *California Historical Quarterly* 53, no. 4 (Winter 1974): 317–32.

9. Kluger, *Simple Justice*, 210, 704.

10. Brown v. Board of Education of Topeka, 347 US 483 (1954); Jack M. Balkin, *What* Brown v. Board of Education *Should Have Said* (New York: New York University Press, 2001), 40; Kluger, *Simple Justice*, 714.

11. Kluger, *Simple Justice*, 714–16.

12. Balkin, *What* Brown, 48.

13. Ibid., 11; James T. Patterson, Brown v. Board of Education: *A Civil Rights Milestone and Its Troubled Legacy* (New York: Oxford University Press, 2001), 68.

14. Balkin, *What* Brown, 11–13, 55–56.

15. Ibid., 64–68.

16. Catherine Fosl, *Subversive Southerner: Anne Braden and the Struggle for Racial Justice in the Cold War South* (New York: Palgrave Macmillan, 2002), 141–55.

17. Hall, *Rest of the Dream*, 142.

18. Fosl, *Subversive Southerner*, 151, 155–73, 175–85, 194–95.

19. Adam Fairclough, *A Class of Their Own: Black Teachers in the Segregated South* (Cambridge, MA: Harvard University Press, 2007), 4–5, 374–75; David S. Cecelski, *Along Freedom Road: Hyde County, North Carolina and the Fate of Black Schools in the South* (Chapel Hill: University of North Carolina Press, 1994), 9–10.

20. Michael Murakami, "Desegregation," in *Public Opinion and Constitutional Controversy*, Nathan Persily et al., eds. (NY: Oxford University Press, 2008), 23.

21. Lee Sigelman and Susan Welch, *Black Americans' Views of Racial Inequality: The Dream Deferred* (NY: Cambridge University Press, 1991), 122.

22. Kluger, *Simple Justice*, 166.

23. W. E. B. Du Bois, "Does the Negro Need Separate Schools?" *Journal of Negro Education* 4, no. 3 (1935): 328–35.

24. Fairclough, *Class of Their Own*, 358.

25. Details of the Hyde County boycott from Cecelski, *Along Freedom Road*.

26. Fight for new building from Thelma Cayne Tilford-Weathers, *A History of Louisville Central High School, 1882–1982* (Louisville, KY: Central High School Alumni Association, 1982), 16–17.

27. Details about Wilson from Hall, *Rest of the Dream*, 133; author interview with Wilson's daughter, Susie Guess, November 4, 2009.

28. Tilford-Weathers, *A History*; Lourena Eaton, "Central High, 'South's Finest,' Nearly Ready," *Louisville Courier-Journal*, June 29, 1952.

29. Eaton, "Central High."

Chapter 8

1. Details of first day of integration: Omer Carmichael and Weldon James, *The Louisville Story* (New York: Simon and Schuster, 1957); Male High School: "Male High School Gets Its Old Name Back; Integration Plans Also Adopted," *Louisville Courier-Journal* (no date); "Louisville Male High School," in *The Encyclopedia of Louisville*, John E. Kleber, ed. (Lexington: University Press of Kentucky, 2000), 558.

2. Peter Irons, *Jim Crow's Children: The Broken Promise of the* Brown *Decision* (New York: Penguin Books, 2002), 165–66, 177.

3. Details of Carmichael's life from Carmichael, *Louisville Story*.
4. Tracy E. K'Meyer, *Civil Rights in the Gateway to the South* (Lexington: University Press of Kentucky, 2009), 47.
5. Carmichael, *Louisville Story*.
6. Kleber, *Encyclopedia of Louisville*, xxix; also see urban renewal in chapter 9.
7. K'Meyer, *Gateway*, 53.
8. Ibid., 54.
9. "Parkland Area Redistricting Asked in Parents' Petition," *Louisville Times*, April 3, 1956.
10. Irons, *Jim Crow's Children*, 165; John D. Mack, "Crowd Turns Back Negroes," *New York Times*, September 11, 1956; K'Meyer, *Gateway*, 53.
11. Brown v. Board of Education, 349 US 294 (1955).
12. Richard Kluger, *Simple Justice: The History of* Brown v. Board of Education *and Black America's Struggle for Equality* (New York: Vintage Books, 2004), 755; Kenneth O'Reilly, "Racial Integration: The Battle General Eisenhower Chose Not to Fight," *Journal of Blacks in Higher Education* 18 (Winter 1997–98): 110–19; "Ike Non-committal on GOP Civil Rights Plank," *Chicago Daily Defender*, August 9, 1956; "Ike Hedges on School Action," *Chicago Daily Defender*, September 6, 1956.
13. See, for example, Josephine Ripley, "President Hopeful of Suez Solution," *Christian Science Monitor*, August 8, 1956; Joseph A. Loftus, "The Farm Problem," *New York Times*, September 10, 1955; "GOP's Farm Belt Support Has Dropped Sharply Since 1952, Poll Indicates," *Washington Post*, September 25, 1956.
14. Bradford Jacobs, "Adlai Chides Ike for Stand on Race Issue," *Baltimore Sun*, September 12, 1956.
15. Carmichael and Eisenhower: "Transcript of Eisenhower's News Conference on Foreign and Domestic Affairs," *New York Times*, September 12, 1956; Bess Furman, "President Doubts Hearing Harms Capital Integration," *New York Times*, September 21, 1956; Anthony Lewis, "President Scores Rioting in South," *New York Times*, September 12, 1956; "Omer Carmichael Is Dead at 66; Head of Schools in Louisville," *New York Times*, January 10, 1960, 86; "Education: How to Integrate," *Time*, September 24, 1956; "Louisville's Integrator: Omer Carmichael," *New York Times*, September 10, 1956.
16. Carmichael, *Louisville Story*; K'Meyer, *Gateway*, 56.
17. History of white resistance to *Brown v. Board of Education*, including use of "school choice" to evade integration, from Davison M. Douglas, *Reading, Writing and Race: The Desegregation of the Charlotte Schools* (Chapel Hill: University of North Carolina Press, 1995); Adam Fairclough, *A Class of Their Own: Black Teachers in the Segregated South* (Cambridge, MA: Harvard University Press, 2007); James T. Patterson, "Southern Whites Fight Back," in Brown v. Board of Education: *A Civil Rights Milestone and Its Troubled Legacy* (NY: Oxford University Press, 2001).
18. Thelma Cayne Tilford-Weathers, *A History of Louisville Central High School, 1882–1982* (Louisville, KY: Central High School Alumni Association, 1982),, 46.
19. Irons, *Jim Crow's Children*, 188–89.
20. Taylor Branch, *Parting the Waters: America in the King Years, 1954–1963* (New York: Simon and Schuster, 1988).
21. "Negro's Fight Must Be Nonviolent, King Says," *Louisville Times*, April 19, 1961.
22. "40 Negro Sit-inners Arrested Downtown," *Louisville Times*, April 19, 1961.
23. Branch, *Parting the Waters*, 271–84.
24. K'Meyer, *Gateway*, 87–88; Wade Hall, *The Rest of the Dream: The Black Odyssey of Lyman Johnson* (Lexington: University Press of Kentucky, 1988), 134–35.
25. Hall, *Rest of the Dream*, 134–35; "Negroes Ask Progress on Integration," *Louisville Times*, February 28, 1961.
26. K'Meyer, *Gateway*, 81.
27. Hall, *Rest of the Dream*, 137–38.

28. F. W. Woolsey, "The Lunch-counter Revolution," *Louisville Courier-Journal Magazine*, March 30, 1980.
29. K'Meyer, *Gateway*, 105.
30. Jim Morrissey, "Integration Timetable," *Louisville Courier-Journal*, June 30, 1963.
31. Ibid.; K'Meyer, *Gateway*, 107–10.
32. "Valley Station," in Kleber, *Encyclopedia of Louisville*, 909.
33. Woolsey, "Lunch-counter Revolution."

Chapter 9

1. Margaret Merrick, "Public Housing," in *The Encyclopedia of Louisville*, John E. Kleber, ed. (Lexington: University Press of Kentucky, 2000), 734.
2. Details of Riccardo X's life from author interviews with Riccardo X.
3. Gerald Henry, "Renewal Affects 5 Pct. Of City; More to Come?" *Louisville Courier-Journal*, February 19, 1967.
4. "Louisvillians Invited to View City Slums," *Louisville Courier-Journal*, March 20, 1957.
5. "Little Africa," in Kleber, *Encyclopedia of Louisville*, 523.
6. "Louisvillians Invited"; Redevelopment Termed Urgent," *Louisville Courier-Journal*, June 14, 1959.
7. Sheldon Shafer, "Changed City Is Left Behind by Chief of Urban Renewal," *Louisville Courier-Journal*, April 2, 1978.
8. Kenneth Jackson, *Crabgrass Frontier: The Suburbanization of the United States* (New York: Oxford University Press, 1985), 210–13.
9. Ibid., 195–215; Douglas Massey and Susan Denton, *American Apartheid: Segregation and the Making of the Underclass* (Cambridge, MA: Harvard University Press, 1993), 54–55.
10. Jackson, *Crabgrass Frontier*, 217.
11. Massey and Denton, *American Apartheid*, 55.
12. Robert Hermann, "Land Buying to Being in July for 2 Downtown Renewal Areas," *Louisville Courier-Journal*, March 28, 1981.
13. Shafer, "Changed City."
14. Rob Deitel, "West Downtown Took 2 Decades," *Louisville Times*, February 7, 1985.
15. Bert Emke, "Urban Renewal: Friend or Foe of the Poor?" *Louisville Times*, September 12, 1969.
16. Deitel, "West Downtown."
17. "Clearing the Way for West End Renewal," *Louisville Courier-Journal*, January 21, 1965.
18. Emke, "Urban Renewal."
19. Author interview with Norbert Logsdon, June 15, 2009; Catherine Fosl and Tracy E. K'Meyer, *Freedom on the Border: An Oral History of the Civil Rights Movement in Kentucky* (Lexington: University Press of Kentucky, 2009), 131.
20. James Braun, "Urban Renewal," in Kleber, *Encyclopedia of Louisville*, 905.
21. David Remnick, *King of the World* (New York: Vintage Books, 1999), 81–82.
22. Ibid., 87–88; Muhammad Ali, *Soul of a Butterfly: Reflections on Life's Journey* (New York: Simon and Schuster, 2004), 11.
23. Remnick, *King of the World*, 81–96.
24. Ali, *Soul of a Butterfly*, 34–39.
25. Remnick, *King of the World*, 105–6.
26. Ibid., 101, 106; Ali, *Soul of a Butterfly*, 29–32.
27. Tilford-Weathers, *A History of Louisville Central High School*, 16–23.
28. Merrick, "Public Housing," 734.
29. "King, Alfred Daniel Williams," in Kleber, *Encyclopedia of Louisville*, 484.
30. Clayborne Carson, foreword to *The Black Panthers Speak*, Philip Foner, ed. (Boston, MA: Da Capo Press, 2002), x–xii.
31. "Oakland Officer Slain in Black Panther Clash," *Los Angeles Times*, October 29, 1967.

32. Remnick, *King of the World*, 205–10.
33. Ali, *Soul of a Butterfly*, 66.
34. Remnick, *King of the World*, 205–10.
35. Ibid., 287.
36. Tracy E. K'Meyer, *Civil Rights in the Gateway to the South* (Lexington: University Press of Kentucky, 2009), 179.
37. Ibid., 179–85.
38. Ibid., 187; "Economic Equality Is Proving Elusive," *Louisville Courier-Journal*, May 29, 1988.
39. K'Meyer, *Gateway*, 187.
40. Ibid., 188–89.
41. Ibid.
42. Carmichael later said he had not been turned away at the airport and denied that he had planned on coming to the rally at all: ibid., 189; Anne Moore, "Carmichael Rumors Helped Start Riots," *Louisville Courier-Journal*, June 16, 1968.
43. K'Meyer, *Gateway*, 188; "Schmied, Kenneth Allen," in Kleber, *Encyclopedia of Louisville*, 789.
44. "Schmied," Kleber, *Encyclopedia of Louisville*, 789; K'Meyer, *Gateway*, 103, 17–129.
45. "Rioting Breaks Out in Louisville," *Louisville Courier-Journal*, May 28, 1968.
46. Ibid.
47. Ibid.
48. David Diaz Jr., "Somebody Threw a Bottle—Then 'Oh Baby . . . It's Really Happening,'" *Louisville Times*, May 18, 1968.
49. Ibid.
50. Paul M. Branzburg, "Looters Took Goods—and Revenge," *Louisville Courier-Journal*, June 16, 1968.
51. Moore, "Carmichael Rumors"; K'Meyer, *Gateway*, 190; "Protesters Ask Removal of Guard," *Louisville Courier-Journal*, May 29, 1968.
52. "Riots Flare Anew in Louisville's West End," *Louisville Courier-Journal*, May 29, 1968.
53. "Restraint Marred by Bloodshed," *Louisville Courier-Journal*, June 16, 1968.
54. Branzburg, "Looters Took"; John Finley, "Anger, Frustration Fanned Riots Despite Carnival Spirit," *Louisville Courier-Journal*, June 16, 1968.
55. "Cortez, 5 Others Indicted as Plotters," *Louisville Courier-Journal*, October 18, 1968.
56. Rudy Johnson, "Negroes in Louisville Are Still Tense and Bitter after May 28 Riot That Left 2 Dead," *New York Times*, June 17, 1968.

Chapter 10

1. Details of Joyce Spond's life from author interview with Joyce Spond, April 14, 2010.
2. "Urban and Rural Population: 1900 to 1990," table, US Census Bureau, October 1995, http://www.census.gov/.
3. Edward Bennett and Carolyn Gatz, *Louisville, Kentucky: A Restoring Prosperity Case Study* (Washington, DC: Brookings Institution, September 2008), 12, http://www.brookings.edu/.
4. C. Vann Woodward, "The Search for Southern Identity," in *Myth and Southern History: Vol. 2, The New South*, Patrick Gerster and Nicholas Cords, eds. (Champaign: University of Illinois Press, 1989), 121; Matthew D. Lassiter and Kevin M. Kruse, "The Bulldozer Revolution: Suburbs and Southern History Since World War II," *Journal of Southern History* 75, no. 3 (2009): 691–706.
5. Douglas Massey and Susan Denton, *American Apartheid: Segregation and the Making of the Underclass* (Cambridge, MA: Harvard University Press, 1993), 148–50; Kenneth Jackson, *Crabgrass Frontier: The Suburbanization of the United States* (New York: Oxford University Press, 1985).

6. James T. Patterson, Brown v. Board of Education: *A Civil Rights Milestone and Its Troubled Legacy* (New York: Oxford University Press, 2001), 124.

7. Rick Perlstein, *Nixonland: The Rise of a President and the Fracturing of America* (New York: Scribner, 2008), 239.

8. Otto Kerner, *Report of the National Advisory Commission on Civil Disorders* (Washington, DC: US Government Printing Office, 1968).

9. Patterson, Brown v. Board, 138–39.

10. James Coleman, *Equality of Educational Opportunity*, (Washington, DC: US Government Printing Office, 1966).

11. Davison M. Douglas, *Reading, Writing and Race: The Desegregation of the Charlotte Schools* (Chapel Hill: University of North Carolina Press, 1995), 125.

12. Green v. County School Board of New Kent County, 391 US 430 (1968).

13. Douglas, *Reading, Writing and Race*, 128.

14. Ibid.

15. Arthur M. Schlesinger Jr., *Robert Kennedy and His Times* (New York: Houghton Mifflin, 2002), 778–800; Taylor Branch, *Parting the Waters: America in the King Years, 1954–1963* (New York: Simon and Schuster, 1988).

16. Perlstein, *Nixonland*, 341–43, 431–35; Joseph Alsop, "Southern Strategy of Nixon Is Seen Likely to Succeed," *Washington Post*, August 12, 1968; Matthew Lassiter, *The Silent Majority: Suburban Politics in the Sunbelt South* (Princeton, NJ: Princeton University Press, 2007).

17. Philip E. Converse et al., "Stability and Change in 1960: A Reinstating Election," *American Political Science Review* 55, no. 2 (1961): 269–80; Mark Stern, "John F. Kennedy and Civil Rights: From Congress to the Presidency," *Presidential Studies Quarterly* 19, no. 4 (1989): 797–823.

18. Perlstein, *Nixonland*, 202, 237–41, 129, 350–51.

19. Nixon in Charlotte: "School Integration in the Election," *Chicago Tribune*, September 16, 1968.

20. Details of *Swann* litigation: Douglas, *Reading, Writing and Race*, 107–29.

21. Swann v. Charlotte-Mecklenburg Board of Education, 402 US 1 (1971).

Chapter 11

1. Peter Irons, *Jim Crow's Children: The Broken Promise of the* Brown *Decision* (New York: Penguin Books, 2002), 225.

2. Mike McKinney, "Central High Must Be Desegregated, City Told by U.S.," *Louisville Courier-Journal*, December 18, 1969.

3. Ibid.

4. Charles Walden, *Southern Cities—Except Louisville—Desegregate Schools: A Report on Public Schools in Louisville, Kentucky and Major Southern Cities, 1968 and 1971* (Louisville: Commission on Human Rights, Commonwealth of Kentucky, May 1972), http://www.eric.ed.gov/.

5. McKinney, "Central High."

6. Thelma Cayne Tilford-Weathers, *A History of Louisville Central High School, 1882–1982* (Louisville, KY: Central High School Alumni Association, 1982), 47.

7. Edward Bennett, "City Schools May Get Desegregation Order," *Louisville Times*, June 26, 1971.

8. Rick Perlstein, *Nixonland: The Rise of a President and the Fracturing of America* (New York: Scribner, 2008), 421, 459; Gary Orfield, "Congress, the President, and Anti-busing Legislation, 1966–1974," *Journal of Law and Education* 81 (1975).

9. Tilford-Weathers, *A History of Louisville Central High School*, 47

10. Ibid., 31–34.

11. Tilford-Weathers, *A History of Louisville Central High School*, 33.

12. McKinney, "Central High."

13. Tilford-Weathers, *A History of Louisville Central High School*, 47

14. Orfield, "Congress," 133.

15. "Can New Plan for Central High Become Model for the Nation?" *Louisville Courier-Journal*, April 10, 1970.

16. "A Chronology of Major Steps in Busing Case," *Louisville Times*, June 17, 1978.

17. "School Bias Suit Names Louisville," *Louisville Courier-Journal*, June 23, 1972.

18. Judy Rosenfield, "Desegregation Suit: The Original 13," *Louisville Times*, July 24, 1975.

19. Linda Raymond, "U.S. Court Asked to Order City School Desegregation," *Louisville Times*, June 22, 1972.

20. Mike McKinney, "City Schools Accept Bid to Talk County Merger," *Louisville Courier-Journal*, December 18, 1969.

21. "The Busing Issue Boils Over," *Time*, February 28, 1972.

22. "Anti-busing Statement Triggers Congressional Criticism of Nixon," *Baltimore African-American*, August 14, 1971.

23. R. W. Apple, "Wallace Again Emerging as Key Campaign Figure," *New York Times*, February 20, 1972; Martin Waldron, "Nixon Margin Big; Governor Captures 75 of 81 Delegates in Dramatic Victory," *New York Times*, March 15, 1972.

24. Roger Wilkins, "To Begin the Birth of a New Nation," *Washington Post*, March 16, 1972.

25. Herbert H. Denton, "Blacks Vote Against Busing," *Washington Post*, March 13, 1972.

26. Leonard Pardue, "Parents Oppose School Racial-Balance Plan," *Louisville Times*, May 28, 1968.

27. David Frum, *How We Got Here: The 70's—The Decade that Brought You Modern Life—For Better or Worse* (New York: Basic Books, 2000), 253.

28. Jean Howerton, "Negro-Pupil Gains Since '56 Reported; Whites Also Up Since Integration," *Louisville Courier-Journal*, March 16, 1980.

29. Johnson and Quay Glass, "Western Louisville: What Does It Think of Busing?" *Louisville Courier-Journal*, September 27, 1975.

30. James Nolan, "School Desegregation Case Begins," *Louisville Courier-Journal*, December 2, 1972.

31. Charles R. Babcock, "National Debate Begins on Court-Ordered Busing," *Louisville Courier-Journal*, October 29, 1975.

32. Details of Judge James F. Gordon's life from interview with Ethel S. White, December 3, 1989, for the Jefferson County Oral History Project, stored in the University of Louisville Archives and Records Center; Jim Adams and Leslie Scanlon, "The Busing Judge: A Reminiscence," *Louisville Courier-Journal*, 1980.

33. Linda Raymond, "School-desegregation Suits Are Dismissed," *Louisville Times*, March 8, 1973.

34. Richard Nixon, "Address to the Nation on Equal Educational Opportunities and School Busing," March 16, 1972, American Presidency Project, http://www.presidency.ucsb.edu/.

35. Irons, *Jim Crow's Children*, 236–40; Gary Orfield and Susan Eaton, eds., *Dismantling Desegregation: The Quiet Reversal of* Brown v. Board of Education (New York: New Press, 1996), 10–11.

36. Gary Orfield, "Segregated Housing and School Resegregation," in Orfield, *Dismantling Desegregation*, 315.

37. Irons, *Jim Crow's Children*, 241.

38. "U.S. Court Orders Desegregation Plan for 3 School Districts in Jefferson County," *Louisville Times*, December 28, 1973.

39. James Nolan, "Judge Orders City and County to Combine Their School Desegregation Plans by Tuesday," *Louisville Courier-Journal*, July 20, 1974.

40. John Finley, "Judge's Decision for a 'Plan X' Surprises Few," *Louisville Courier-Journal*, July 20, 1974.

41. James Nolan, "Louisville-Area School Plan Canceled as Most Cross-district Busing

Barred," *Louisville Courier-Journal*, July 26, 1974; Milliken v. Bradley, 418 US 717 (1974), http://supreme.justia.com/.

42. Irons, *Jim Crow's Children*, 242–49.

43. "Any Busing Here Is Stalled Past Oct. 14," *Louisville Times*, August 9, 1974.

44. Albert Sehlstedt Jr., "Ford Bid in 1976 Probable; Education Bill, with Busing Curb, Is Signed," *Baltimore Sun*, August 22, 1974.

45. Orfield, "Congress," 131; 133–34.

46. Ronald P. Formisano, *Boston against Busing: Race, Class, and Ethnicity in the 1960s and 1970s* (Chapel Hill: University of North Carolina Press, 1991); "This Is Testing Our Sense of Humid," *Louisville Courier-Journal*, July 20, 1974.

47. James Nolan, "Racial Balance of City's Schools Tips to Blacks," *Louisville Courier-Journal*, October 17, 1972; Edward Bennett, "City Schools May Get Desegregation Order," *Louisville Times*, June 28, 1971; "Pupils in Integrated Schools Gain Here," *Louisville Courier-Journal*, October 2, 1957.

48. David McGinty, "Local Desegregation Battle to Resume," *Louisville Times*, October 14, 1974.

49. Dennis Polite, "Desegregation Order to Be Appealed," *Louisville Times*, January 7, 1975.

50. David McGinty, "Judge Gordon to Draft Own Plan to Desegregate Schools," *Louisville Times*, July 18, 1975; David McGinty, "Gordon's Integration Plan Will Bus 23,000," *Louisville Times*, July 23, 1975.

51. "Justice Blackmun Denies SOCS Attorneys' Plea to Delay Busing Order," *Louisville Times*, September 4, 1975; Linda Stahl, "Powell Is Asked to Stay Order on School Busing," *Louisville Courier-Journal*, August 29, 1975.

52. Larry Werner, "Hotline: Volunteers Answer Questions on Busing," *Louisville Courier-Journal*, July 31, 1975.

53. Mike Brown, "As the 'General' of a Small Army, There Are Few Free Moments for . . . an Antibusing Leader," *Louisville Courier-Journal*, September 13, 1975.

54. Larry Werner and John Filiatreau, "85 White Students State 'Sit-in,'" *Louisville Courier-Journal*, November 7, 1975.

55. Formisano, *Boston Against Busing*, 114, 115, 143, 150, 153.

56. Jim Adams, "Concerned Parents Rally Canceled for Prayer Vigil," *Louisville Courier-Journal*, August 18, 1975; Jim Adams, "Downtown Protest Attracts 2,500," *Louisville Courier-Journal*, September 5, 1975.

Chapter 12

1. John Flynn, "'The South End Is a Feeling, Not a Place,'" *Louisville Courier-Journal*, September 14, 1975; Dick Kaukas, "Women Stage Okolona March against Busing," *Louisville Courier-Journal*, October 10, 1975.

2. Jim Adams, "Downtown Protest Attracts 2,500," *Louisville Courier-Journal*, September 5, 1975.

3. "Protesters Delay Buses at Fairdale," *Louisville Times*, September 5, 1975.

4. "Dozens Hurt, 192 Arrested in Riots," *Louisville Times*, September 6, 1975.

5. Paul Bulleit, "Slingshot Defendant Acquitted," *Louisville Courier-Journal*, March 31, 1976.

6. "Ballard High Principal Has Suspended 20 Black Students Since Monday," *Louisville Courier-Journal*, September 11, 1975.

7. "Rumor of Rapes False, Six School Principals Say," *Louisville Courier-Journal*, September 11, 1975.

8. "How Did the Black Community Handle First Seven Days of School Desegregation?" *Louisville Defender*, September 11, 1975.

9. Ben Johnson, "Small Woman Shouts Loudly on Behalf of Black Students," *Louisville Courier-Journal*, September 5, 1975.

10. Johnson and Quay Glass, "Western Louisville: What Does It Think of Busing?" *Louisville Courier-Journal*, September 27, 1975.

11. "Black Students Say the Hate Was Unexpected," *Louisville Courier-Journal*, September 11, 1975.

12. Ira Simmons, "The Whitening of Central: Black Students Feel It Isn't 'Their' School Anymore," *Louisville Times*, 1976.

13. Thelma Cayne Tilford-Weathers, *A History of Louisville Central High School, 1882–1982* (Louisville, KY: Central High School Alumni Association, 1982), 34.

14. "Central Was All We Had," *Louisville Courier-Journal*, June 27, 1982; Tilford-Weathers, *A History of Louisville Central High School*, 49.

15. Simmons, "The Whitening of Central."

16. W. E. B. Du Bois, *The Souls of Black Folk* (New York: Barnes and Nobles Classics, 2005), 9.

17. Douglas Massey and Susan Denton, *American Apartheid: Segregation and the Making of the Underclass* (Cambridge, MA: Harvard University Press, 1993), 4, 59.

18. Anti-Discrimination Center, Dynamic Census Mapping, http://www.antibiaslaw.com/.

19. Massey and Denton, *American Apartheid*, 60–82.

20. Linda Stahl, "Private Schools Are Losing Students; Reasons Include New Faith in Public Schools," *Louisville Courier-Journal*, August 25, 1985.

21. "Changes in Racial Attitudes in Jefferson County," *Louisville Times*, May 12, 1980.

22. Photo caption, *Louisville Times*, May 16, 1980.

23. Linda Raymond, "Test-Score Trends: Blacks Gain, Whites Hold Steady," *Louisville Times*, May 13, 1980.

24. Frank Knorr, ed., "Fulfilling the Letter and Spirit of the Law: Desegregation of the Nation's Public Schools" (Washington, DC: US Commission on Civil Rights August 1976), 83, 161, http://www.eric.ed.gov/.

Chapter 13

1. Elinor J. Brecher and Leslie Ellis, "Grayson Plans Counterattack in Bid to Keep Job," *Louisville Courier-Journal*, July 24, 1980; "Grayson Sues Board, Alleging Conspiracy, Attempted Bribery," *Louisville Times*, July 24, 1980.

2. "Chronology of the Grayson Controversy," *Louisville-Times*, July 25, 1980.

3. Elinor J. Brecher, "School Officials Considering Busing of Whites in More Grades," *Louisville Courier-Journal*, November 14, 1979.

4. Elinor J. Brecher, "Board Approves Voluntary Busing Plan amid Criticism," *Louisville Courier-Journal*, November 27, 1979.

5. "Six Men Who Would Be Superintendent Tell Why—And How," *Louisville Courier-Journal*, January 19, 1981.

6. " 'Low-Income Pupils Threaten Education of Others,' Gamboa Says," *Louisville Courier-Journal*, January 23, 1981.

7. "Gamboa Rapped for Linking Poverty, Pupil Attitudes," *Louisville Times*, January 23, 1981; "Black Leaders Want Gamboa, DeRuzzo Out," *Louisville Courier-Journal*, January 27, 1981.

8. "Californian Ingwerson Is Persuasive and Poised," *Louisville Courier-Journal*, February 24, 1981.

9. Details of Donald Ingwerson's life from author interview with Ingwerson, February 11, 2010; "Californian Ingwerson"; "Job Pressures May Have Led to Departure," *Louisville Courier-Journal*, March 5, 1993.

10. Kristina Steward Ward, "The Outsider," *Vogue*, December 2007; multiple articles in the *Orange County Register*, e.g., "Yorba Linda Rejects for Buddhist Temple," *Orange County Register*, March 6, 1997.

11. Rosalva Hernandez, "Ruling on Census Raises Few Eyebrows in County," *Orange County Register*, March 21, 1996.

12. Daniel Rubin and Leslie Scanlon, "Both Races Show Gains on Test, but an Analysis Shows an Achievement Gap," *Louisville Courier-Journal*, August 25, 1985.

13. Daniel Rubin, "Turmoil of Early Years Is Over, but Suspensions Are Still Causing Concern," *Louisville Courier-Journal*, August 25, 1985.

14. Daniel Rubin, "Both Blacks and Whites Are Missing Fewer Classes and Dropping Out Less Often," *Louisville Courier-Journal*, August 25, 1985.

15. Dianne Aprile, "Troubled Waters Calm Now at Fairdale and Shawnee," *Louisville Times*, May 14, 1980.

16. Rubin, "Turmoil of Early Years."

17. Linda Stahl, "Integration Order Changed to Aid 'Advance' Pupils," *Louisville Courier-Journal*, August 16, 1975; Leslie Scanlon and Daniel Rubin, "Systemwide Race Ratios Aren't Holding Up in Special Programs and Tough Courses Like Physics," *Louisville Courier-Journal*, August 25, 1985.

18. Jeannie Oakes, *Keeping Track: How Schools Structure Inequality* (New Haven, CT: Yale University Press, 2005), 278; "The History of Gifted and Talented Education," National Association of Gifted Children, http://www.nagc.org/; Stephen J. Caldas and Carl L. Bankston, *Forced to Fail: The Paradox of School Desegregation* (Westport, CT: Praeger, 2005); Kenneth J. Meier, Joseph Steward, and Robert E. England, *Race, Class and Education: The Politics of Second-Generation Discrimination* (Madison: University of Wisconsin Press, 1989), 81–99.

19. Michael Days and Mervin Aubespin, "Blacks See Their Hopes on Busing Swept Aside," *Louisville Courier-Journal*, May 4, 1981.

20. Michael Wines, "Busing: 5 Years Later," *Louisville Times*, May 12, 1980; Linda Stahl, "Private Schools Are Losing Students," *Louisville Courier-Journal*, August 25, 1985.

21. Wines, "Busing: 5 Years Later."

22. Days, "Blacks See Their Hopes."

23. Bob Deitel, "Central High's Enrollment Drop Underscores Problem, Officials Say," *Louisville Times*, October 19, 1983.

24. Saundra Keyes, "Bused Students Seek More Medical Transfers," *Louisville Courier-Journal*, September 26, 1983.

25. Days, "Blacks See Their Hopes."

26. Dianne Aprile, "Pupils Who Live It Say Prejudices Fading," *Louisville Times*, May 16, 1980.

27. Aprile, "Troubled Waters."

28. Wines, "Busing: 5 Years Later."

29. Saundra Keyes, "Programs, No Numbers, May Be Key to Busing Plan," *Louisville Courier-Journal*, November 26, 1983.

30. Leslie Scanlon, "Many Doubt That Central Would Attract East End Students," *Louisville Courier-Journal*, January 21, 1984.

31. National Commission on Excellence in Education, *A Nation at Risk: The Imperative for Educational Reform*, (Washington, DC: US Government Printing Office, 1983).

32. George H. Gallup and Stanley Elam, "The 13th Annual Gallup Poll of the Public's Attitudes toward the Public Schools," *Phi Delta Kappan* 63, no. 1 (1981).

33. "For the Record: President Reagan, Responding to Reporters' Questions during a White House News Conference on May 17," *Education Week*, May 25, 1983.

34. Katherine Magnuson and Jane Waldfogel, eds., *Steady Gains and Stalled Progress* (New York: Russell Sage Foundation, 2008).

35. David Grissmer, Ann Flanagan, and Stephanie Williamson, "Why Did the Gap Narrow in the 1970s and 1980s?" in *The Black-White Test Score Gap*, Christopher Jencks and Meredith Philips, eds. (Washington, DC: Brookings Institution Press, 1998), 195.

36. Ibid.

Chapter 14

1. Details of Carman Weathers's life from author interviews with Weathers.
2. Roscoe Nance, "Jackson State Celebrates 100 Years of Football," *Southwestern Athletic Conference*, November 7, 2011, databaseFootball.com.
3. Khristopher Brooks, phone interview with Marshall Gray, chairman of the Crispus Attucks Community Association, January 23, 2012, http://attucks.org.
4. James Nolan, "Pupil Assignments Still to Be Made," *Louisville Courier-Journal*, July 24, 1974.
5. Greg Toppo, "Thousands of Black Teachers Lost Jobs," *USA Today*, April 28, 2004.
6. Michael Fultz, "The Displacement of Black Educators Post-*Brown:* An Overview and Analysis," *History of Education Quarterly* 44, no. 1 (2004): 14.
7. National Education Association, "Report of NEA Task Force III," in *School Desegregation: Louisiana and Mississippi* (Washington, DC: NEA, November 1970), cited in Fultz, "Displacement of Black Educators," 14.
8. Fultz, "Displacement of Black Educators," 26–28.
9. Charles Walden, *Southern Cities—Except Louisville—Desegregate Schools: A Report on Public Schools in Louisville, Kentucky and Major Southern Cities, 1968 and 1971* (Louisville: Commission on Human Rights, Commonwealth of Kentucky, May 1972), http://www.eric.ed.gov/.
10. Fultz, "Displacement of Black Educators," 28.
11. Mary Margaret Bell, "Ahrens High School," "Shawnee Junior High," "Johnston School," Jefferson County Public Schools History blog, http://media.jefferson.k12.ky.us/; "Ahrens, Shawnee Middle, 6 Elementaries May Close," *Louisville Courier-Journal*, January 9, 1979.
12. "Hearing Is Rally for Threatened Schools," *Louisville Times*, January 24, 1980.
13. "County Board Gets Three Alternatives on Middle Schools," *Louisville Courier-Journal*, January 22, 1980.
14. Leslie Scanlon, "DeRuzzo Details School Cutbacks," *Louisville Courier-Journal*, January 8, 1981.
15. "Debt Helps Spare Fern Creek High from Closing Plan," *Louisville Courier-Journal*, January 18, 1981.

Chapter 15

1. Saundra Keyes, "Black Leaders Condemn Ingwerson Plan," *Louisville Courier-Journal*, March 20, 1984.
2. Leslie Scanlon, "Many Doubt That Central Would Attract East End Students," *Louisville Courier-Journal*, January 21, 1984.
3. Saundra Keyes, "Endorsing Central as 'Magnet' School Skirted Real Issue," *Louisville Courier-Journal*, January 16, 1984.
4. Saundra Keyes, "Citizens' Panel Suggests Compromise on Central," *Louisville Courier-Journal*, January 20, 1984; Saundra Keyes and Leslie Scanlon, "Compromise Offer on Busing Plan Getting Hard Look," *Louisville Courier-Journal*, March 30, 1984.
5. "Highlights of Ingwerson's Desegregation Plan," *Louisville Times*, February 14, 1984; Saundra Keyes, "Majority of Ingwerson's Committee Urges Withdrawal of Busing Plan," *Louisville Courier-Journal*, March 24, 1984; Leslie Scanlon and Saundra Keyes, "Anatomy of a Controversy," *Louisville Courier-Journal*, April 15, 1984.
6. Leslie Scanlon and John C. Long, "Advisory Panel Greets Plan with Wrath, Pleasure," *Louisville Courier-Journal*, February 15, 1984; "Negotiators Praise Busing-Plan Accord," *Louisville Courier-Journal*, March 31, 1984.
7. Leslie Scanlon, "Ingwerson Denies Plan Is 'One-Way Busing,'" *Louisville Courier-Journal*, February 11, 1984.

8. Saundra Keyes, "Black Leaders Condemn Ingwerson Plan," *Louisville Courier-Journal*, March 20, 1984; Saundra Keyes, "Revised Busing Plan Stirs Fear Central's Enrollment Will Fall," *Louisville Courier-Journal*, March 15, 1984.

9. Saundra Keyes and Leslie Scanlon, "Busing Plan Hearing at Central Filled with Emotion," *Louisville Courier-Journal*, March 7, 1984.

10. Keyes, "Majority of Ingwerson's Committee"; Saundra Keyes, "Black Ministers Plan Petition Drive against Busing Plan," *Louisville Courier-Journal*, February 22, 1984.

11. Scanlon, "Anatomy of a Controversy."

12. Saundra Keyes, "School Board Approves Busing Plan," *Louisville Courier-Journal*, April 5, 1984.

13. "Desegregation Plan at a Glance," *Louisville Courier-Journal*, April 5, 1984.

14. Al Cross, "Judge Frees Schools from Busing-Change Review," *Louisville Courier-Journal*, September 26, 1985.

15. Bob Deitel, "Central High's Enrollment Drop Underscores Problem, Officials Say," *Louisville Times*, October 19, 1983; Cheryl Devall, "Central's Attendance Is Too Low, Panel Fears," *Louisville Courier-Journal*, September 20, 1984.

16. Daniel Rubin, "Schools Are Taking Aim at Better Attendance," *Louisville Courier-Journal*, April 11, 1985.

17. Kit Lively, "Central High School Dealing with Many Changes This Year," *Louisville Times*, February 8, 1985.

18. Al Cross, "Plan to Improve Central High School Approved," *Louisville Courier-Journal*, July 16, 1985.

19. Alan Judd, "Central to Use Its Urban Setting, New Stability, to Sharpen Its Focus," *Louisville Courier-Journal*, August 25, 1984.

20. Saundra Keyes, "Committee Is Urged to Reconsider 'Magnet' Plan for Central High," *Louisville Courier-Journal*, January 18, 1984.

21. Daniel Rubin and Kit Lively, "Revised School Plan Greeted as Both Boon, Bust for West End," *Louisville Courier-Journal*, March 13, 1986.

Chapter 16

1. Daniel Rubin and Leslie Scanlon, "Both Races Show Gains on Test, but an Analysis Shows an Achievement Gap," *Louisville Courier-Journal*, August 25, 1985.

2. John R. Logan and Mark Schneider, "Racial Segregation and Racial Change in American Suburbs, 1970–1980," *American Journal of Sociology* 89, no. 4 (1984): 874–88; Kenneth Jackson, *Crabgrass Frontier: The Suburbanization of the United States* (New York: Oxford University Press, 1985), 393.

3. Gary Orfield, "Turning Back to Segregation," in *Dismantling Desegregation: The Quiet Reversal of* Brown v. Board of Education, Gary Orfield and Susan Eaton, eds. (New York: New Press, 1996), 16–19.

4. Merrill Hartson, "Attorney General Doubts Value of Court-Ordered School Busing," Associated Press, March 15, 1985.

5. Susan E. Eaton and Christina Meldrum, "Broken Promises: Resegregation in Norfolk, Virginia," in Orfield, *Dismantling Desegregation*, 115.

6. Stephen Engelberg, "Norfolk Busing Case Viewed as Key to Keeping U.S. Schools Integrated," *New York Times*, February 3, 1985.

7. Eaton, "Broken Promises."

8. Lena Williams, "Controversy Reawakens as Districts End Busing," *New York Times*, March 25, 1989.

9. Stuart Taylor Jr., "Court Won't Hear 2 Busing Appeals," *New York Times*, November 4, 1986; Lena Williams, "Norfolk Can Halt Busing of Pupils," *New York Times*, February 8, 1986.

10. David G. Savage, "Rulings Displeased Both Right, Left," *Los Angeles Times*, July 7, 1986.
11. Jeffrey Toobin, *The Nine: Inside the Secret World of the Supreme Court* (New York: Anchor Books, 2007), 33–37.
12. William Rehnquist, "A Random Thought on the Segregation Cases," memo, 1952, PBS, *The Supreme Court*, "Primary Sources," http://www.pbs.org/; Peter Irons, *Jim Crow's Children: The Broken Promise of the* Brown *Decision* (New York: Penguin Books, 2002), 242.
13. Sharon LaFraniere, "At Justice, a Shift on School Desegregation; Department Not Attacking Court-Ordered Plans, Despite Recent Case," *Washington Post*, January 24, 1991; Orfield, *Dismantling Desegregation*, 17.
14. Associated Press, "Supreme Court Rules on Busing; Districts May Sometimes Choose," *Seattle Post-Intelligencer*, January 16, 1991.
15. David Savage, "Cases May Chart Future of School Desegregation," *Los Angeles Times*, December 17, 1990.
16. Board of Education of Oklahoma City v. Dowell, 498 US 237, (1991); Anti-Discrimination Center, Dynamic Census Mapping, http://www.antibiaslaw.com.
17. *Oklahoma City*; Linda Greenhouse, "Justices Rule Mandatory Busing May Go, Even if Races Stay Apart," *New York Times*, January 16, 1991.
18. Irons, *Jim Crow's Children*, 269.
19. Robert Anthony Watts, "High Court Takes DeKalb School Case," *Atlanta Journal and Constitution*, February 19, 1991.
20. Robert Anthony Watts, "Feds: Racial Balance OK in Schools in DeKalb," *Atlanta Journal and Constitution*, May 4, 1991.
21. Robert Anthony Watts, "Stakes High in DeKalb School Desegregation Case," *Atlanta Journal and Constitution*, October 6, 1991.
22. Robert Anthony Watts, "Faced with Busing, DeKalb Weighs the Impact of Its Magnet Force," *Atlanta Journal and Constitution*, May 6, 1991.
23. Watts, "Stakes High."
24. Irons, *Jim Crow's Children*, 271–73.
25. Ibid., 274; Howard Ball, *A Defiant Life: Thurgood Marshall and the Persistence of Racism in America* (New York: Crown, 1998); "Retirement of Justice Marshall," C-SPAN Video Library, June 28, 1991, http://www.c-spanvideo.org/.
26. Mary McGrory, "Bush's Enigmatic Nominee," *Washington Post*, July 9, 1991.
27. Ibid.
28. John E. Yang and Sharon LaFraniere, "Bush Picks Thomas for Supreme Court; Appeals Court Judge Served as EEOC Chairman in Reagan Administration," *Washington Post*, July 2, 1991.
29. R. W. Apple Jr., "The Thomas Confirmation: Senate Confirms Thomas, 52-48, Ending Week of Bitter Battle," *New York Times*, October 16, 1991.
30. Irons, *Jim Crow's Children*, 273–77.
31. Freeman v. Pitts, 503 US 467 (1992).
32. Robert Anthony Watts, "High Court Upholds DeKalb in School Desegregation Case," *Atlanta Journal and Constitution*, March 31, 1992.
33. Lee Sigelman and Susan Welch, *Black Americans' Views of Racial Inequality: The Dream Deferred* (NY: Cambridge University Press, 1991), 123.
34. Ibid., 126.
35. Dennis Kelly, "Less than World-Class; U.S. Pupils Rank Low in Global Test," *USA Today*, February 6, 1992; Andrew Pollack, "Tokyo Journal: Students Get a Saturday Off: Can They Handle It?" *New York Times*, September 11, 1992.
36. Brian M. Stecher and Sheila I. Barron, *Quadrennial Milepost Accountability Testing in Kentucky: CSE Technical Report 505* (Los Angeles: Graduate School of Education & Information Studies, University of California and RAND Education, June 1999), 2.

37. Ibid., 6.

38. Roger S. Pankratz, "The Legal and Legislative Battles," in *All Children Can Learn: Lessons from the Kentucky Reform Experience*, Roger S. Pankratz and Joseph M. Petrosko, eds. (San Francisco: Jossey-Bass, 2000), 11.

39. Eaton, "Broken Promises," 130–33.

Chapter 17

1. Mary Margaret Bell, "Buechel Metropolitan High School," Jefferson County Public Schools History blog; "Buechel Metropolitan High," school profile, Jefferson County Public Schools, http://www.jefferson.k12.ky.us/.

2. Bell, "Buechel."

3. Mary Margaret Bell, "Liberty High School," Jefferson County Public Schools History blog.

4. "'Low-Income Pupils Threaten Education of Others,' Gamboa Says," *Louisville Courier-Journal*, January 23, 1981.

5. Carman Weathers, "A Choice for African Americans," *Louisville Courier-Journal*, December 17, 1991.

6. Roger Pankratz, "The Legal and Legislative Battles," in *All Children Can Learn: Lessons from the Kentucky Reform Experience*, Roger S. Pankratz and Joseph M. Petrosko, eds. (San Francisco: Jossey-Bass, 2000), 23.

7. Jack Foster, "A New Vision for Public Schooling," in ibid., 53–58.

8. Stephen K. Clements, "Linking Curriculum and Instruction to Performance Standards," in ibid., 109.

9. Brian M. Stecher and Sheila I. Barron, *Quadrennial Milepost Accountability Testing in Kentucky: CSE Technical Report 505* (Los Angeles: Graduate School of Education & Information Studies, University of California and RAND Education, June 1999), 31.

10. James Raths, "Challenges in Implementing Kentucky's Primary School Program," in Pankratz, *All Children Can Learn*, 116–17.

11. "Jefferson May Rethink School Busing," *Louisville Courier-Journal*, September 21, 1991.

12. "Busing of Elementary Students May End; County Seeks New Ways to Attain Racial Balance," *Louisville Courier-Journal*, September 24, 1991.

13. Larry Bleiberg, "School Board Elects Cosby as Chairman," *Louisville Courier-Journal*, April 12, 1988.

14. Bruce Allar, "The Gospel According to Kevin Cosby," *Louisville Magazine*, September 1993.

15. "Boysen Says Jefferson Need Not Stop Busing," *Louisville Courier-Journal*, September 25, 1991.

16. Ibid.

17. "Forum of Protest; School Plan to End Busing Called Racist," *Louisville Courier-Journal*, October 4, 1991.

18. Allar, "Gospel According to Kevin Cosby."

19. "Forum of Protest."

20. Ibid.

21. "Blacks' Old, New Guards Emotionally Torn over School Plan," *Louisville Courier-Journal*, October 13, 1991.

22. "Meeting's Speakers United in Support for End to Busing," *Louisville Courier-Journal*, October 11, 1991.

23. "Consultants Collect $70,400 for Work on School Plan," *Louisville Courier-Journal*, January 30, 1992.

24. "Meeting's Speakers."

25. "Powers, Ingwerson Cover No New Ground at Meeting on Plan to End Busing," *Louisville Courier-Journal*, November 2, 1991.

26. "Busing Revisited; Angry Parents Say Forums Designed to Stifle Debate," *Louisville Courier-Journal*, October 15, 1991; "Desegregation's New Direction; Parents Left Waiting, Worrying as Schools Decide What's Best," *Louisville Courier-Journal*, November 17, 1991.

27. "Ingwerson Would Resume Busing to Meet Racial Goals," *Louisville Courier-Journal*, October 31, 1991; "Sen. Neal Opposes Proposed Student-Assignment Plan," *Louisville Courier-Journal*, December 15, 1991.

28. "Readers' Forum . . . The Busing Proposal 'Community Input,'" *Louisville Courier-Journal*, November 25, 1991.

29. Ibid.

30. "NAACP to Ask Ingwerson to Withdraw Busing Plan," *Louisville Courier-Journal*, December 7, 1991.

31. "Revised School Plan Approved," *Louisville Courier-Journal*, December 20, 1991.

32. "Educators Still Sorting out Details of New Busing Plan," *Louisville Courier-Journal*, December 21, 1991.

33. "Facts on School Plan Scare Confusing," *Louisville Courier-Journal*, February 11, 1992.

34. "Ingwerson Is Superintendent of the Year," *Louisville Courier-Journal*, February 22, 1991; "Some Hoping to Foil Ingwerson's Chance for National Award," *Louisville Courier-Journal*, February 13, 1992.

35. "Integration Goal Reached," *Louisville Courier-Journal*, May 23, 1992.

36. For the composition of the monitoring committee, see monitoring committee documents from Robert Douglas, private collection; "Groups Jockey for Slots on Panel to Monitor School-Assignment Plan," *Louisville Courier-Journal*, June 18, 1992.

37. Details of Joseph McMillan's life from author interview with McMillan, January 11, 2010.

38. "Push to Persuade Ingwerson to Stay Unlikely to Work," *Louisville Courier-Journal*, September 5, 1992; "Ingwerson Quits to Lead Educational Institute," *Louisville Courier-Journal*, March 5, 1993.

39. "Job Pressures May Have Led to Departure," *Louisville Courier-Journal*, March 5, 1993.

40. "Schools Accused of Resegregating," *Louisville Courier-Journal*, February 25, 1993.

41. Beverly Bartlett, "Panel Raises Possibility of Mostly Black Academy," *Louisville Courier-Journal*, March 12, 1996.

42. Carman Weathers, "Separation Not Necessarily Evil," *Louisville Courier-Journal*, August 5, 1994.

43. "Racial Imbalance Forces 10 Blacks to Leave Central," *Louisville Courier-Journal*, September 23, 1994.

44. Veda Morgan, "The Fourth 'R': How Race Affects School Choices under Jefferson County's Project Renaissance," *Louisville Courier-Journal*, June 16, 1996.

45. Veda Morgan, "District Expands Some Schools Despite Enrollment Being Flat," *Louisville Courier-Journal*, June 17, 1996.

46. Veda Morgan, "School Integration Incentives Proposed," *Louisville Courier-Journal*, August 13, 1996; Veda Morgan, "Daeschner Backs Revised Version of School Plan," *Louisville Courier-Journal*, August 23, 1996.

47. Details of Deborah Stallworth's life from author interview with Stallworth, May 20, 2009.

48. Author interview with Sandra Hampton, August 19, 2009.

Chapter 18

1. Interviews with Robert Douglas, Carman Weathers, Riccardo X, Fran Thomas.

2. Details of Teddy Gordon's life from author interviews with Gordon, March 31, 2009, and January 21, 2010, except where other sources cited.

3. "Woman Injured on Waterslide at Kentucky Kingdom," *Louisville Courier-Journal*, July 24, 1992.

4. "Officer Sues for Promotion, Cites Reverse Discrimination," *Louisville Courier-Journal*, November 27, 1990; "Appeals Court Rejects White Police Officer's Promotion-Bias Claim," *Louisville Courier-Journal*, April 2, 1993.

5. "Oldham Suit over Racial Harassment Is Resolved," *Louisville Courier-Journal*, March 10, 1995.

6. "Judge Declares Alderman's Seat Vacant," *Louisville Courier-Journal*, April 21, 1998.

7. Rick McDonough, "Court Orders Alderman Removed," *Louisville Courier-Journal*, April 18, 1998; "Representative Reginald Meeks (D)," Kentucky Legislature, http://www.lrc.ky.gov/.

8. Bill Billiter, "The Voter Is King, and Candidate," *Louisville Courier-Journal*, May 18, 1971.

9. "The Candidate Who Wasn't There Is a Sure Loser," *Louisville Times*, May 25, 1971.

10. Andrew Wolfson and Chris Kenning, "Court to Hear Unlikely Advocate," *Louisville Courier-Journal*, December 4, 2006; "32nd District," *Louisville Courier-Journal*, October 24, 1979; "5th District," *Louisville Courier-Journal*, October 20, 1983; Alan Judd, "Democratic Candidates for Prosecuting Attorney Have Varied Backgrounds," *Louisville Courier-Journal*, May 21, 1987.

11. Author interviews with Harold Fenderson, January 14, 2010, and Daniel Withers, principal of Central High School, November 2, 2009.

12. Veda Morgan, "Suit Attacks Schools' Way of Integrating: 6 Black Parents Challenge Limits at Central High," *Louisville Courier-Journal*, April 23, 1998.

13. Ibid.

14. Ibid.

15. *Hampton*, Complaint, April 22, 1998.

16. Details of Judge John Heyburn's life from author interview with Heyburn, August 20, 2009, and author communication with Heyburn, January 13, 2012.

17. Mary Margaret Bell, "Chenoweth Elementary School," Jefferson County Public Schools History Blog,.

18. Details about Frank Mellen from author interview with Mellen, April 3, 2009.

19. Details about Byron Leet from author interview with Leet, November 9, 2009.

20. *Hampton*, Answer of the Defendants, May 13, 1998.

21. Mark Schaver, "Black Parents Seek End to Court Order Issued in '75," *Louisville Courier-Journal*, January 30, 2000; *Hampton*, Intervening Complaint, Virgil C. Fitzpatrick, October 14, 1998.

22. Some details about QUEST from author interview with Steve Porter, January 15, 2010.

23. *Hampton*, Intervening Complaint.

Chapter 19

1. Fern Creek High School was eligible for a federal school-improvement grant for the nation's worst schools in 2009 after years of poor performance on state tests. Lonnie Harp, "School Ratings Give a First Look at New System," *Louisville Courier-Journal*, January 27, 2000; author interview with Houston Barber, principal at Fern Creek, April 8, 2010; also see Cary Stemle, "Get under the Bus?" *Leo (Louisville Eccentric Observer) Weekly*, August 4, 2010.

2. Veda Morgan, "2 Groups Seek Dismissal of Central Suit," *Louisville Courier-Journal*, September 15, 1998.

3. Details of first *Hampton* trial from *Hampton v. Jefferson County* transcripts, April 13, 14, and 21, 1999; author interviews with Teddy Gordon, Byron Leet, Frank Mellen, Judge Heyburn, and CEASE members.

4. Regents of the University of California v. Bakke, 438 US 265 (1978).

5. W. E. B. Du Bois, *The Souls of Black Folk* (New York: Barnes and Nobles Classics, 2005), 9.

6. Author interview with Stephen Daeschner, January 13, 2010.
7. *Hampton*, Memorandum and Order, April 22, 1999.
8. Michael Jennings, "Balancing Races Is Hard, Schools Say," *Louisville Courier-Journal*, April 15, 1999.

Chapter 20

1. Hampton v. Jefferson County, Response, April 26, 1999.
2. Hampton v. Jefferson County, Second Amended Complaint, May 10, 1999.
3. Hampton v. Jefferson County, 72 F. Supp. 2d 753 (1999), Opinion, June 10, 1999.
4. Carman Weathers, "Debating Integration's Value," *Louisville Courier-Journal*, August 19, 1997.
5. Author interview with Robert Douglas.
6. Michael Jennings, "Parents Seek to End School Decree," *Louisville Courier-Journal*, June 16, 1999.
7. Jeffrey Rosen, "The Lost Promise of School Integration," *New York Times*, April 2, 2000.
8. Terry Belk v. The Charlotte-Mecklenburg Board of Education, 269 F.3d 305 (4th Cir. 2001); Alison Morantz, "Desegregation at Risk: Threat and Reaffirmation in Charlotte," in Gary Orfield and Susan Eaton, eds., *Dismantling Desegregation: The Quiet Reversal of Brown v. Board of Education* (New York: New Press, 1996), 179–206.
9. Rosen, "Lost Promise"; Julia A. McLaughlin v. Boston School Committee, 938 F. Supp. 1001 (US Dist. 1996).
10. Rosen, "Lost Promise"; Brian Ho v. San Francisco Unified School District, 965 F. Supp. 1316 (US Dist. 1997).
11. Rosen, "Lost Promise."
12. Ibid.
13. Peter Applebome, "New Choices for Parents Are Starting to Change U.S. Education Landscape," *New York Times*, September 4, 1996; Alan Wolfe, ed., *School Choice: The Moral Debate* (Princeton, NJ: Princeton University Press, 2003).
14. Susan Chira, "A Sea of Doubt Swells Around Bush's Education Plan," *New York Times*, July 22, 1991.
15. Applebome, "New Choices"; Adam Nagourney, "Dole Backs School Choice through Vouchers," *New York Times*, July 19, 1996.
16. Applebome, "New Choices."
17. Peter Cookson, *School Choice: The Struggle for the Soul of American Education* (New Haven, CT: Yale University Press, 1994).
18. Andrea Billups, "Poll Finds Ignorance on School Choice," *Washington Times*, November 17, 1999.
19. Rosen, "Lost Promise."

Chapter 21

1. Larry Weisman, "Surprising Rams, Titans Duel to Finish," *USA Today*, January 31, 2000.
2. Liz Clarke, "Hardy Warner Takes Home a Final Laurel; Unlikely Hero Finishes with MVP Performance," *Washington Post*, January 31, 2000.
3. Details of the second *Hampton* trial from *Hampton v. Jefferson County* transcripts, January 31, February 1, 2, 17, 18, and 24, and March 17 and 28, 2000.
4. Idris Ghani, "Judge Confirms Victory of Handy over Williams in 42nd District Race," *Louisville Times*, August 7, 1984; Mervin Aubespin, "Local NAACP Elects Attorney as President," *Louisville Courier-Journal*, December 7, 1976.
5. Carol Marie Cropper, "Aubrey Williams Fired from State Director's Job," *Louisville Courier-Journal*, September 3, 1987.

6. Courtroom dialogue here and below comes from the transcripts, Hampton v. Jefferson County, 72 F. Supp. 2d 753 (1999), US District Court-Western District of Kentucky.

7. Details of John Whiting's life from author interview with Whiting, January 13, 2010, in addition to transcripts.

8. Mark Schaver, "Schools Will Talk about Settlement of Central Lawsuit," *Louisville Courier-Journal*, January 22, 2000.

9. Mark Schaver, "Settlement in Central High Case Looks Unlikely," *Louisville Courier-Journal*, March 28, 2000.

10. Details of Pat Todd's life from author interviews with Todd, November 4, 2009, and January 14, 2010.

Chapter 22

1. Chris Poynter, "The Plaintiffs: Elated CEASE Members Say They Feel Vindicated," *Louisville Courier-Journal*, June 21, 2000.

2. Hampton v. Jefferson County, 102 F. Supp. 2d 358 (U.S. Dist. 2000), Opinion, June 20, 2000.

3. Poynter, "The Plaintiffs"; Holly Coryell, "Group Hails End of Racial Limits," *Louisville Courier-Journal*, June 23, 2000.

4. Andrew Wolfson, "Schools and Race: Attitudes Changing," *Louisville Courier-Journal*, June 25, 2000.

5. Holly Coryell, "Schools Won't Fight Ruling in Race Case," *Louisville Courier-Journal*, June 27, 2000.

Chapter 23

1. Details about Crystal Meredith from court transcripts and interviews with Teddy Gordon and an anonymous source. See also Jan Crawford-Greenburg and Howard Rosenberg, "Two Women Come Together to Oppose Busing: Plaintiff Crystal Meredith and Civil Rights Activist Mattie Jones Say Program Failed Their Children," *Nightline*, ABC News, June 28, 2007.

2. McFarland v. Jefferson County, Civil Docket for Case, http://www.clearinghouse.net/.

3. Details about the McFarlands from court transcripts and author interview with David McFarland, August 20, 2009.

4. McFarland v. Jefferson County, Civil Docket.

5. Details about the McFarland trial from *McFarland v. Jefferson County* transcripts, December 8, 9, 10, 11, and 12, 2003.

6. Jennifer Gratz v. Lee Bollinger, 539 U.S. 244 (2003).

7. Barbara Grutter v. Lee Bollinger, 539 U.S. 306 (2003).

8. Orfield and Eaton, *Dismantling Desegregation*; Charles T. Clotfelter, *After Brown: The Rise and Retreat of School Desegregation* (Princeton, NJ: Princeton University Press, 2004).

9. Richard Fry, *The Changing Racial and Ethnic Composition of U.S. Public Schools* (Washington, DC: Pew Hispanic Center, August 30, 2007), http://www.pewhispanic.org/.

10. Marjorie Coeyman, "Charter Schools Build on a Decade of Experimentation," *Christian Science Monitor*, January 7, 2003.

11. Howard S. Bloom, Saskia Levy Thompson, and Rebecca Unterman, *Transforming the High School Experience: How New York City's New Small Schools Are Boosting Student Achievement and Graduation Rates* (New York: MDRC and the Bill & Melinda Gates Foundation, June 2010), http://eric.ed.gov/.

12. Paul E. Peterson and Martin R. West, eds., *No Child Left Behind? The Politics and Practice of School Accountability* (Washington, DC: Brookings Institution, 2003).

13. Kentucky and national achievement gap data are based on 2005 National Assessment of

Education Progress scores, which were compiled by the Education Trust, www.edtrust.org.

14. Chris Kenning, "Jefferson County School Board: Three Incumbents Retain Seats," *Louisville Courier-Journal*, November 3, 2004; Chris Kenning, "School Race-Policy Foe Runs for Board," *Louisville Courier-Journal*, August 11, 2004.

Chapter 24

1. Chris Kenning, "School Desegregation Plan on Trial," *Louisville Courier-Journal*, December 8, 2003.

2. Chris Kenning, "Three Magnet Schools See Declining Diversity," *Louisville Courier-Journal*, November 5, 2006.

3. Chris Kenning, "Central High Principal Dismissed," *Louisville Courier-Journal*, November 13, 2002.

4. Chris Kenning, "Supporters Rally for Ousted Central High Principal," *Louisville Courier-Journal*, November 19, 2002.

5. From transcripts, Hampton v. Jefferson County, 72 F. Supp. 2d 753 (1999), US District Court-Western District of Kentucky.

6. Ibid.

7. Details about Harold Fenderson's life from author interview with Fenderson, January 14, 2010.

8. Kenning, "Supporters Rally."

9. Chris Kenning, "Fenderson Appeals His Dismissal," *Louisville Courier-Journal*, November 16, 2002.

10. Teddy B. Gordon, "Petition for Writ of Certiorari, Petitioner Crystal D. Meredith," US Court of Appeals, Sixth Circuit, July 21, 2005, in Teddy Gordon, "Federal Appellate Practice, a/k/a Ted Gordon's Incredible Adventure," unpublished manuscript provided by Gordon to the author.

11. Andrew Wolfson and Chris Kenning, "Court to Hear Unlikely Advocate: Lawyer Challenges Jefferson Desegregation Policy," *Louisville Courier-Journal*, December 4, 2006.

12. Toobin, *The Nine*, 2–9, 293–95, 323–74.

13. Douglas Judge, "Housing, Race and Schooling in Seattle: Context for the Supreme Court Decision," *Journal of Educational Controversy* (Western Washington University) 2, no. 1 (Winter 2007), http://www.wce.wwu.edu/.

14. Parents Involved in Community Schools, www.piics.org.

15. Davis Wright Tremaine LLP, www.dwt.com.

16. Linda Shaw, "Integration No Longer a Top Priority for District," *Seattle Times*, June 3, 2008.

17. Brief of 553 Social Scientists as *Amici Curiae* in Support of Respondents, Parents Involved in Community Schools v. Seattle School District No. 1, 551 U.S. 701 (2007), and Meredith v. Jefferson County.

18. Eric A. Hanushek, John F. Kain, and Steven G. Rivkin, "How Much Does School Integration Affect Student Achievement?" paper presented at the Annual Meeting of the American Economic Association, New Orleans, January 2001.

19. Robert Rodosky, unpublished survey cited in transcripts, Hampton v. Jefferson County, 72 F. Supp. 2d 753 (1999), US District Court-Western District of Kentucky.

20. Brief Amicus Curiae of Pacific Legal Foundation, American Civil Rights Institute, and Center for Equal Opportunity in Support of the Petitioner, Meredith v. Jefferson County.

21. Robert Barnes, "Court Hears Cases on Schools and Race," *Washington Post*, December 5, 2006.

22. Notes included in in Teddy Gordon, "Federal Appellate Practice, a/k/a Ted Gordon's Incredible Adventure," unpublished manuscript provided by Gordon to the author.

23. Details of oral arguments from *Meredith*.

24. Parents Involved in Community Schools v. Seattle, transcript of oral arguments, December 4, 2006.

Chapter 25

1. Nancy C. Rodriguez, "Court Rejects Louisville Student Assignment Plan," *Louisville Courier-Journal*, June 29, 2007.
2. Meredith v. Jefferson County, Opinion, June 28, 2007.
3. "High Court Rejects School Integration Plans," *Seattle Times*, June 28, 2007.
4. Chris Kenning, "Woman Kept 'My Promise' to Son," *Louisville Courier-Journal*, June 29, 2007.
5. Chris Kenning, "Three Magnet Schools See Declining Diversity," *Louisville Courier-Journal*, November 5, 2006.
6. Harris Cooper et al., "The Effects of Summer Vacation on Achievement Test Scores: A Narrative and Meta-analytic Review," *Review of Educational Research* 66, no. 3 (1996); National Summer Learning Association, http://www.summerlearning.org/.
7. Central High School Report Card, 2009–10, 2008–9, 2007–8, 2006–7, Commonwealth of Kentucky, http://applications.education.ky.gov/.
8. Barack Obama, "Obama: Supreme Court Ruling an Obstacle to Opportunity," State News Service, Washington, DC, July 2, 2007; also see Russell Berman, "Democratic Candidates Criticize Roberts Court on Race Decision," *New York Sun*, June 29, 2007.
9. Emily Bazelon, "The Next Kind of Integration," *New York Times Magazine*, July 20, 2008; Andrew Wolfson and Deborah Yetter, "New Suit Challenges Jefferson Student Assignment Plan," *Louisville Courier-Journal*, July 2, 2009; Chris Kenning, "Elementary School Assignments Leave Some Unhappy," *Louisville Courier-Journal*, August 9, 2009.
10. Bazelon, "Next Kind of Integration"; Jordan Schrader, "Districts Try to Spread out Poor Students: Income, Not Race Becoming Basis for Busing," *USA Today*, November 2, 2009; Richard D. Kahlenberg, *Economic School Integration: An Update* (New York: Century Foundation, September 16, 2002), http://www.eric.ed.gov/.
11. Lloyd Grieger and Jessica Wyse, *The Growing Racial Divide in U.S. Children's Long-Term Poverty at the End of the Twentieth Century* (Ann Arbor, MI: Population Studies Center, University of Michigan, November 2008), http://www.psc.isr.umich.edu/.
12. Rakesh Kochhar, Richard Fry, and Paul Taylor, *Wealth Gaps Rise to Record Highs Between Whites, Blacks, Hispanics: Twenty-to-One* (Washington, DC: Pew Research Center, July 26, 2011), http://pewresearch.org/.
13. Michael J. Puma et al., *Prospects: The Congressionally Mandated Study of Educational Growth and Opportunity, The Interim Report* (Washington, DC: US Government Printing Office, July 1993); but also see: Sharon Lewis, Candace Simon, Renata Uzzell, Amanda Horwitz, and Michael Casserly, *A Call for Change: The Social and Educational Factors Contributing to the Outcomes of Black Males in Urban Schools* (Washington, DC: Council of the Great City Schools, October 2010), http://cgcs.schoolwires.net/.
14. Wolfson, "New Suit"; Chris Kenning, "Second Parent Asks to Join Student Assignment Suit," *Louisville Courier-Journal*, July 23, 2009.
15. See, for example, Wake County's retreat from an income-based plan: Stephanie McCrummen, "Republican School Board in N.C. Backed by Tea Party Abolishes Integration Policy," *Washington Post*, January 12, 2011.
16. Linda Shaw, "Integration No Longer a Top Priority for District," *Seattle Times*, June 3, 2008.

Epilogue

1. David Grissmer, Ann Flanagan, and Stephanie Williamson, "Why Did the Gap Narrow in the 1970s and 1980s?" in *The Black-White Test Score Gap*, Christopher Jencks and Meredith Philips, eds. (Washington, DC: Brookings Institution Press, 1998), 182–223; Kath-

erine Magnuson, Dan T. Rosenblum, and Jane Waldfogel, "Inequality and Black-White Achievement Trends in the NAEP," in Katherine Magnuson and Jane Waldfogel, eds., *Steady Gains and Stalled Progress* (New York: Russell Sage Foundation, 2008), 33–64; Jacob L. Vigdor and Jens Ludwig, "Segregation and the Test Score Gap," in Magnuson, *Steady Gains*, 181–208; Paul Barton and Richard J. Coley, *The Black-White Achievement Gap: When Progress Stopped*, Educational Testing Services, http://www.ets.org/; Amy Stuart Wells, Jennifer Jellison Holme, Anita Tijerina Revilla, and Awo Korantemaa Atanda, *Both Sides Now: The Story of School Desegregation's Graduates* (Berkeley: University of California Press, 2009), 19.

2.   Douglas N. Harris, *Lost Learning, Forgotten Promises: A National Analysis of School Racial Segregation, Student Achievement, and 'Controlled Choice' Plans* (Washington, DC: Center for American Progress November 24, 2006), http://www.americanprogress.org/; Harris, "Educational Outcomes of Disadvantaged Students: From Desegregation to Accountability," in *AEFA Handbook of Research in Education Finance and Policy*, Helen Ladd and Edward Fiske, eds. (Hillsdale, NJ: Laurence Erlbaum, 2008); Roslyn Arlin Mickelson and Martha Bottia, "Integrated Education and Mathematics Outcomes: A Synthesis of Social Science Research," *North Carolina Law Review* 88, no. 3 (2010); Eric A. Hanushek, John F. Kain, and Steven G. Rivkin, "How Much Does School Integration Affect Student Achievement?" paper presented at the Annual Meeting of the American Economic Association, New Orleans, January 2001.

3.   Wells, *Both Sides Now*, 22–24.

4.   Center for Research on Education Outcomes, *Multiple Choice: Charter School Performance in 16 States* (Stanford, CA: Stanford University Press, June 2009), http://credo.stanford .edu/; Bruce Fuller, ed., *Inside Charter Schools: The Paradox of Radical Decentralization* (Cambridge, MA: Harvard University Press, 2002).

5.   Stefanie Chambers, *Mayors and Schools: Minority Voices and Democratic Tensions in Urban Education* (Philadelphia: Temple University Press, 2006); also see Jeffrey R. Henig and Wilbur C. Rich, *Mayors in the Middle: Politics, Race and Mayoral Control of Urban Schools* (Princeton, NJ: Princeton University Press, 2004).

6.   For example, William L. Sanders, S. Paul Wright, and Sandra P. Horn, "Teacher and Classroom Context Effects on Student Achievement: Implications for Teacher Evaluation," *Journal of Personnel Evaluation in Education* 11, no. 1 (1997).

7.   Sarah Carr, *Hope Against Hope* (New York: Bloomsbury, forthcoming).

8.   "NYC's Disappearing Black/Latino Public School Teachers," *Black Educator* blog, December 19, 2006, http://blackeducator.blogspot.com/.

9.   Bill Turque, "Fired DC Principals Go to Court Again," *Washington Post*, October 27, 2009.

10. Joel Hood, "Chicago Teachers Union Accuses CPS of Discriminating Against African-American Teachers," *Chicago Tribune*, February 8, 2012.

11. Laura Pappano, "Closing Time," *Ed.: The Magazine of the Harvard Graduate School of Education* (Summer 2011).

12. Joel Hood and Noreen Ahmed-Ullah, "Protesters Send CPS Board Members Scurrying," *Chicago Tribune*, December 14, 2011; Yirmeyah Beckles, "OUSD Meeting Turns into Emotional Protest," *Oakland North* website, September 21, 2011; Lindsey Christ, "Parents Protest DOE Official's Threats to Close 47 City Schools," *NY1*, November 22, 2011; Ann Doss Helms, "Claims of Racial Bias Rattle Charlotte-Mecklenburg Schools," *Charlotte Observer*, October 24, 2010.

13. Pappano, "Closing Time."

14. For example, "Governor Chris Christie Designates Week of January 22rd [*sic*], 2012 School Choice Week in New Jersey," State of New Jersey, January 23, 2012, http://nj .gov/governor/.

15. Concept of black and white double-consciousness: Wells et al., *Both Sides*, 26–35.

16. Jeffrey Passel and D'Vera Cohn, *U.S. Population Projections: 2005–2050* (Washington, DC: Pew Hispanic Center, February 11, 2008), http://www.pewhispanic.org/.

17. Richard Fry, *The Changing Racial and Ethnic Composition of U.S. Public Schools* (Washington, DC: Pew Hispanic Center, August 30, 2007), http://www.pewhispanic.org/.

18. Office of Public Affairs, "New Guidance Supports Voluntary Efforts to Promote Diversity and Reduce Racial Isolation in Education" (Washington, DC: Department of Justice, December 2, 2011), http://www.ed.gov/.

19. Richard Fry, *Sharp Growth in Suburban Minority Enrollment Yields Modest Gains in School Diversity* (Washington, DC: Pew Hispanic Center, March 31, 2009) http://www.pewhispanic.org/.

20. Meredith P. Richards, Kori J. Stroub, and Jennifer Jellison Holme, "Can NCLB Choice Work? Modeling the Effects of Interdistrict Choice on Student Access to Higher-Performing Schools" (New York: Century Foundation, May 31, 2011), http://tcf.org/.

21. Erica Frankenberg, Genevieve Siegel-Hawley, and Jia Wang, *Choice Without Equity: Charter School Segregation and the Need for Civil Rights Standards* (Los Angeles: Civil Rights Project, UCLA Graduate School of Education and Information Studies, January 2010), http://civilrightsproject.ucla.edu/.

22. Purpose Built Communities, http://purposebuiltcommunities.org/.

23. See the *Brown* decision and Irons, *Jim Crow's Children*, 162–63: "The primary role of public education lies in fostering 'cultural values' and 'good citizenship' among children."

INDEX